A SINGAP...

Also by Peter Broadbent
HMS GANGES DAYS
HMS BERMUDA DAYS

A SINGAPORE FLING

An AB's Far-Flung Adventure

PETER BROADBENT

CHAPLIN BOOKS

www.chaplinbooks.co.uk

ISBN 978-1-911105-00-8

A CIP catalogue record for this book is available from The
British Library

Design by Michael Walsh at The Better Book Company
Printed by Imprint Digital

Chaplin Books
1 Eliza Place
Gosport PO12 4UN
Tel: 023 9252 9020
www.chaplinbooks.co.uk

CONTENTS

FOREWORD

Having survived the notorious Training Establishment *HMS Ganges* and 'cut my teeth' onboard the infamous Battle Cruiser *HMS Bermuda*, I believed that – as an Ordinary Seaman Radar Plotter – I was equipped for anything the Royal Navy could throw at me.

For 18 incident-filled months (1962-64) I 'did my bit' onboard *HMS Lincoln* caught up in an Oriental squabble on the other side of the world known as the 'Malaysian Crisis'. Although our homeport was Singapore, we spent time in Hong Kong, Osaka, Kobe, Manila, Tawau, Jesselton, Sandakan, Lahad Datu, Semporna, Lankawi and the Indian Ocean RAF station at Gan. On Kumpit Patrol, we ploughed our lonely furrow through the Andaman, South China, Sulu, Banda, Flores, Java, and Sulawesi Seas … but crossed the Equator only once. I cavorted myself down Hong Kong's Lockhart, Hennessy, Cameron and Hankow Roads, and in the many Wan-Chai side streets and go-downs. I horsed around in Singapore's Sembawang village, niftily defying the advances of 'Suzie Right', 'Lilly the legs', 'Calamity Jayne' and a girl with bad teeth known as 'Piano'. In Japan I was bathed to within an inch of my life by the origami-gifted Harumi.

During Borneo Patrol, I was a member of the front-line 'Kumpit Boarding Party' that stopped and searched 'enemy' vessels. I spent an interesting week with the Gurkhas at Kota Tinggi in the Malayan jungle. Finally, with good friends and an ice-cold Tiger beer at my elbow, I saw the sun come up over Singapore's notorious Bugis Street the night before returning to the UK.

My return, in early 1964, coincided with the appearance on the streets of that design classic … the mini-skirt. I had just celebrated my twentieth birthday and the girls of the United Kingdom voluntarily hoisted their hemlines in acknowledgment.

Unfortunately, I'd missed hearing The Beatles for the first time. On the downside, returning to the UK sporting a well-ingrained suntan was not welcomed by everyone ... in particular an intolerant bar owner in central Bradford.

The only real person in my story is me: none of the book's characters represent, or are based on, actual crewmembers. I gratefully acknowledge those who served onboard *HMS Lincoln* with me, all of whom made my first trip to the Far East the most memorable period of my young life.

Peter Broadbent
Ex Junior Seaman 2nd Class (P/053653)
Hondón de Las Nieves, Spain
January 2015

1

GO EAST, YOUNG MAN

'Name?'

'Broadbent.'

'PARDON?'

'Broadbent, PO.'

'Rate?'

'Ordinary Seaman.'

The sullen Petty Officer on the opposite side of the chest-high counter flicks through a tray of index cards.

I am at the front of a short queue of three joining *HMS Dryad* this morning.

The Petty Officer looks up at me with bored, unfriendly eyes. 'You tired, lad?'

'No.'

'No WHAT?'

'No, PO.'

'Then don't lean on my counter.'

I straighten up.

He looks at my arm badge. 'Still a basic Radar Plotter I see.'

I nod. 'Yes, PO.'

He extracts a card from his tray, 'Got ya.' He scans the card. 'You have failed your simple starring exam three times, Ordinary Seaman Broadbent.'

'That's correct ... yes, PO.'

Without looking at me he reads from my card. 'You have a draft chit already, young man. *HMS Lincoln* will have the pleasure of your lack of knowledge in October. Until then you will work on the Buffers Party. We can't allow anyone who struggles to pass a simple starring exam to work near anything remotely technical, can we?'

I nod in agreement. 'No, PO.'

He places a sheet of paper in front of me. 'Joining routine: have it back here completed by 15:30 today. You're in Ross 6 mess. See the Killick of the mess for your locker key. Next.'

I collect my kit bag from outside the clock tower and carry it down to Ross 6 mess. It's my second time at *HMS Dryad* and I know the way.

I am surprised to discover that the Killick of Ross 6 mess is Leading Seaman Lee who was on *HMS Bermuda* with me.

As he hands me my locker key I say. 'I've got a draft chit already.'

'Where?' he asks.

'*HMS Lincoln.*'

He stops what he is doing and looks directly at me. 'Well, there's a coincidence.'

'Eh?'

'Me too.'

'What is it and where is it – do you know?' I ask.

'Frigate in Singapore.'

Singapore! I toss my locker key in the air and try to catch it, but miss. I'm tingling all over. 'Really ... Singapore?'

'Yep.'

'I go in October.' I pick my locker key up.

'I suppose we'll all be flying out together,' says Tansy. 'Unpack your kit then, young 'un and get on with your joining routine.'

As I wander around *Dryad* getting my joining sheet stamped and signed, I can't stop thinking about Singapore. Since that day in the Leeds Recruiting Office, I've dreamt of far distant tropical places, relaxing under cloudless blue skies and getting myself a proper suntan.

Back in the mess 'Lash' Trainer, a mate from *Ganges* and *Bermuda*, says that he's also drafted to *HMS Lincoln*.

'Third ship together then, mate,' I say, pleased that I will know at least two people onboard.

Wilco and I exchanged letters, containing overtly sexual promises and guarantees, while I was onboard *HMS Bermuda*. I don't expect her to make a public fuss in the canteen ... but she does.

I'm third in the canteen queue when she spots me. She overfills someone's tea, plonks her large NAAFI kettle down and slithers over the top of her counter, flashing her nyloned legs in the process. She throws one of her arms around my shoulder and squeezes my bottom with the other. 'Peter ... welcome back.'

The blokes in the queue watch with interest as she holds me at arm's length and licks her crimson lips. She hasn't changed: still sensuously gorgeous. The top button of her NAAFI overall is undone, allowing it to gape a little.

'Did you enjoy my letters?' she asks.

'Certainly did.'

'What about the naughty bits?'

'Particularly those ... yeah.'

'Thought you'd like 'em.' She wraps her arms around herself. 'How long you here for?'

'Till October. I've got a draft to Singapore.'

'Oh no!' She drapes both arms over my shoulders and presses her breasts firmly into my chest. 'I'll see if there are any NAAFI jobs going in Singapore then.'

'That'd be good,' I reply. My head is ringing. Wilco in Singapore. Wilco in the sunshine. Wilco in, or out of, a bikini ...

The bloke at the front of the queue slaps the counter. 'I've only got ten minutes to drink mi tea, love.'

She gives me a kiss on my cheek and slithers back over her counter. 'Tea and one sugar is it?' she asks.

'After watching that performance, love ... I'll 'ave three sugars.'

The detail of Wilco's greeting flies around *Dryad* and my reputation rockets.

The first muster at the Buffer's cabooch is always a worry: as a new arrival you never know what kind of a job you'll be given. I wonder if the Petty Officer in the Ship's Office has told the Buffer that I have to be kept away from anything remotely technical. Lash and I stand to one side while everybody else is given their jobs around the Southwick Estate.

The Buffer looks at Lash. 'What jobs have you done at *Dryad* before, Trainer?'

'Err ... did some grass cutting down the back drive year before last, Chief,' says Lash unenthusiastically.

'Just the lad I'm looking for then.' He rubs his hands. 'Report to Leading Seaman Potter. For the next fortnight, you are part of the dredging party cleaning out the river over by the Estate boundary. You'll need to draw seaboots and a shovel.'

Lash nods. He looks at me with downcast eyes.

He turns his attention to me. 'Now what can I find to suit your talents, Ordinary Seaman Broadbent?'

I gulp. I think he's being sardonic.

'Having given it some considerable thought ...'

I think I know where this is going.

'Having given it some considerable thought ... Sullage Party is the place for you, young man. You'll need to draw a couple of extra pairs of overalls and report to Leading Seaman Collier in the laundry after dinner today. For the rest of the morning you can grab a broom and help my gang of specialist technicians sweep the Parade Ground. Capiche?'

'Yes, Chief. Thank you, Chief.'

Sullage Party doesn't sound glamorous, but it proves to be a job that I'm perfectly suited to. As it involves working odd hours, it is termed a 'blue card' job, which means that I don't keep normal duty watches and avoid being part of the dreaded Emergency Party and sleeping fully clothed in the old Nissen hut behind the main gate.

My working day starts at 05:30 each morning, well before the rest of the camp are awake. Four of us, under the guidance of three-badge Leading Seaman Collier, 'trolley' bins full of the previous day's uneaten food from the main and wardroom galleys to a small building near to the main boiler room where we empty the food into large heating bins. We scoop out the previous day's pulp that has been cooking for 24 hours into filthy, sticky dustbins and 'trolley' the obnoxious stuff up to the pigsties where the grunting occupants are awake and waiting for us. By the time we return our empty dustbins to the main galley we have absorbed that peculiar, pig-swill smell. We dump our overalls in the laundry, shower and change into a fresh pair of overalls before tucking into breakfast at our designated dining hall table located a good distance away from everybody else. After breakfast, when all the classes have marched away to school, we tour the camp on the back of a wagon collecting and emptying all the rubbish bins. Once *Dryad* is cleared, we drive along the top of Portsdown Hill and collect the gash from five of the Forts before going down to the main rubbish tip in Portsmouth before dinner. Our day is effectively over at dinnertime and we have every afternoon off. I shower again after dinner and infuse myself with Old Spice talcum powder. After the afternoon Stand-easy, the Canteen shutters are dropped and two or three times a week, Wilco and I enjoy some time private time together in her NAAFI quarters.

Southwick village is a quiet, sophisticated Hampshire village with a couple of pubs. At the bottom of the main drive is the Golden Lion; at the village end of the back drive is the Red Lion. With typical Naval brevity they are known respectively as the 'Gold' and the 'Red'. While relatively similar in both decor and standard of service, they attract quite different clientele. The Gold is the preferred place for those who live in Married Quarters as it has a room where children can play. The Red is the place for us hardened drinkers as it sells Scrumpy for less than a bob a pint.

Lash and I are enjoying a couple of pints of 'Scrumps' at the Red.

'You'll never guess who the killick in charge of the dredging party is,' says Lash between gulps.

'Who?'

'Potter the Plotter.' Lash burps. 'Remember, the bloke who welcomed us to Dryad in sixty one? The bloke on the bus wearing the eye patch and pretending to be Long John Silver.'

'Yeah.'

'He's medically unfit for sea and has been in *Dryad* for the last three and a half years.'

I buy our third round. The woman behind the bar gives me change without looking up. She's nothing much to look at herself.

Lash takes his normal large slurp of his fresh pint and taps the table top. 'Is Wilco duty tonight then?'

'Lash, I enjoy your ferkin company, but do you honestly think I would be here now if she wasn't working?'

'Not really.'

'Nothing personal, you understand.'

'I understand.'

'So Potter the Plotter is a bit of a Sick Bay ranger then?' I ask.

'Appears to be – claims he suffers from acute sea-sickness.'

'And he gets away with that?'

'Apparently.'

A group of well-oiled lads swing into the bar fresh from their stroll down the back drive. One of them points an arm at me as he slumps down into a chair opposite. 'Wilco not wiv ya then?'

'Don't be a ferkin idiot,' says one of his mates. 'Who do you think has been pulling pints for you in the *Dryad* Canteen for the past hour and a half?'

Someone turns the jukebox volume up as another group staggers in.

It is a brilliant evening. Many powerful toilet stops punctuate the return journey up the back drive.

Along with a group of others who are soon to join ships in the tropics, I am sent down to Portsmouth to be issued with my tropical kit. In a Store Room in the bowels of *HMS Victory* barracks, an unsmiling civilian wearing a grubby brown overall coat issues me with my tropical kit. Two uniform white duck jackets incorporating a blue collar, two pairs of white bell-bottomed duck trousers, two pairs of white shorts, four pairs of long white socks, a pair of white canvas shoes and a couple of additional white fronts.

Then, as a motley group carrying bundles of badly folded tropical uniforms, we are shepherded over to the Sick Bay.

I'm not prepared for this. I'm jabbed a number of times: one is particularly painful as it's badly administered by a bespectacled, spotty individual with a persistent cough. Before I leave, I'm issued with a folded yellow paper that catalogues all my jabs.

Back in Ross 6 mess I examine my Tropical kit more closely. The uniform jacket and trousers are yellow-white and extremely stiff. Tansy suggests I give them to my mother when I go home on leave. Apparently washing out the yellow is best left to the professionals.

It's only a week until Summer Leave. My perforated arm is bruised.

I show Wilco all my inoculation marks and my yellow folded certificate later that evening. She calls me her hero and tells me to 'Lie back and think of England'. So that's exactly what I do.

Before I go on leave, Wilco tells me that she has officially made inquiries about a transfer to the NAAFI in Singapore. Apparently she's not the only NAAFI girl who fancies a tropical posting and is now tagged on the end of a rather lengthy NAAFI queue.

I buy myself one of those green Pusser's suitcases with reinforced brown leather corners. I need it to take all my tropical kit home.

At home in Pudsey, everything is relatively normal. I give Mum the four quid 'bed and board' money. Both Mum and Tony are speechless when I tell them that I'm going to Singapore in October.

'Will you be sailing all the way there?' Mum asks.

I'd not thought about that. 'Dunno.'

'Where is Singapore then?' asks Tony.

'Somewhere tropical,' I know it's on the end of Malaya about a sixteenth of an inch north of the equator on page 76 of our Reader's Digest World Atlas, but I don't want to sound too knowledgeable.

'It's an island at the bottom of the Malayan Peninsular isn't it?' Tony asks.

'Somewhere near there, yeah.'

At Mum's insistence, I struggle into my white tropical uniform. Surprisingly, the 'off the cuff' measurements I had given the bloke in *Victory* were reasonably accurate, as it fits with a little room for growth. The jacket doesn't have a front zip and the trousers incorporate a ridiculously complicated front flap design. Both the trousers and jacket smell of long, musty storage.

Mrs Shufflebottom, a purple-haired lady who owns the local haberdashery shop and is a whiz with needle and thread, is contracted to make my tropical uniform fit me like a glove ... once it has been washed.

Mum is confident that she can get the altered uniforms sparkly clean and in contravention of a Pudsey tradition, does a special wash for me on a Thursday morning. At dinnertime, our washing line is hoisted to display two tropical white uniforms, two pairs of white shorts, four pairs of knee-length white stockings, four white fronts and a couple of pairs of white 'Y' fronts. They all swing and drip in a sultry mid-week summer breeze for everybody to see. Residents of Robin Lane look on in disbelief at a full Thursday washing line. A photographer from the *Pudsey Evening News* is summoned.

Mrs Shufflebottom, known to us lads as something quite different, licks her lips as she snaps her tape measure. She coughs nervously as she kneels down in front of me to measure my inside leg. She measures it twice just to make sure she has it right. 'That's a good inside leg you have there, Peter my lad.'

'Thanks.'

'The best 31½" I've have the pleasure of measuring since ... since I don't remember when.'

'Really?'

'I will see you in your uniform after I've made the alterations, won't I?'

'Of course.'

On Saturday morning, she scuttles up to the shop to see me in my washed, ironed and altered uniform. I look a little like the blokes I'd seen in the recruitment posters all those years ago ... without the eye-catching sun tan of course.

She claps her hands joyfully. 'My my oh ... my!'

Mum looks on, proudly silent. 'He's going to Singapore in October.'

'Singapore, really?' says Shufflebottom. 'Where is that exactly?'

'It's near Malaya,' says Mum.

'Only a few miles north of the equator,' I add.

'Bet it's ferkin hot there then,' says Shufflebottom.

We all look at her in disbelief. Shufflebottom swears!

'Just look at how those trousers hang ... absolutely perfect,' she says. 'Absolutely ferkin perfect.'

The shop bell rings. Mum scuttles away and I am alone with Shufflebottom.

'Thanks for the alterations Mrs Shuffle ... err ... Shufflebottom.'

'You are most welcome,' she grabs me around the shoulders and gives me a kiss on my starboard cheek. Her lips stick briefly. 'You are most welcome. I'm glad to have done my bit to help you brave boys travelling to the other side of the world to protect our interests.'

Thankfully she has nothing else to say and she shuffles away.

Mum returns, having quickly dealt with her customer. 'What's that on your cheek?' she asks.

'Shufflebottom gave me a kiss.'

'I'll have a word with her later,' says a serious looking Mum. 'She has a mouth on her as well, swearing like that ... disgusting. Where does she think she is?'

'Pudsey.'

As I'm due to be travelling to exotic places, I buy myself a grey made-to-measure suit with scarlet lining from John Collier's, the current Tailors of Distinction, in Leeds. They make a special, extra ten-shilling effort to have the suit fitted and ready before my leave ends.

Leaving home for eighteen months isn't that much of a wrench. Apart from family, I no longer have any real friends in Pudsey and the fact that I'm going to Singapore helps me leave with an expectant spring in my step. I shall miss Wilco of course, but if she manages to get a transfer to Singapore ... well.

I promise Mum that I will look after myself and that I will write regularly.

'Watch that foreign sun, Peter.'

'I will Mum,' I reply, and I really mean it. I'm going to love all the sun that Singapore can throw at me.

Tony is a bit jealous.

I'm careful how I fold my tropical uniform up in my suitcase.

'You didn't bring your Seamanship book home this time,' says Mum.

In the privacy of her small self-contained unit, with the curtains drawn and the door locked and bolted, Wilco brings me up to date with all the latest NAAFI news. She hangs her overall on a wire hanger and hooks it over the curtain rail. Wilco out of her NAAFI overall is a sight-and-a-half. She bounces onto the bed and runs a well-manicured fingernail down the centre of my bared chest. 'We're going to get a jukebox.'

'Who ... you and me?' I ask, wide eyed.

'No. The NAAFI, silly.'

'What, for the canteen?'

'Naah. We're going to put it in the centre of the Parade Ground.'

'Really?'

'Peter!'

I can become a bit befuddled when faced with a semi-naked female. 'I don't really ...'

'For the Canteen ... but we're only allowed to plug it in during stand-easy and between 19:00 and 22:00 in the evening ... and never on a Sunday.'

'Never on a Sunday eh?' I twang something pink and elasticated. Jukebox discussion over and done with.

The jukebox is set up by a team of NAAFI installation Engineers the following Sunday. During Monday morning's stand-easy a queue forms, eager to pay for the rest of us to listen to the most popular records of the time: according to NAAFI. 'Telstar' by The Tornadoes is played more than once. It's nice to have music to accompany NAAFI tea and a cheese roll.

At exactly 10:30 Wilco marches over to the machine and unplugs it mid way through 'Loco-Motion' by Little Eva.

There is a chorus of polite boos and hissing.

'Only doing what I'm told,' she says, her arms held wide in supplication.

'NAAFI rules are NAAFI rules,' says 'Potter the Plotter' as he tries to usher everybody out.

The following week I join all the other Radar Plotters drafted to *HMS Lincoln* for Pre Commissioning Training. We spend time playing simulated war-games in dark claustrophobic rooms designed to look like those that we will experience onboard. As a Basic Radar Plotter, my contribution is relatively unimportant. We visit *HMS Vernon* (the Anti-Submarine School in Portsmouth) and *HMS Mercury* (the Communication School at Petersfield).

Our Senior Radar Plotter is a Petty Officer called Rogers who, despite his rank, appears to be a reasonably considerate bloke. My Radar Plotting skills don't impress anybody.

I spend the whole of my final night at *Dryad* with Wilco. Being together overnight is a risky business: I am in breach of a stack of Queen's Regulations, Admiralty Instructions and *HMS Dryad* standing orders. Wilco, for her part, flouts a whole catalogue of NAAFI rules and if discovered, would lose her job. But we're reasonably quiet about things and we get away with it.

In the morning, there are gushing tears. Wilco dries my eyes on a wodge of NAAFI napkins before we hug and say a final farewell. We both double check that the coast is clear as I sneak out before 'Charlie'.

'I'm definitely going to find myself a job in Singapore,' she whispers.

'That will be brilliant.'

'Keep an eye out for me.'

'I will.' I sneak one last kiss.

'I'll write you loads of sexy letters.'

'Please do.'

In the dining hall I say a fond farewell to Tug who has been a friend since those early days in the *Ganges* Annexe. He doesn't have a draft yet. Misty Melrose has a draft to *HMS Albion* next week and we hope to meet up sometime in Singers.

Resplendent in my new John Collier's suit with my passport in my pocket, I muster outside the clock-tower with my kit bag. In the distance I spot a NAAFI-uniformed Wilco waving me farewell. There are a few unrepeatable comments from my new shipmates standing alongside me. Self-consciously I wave back.

An unknown someone places an arm around my shoulder. 'All good things come to an end, young 'un.'

Along with others drafted to *HMS Lincoln* I throw my tagged kit bag and suitcase, containing everything I own, into the back of a Naval truck and board a blue Naval bus bound for *RAF Stansted*. It's a dull, overcast day. My Far East adventure begins in a Pusser's blue bus with a less than perfect gearbox.

It's a relatively subdued and quiet journey. I try to catch up on last night's lost sleep but I can't: I'm too excited.

RAF Stansted is a small collection of Nissan huts among the flat Essex countryside. On arrival we unload our kit bags and suitcases into a paler blue RAF truck before being ushered into a Briefing Room. Lash and I sit next to each other. There is a small group of individuals taking the forthcoming journey in its stride and making merry. During the following hours, others join us. Altogether, I suppose, there are over a hundred of us. Petty Officer Rogers and the other Senior Rates have to tell us more than once to calm down as we are getting bored just sitting around smoking.

Eventually a bloke wearing an RAF uniform, with sergeant's stripes, faces us. 'Welcome to RAF Stansted. Have any of you flown before? Not necessarily with the Royal Air Force but with anybody?'

Almost all of the Senior Rates on the front row put their hands up.

The Sergeant smiles. 'You will be accommodated here overnight as your flight is scheduled for an early morning departure tomorrow. A late lunch-stroke-tea will be available in the dining halls for the remainder of the afternoon. A late supper will be available from 20:00 hours. Breakfast will be provided from 04:30 hours in the morning. I suggest that you control the amount of alcohol intake this evening. Dehydration during a long flight can be very uncomfortable.'

'What time are we scheduled to take off tomorrow, Sergeant?' asks a front-row Petty Officer.

'Approximately 06:00 hours. Your aircraft for the flight to Singapore is a Bristol Brittania that has a cruising speed of 350 knots, has a service ceiling of 24,000 feet and a range of 4,400 miles. Any other questions?'

Someone behind me coughs to clear his throat. 'Will we have any air hostesses onboard?'

The Sergeant smiles. 'The Royal Air Force will do everything we can to make your flight with us as enjoyable as possible.'

'Will there be alcohol available onboard the aircraft?' someone else asks.

'No.'

One of the Petty Officers stands. 'Singapore is much further away than the range of your aircraft, so where will we be refuelling?'

The Sergeant consults his clipboard. 'As far as I know, tomorrow's flight is scheduled to stop at Istanbul and Bombay ... but that is subject to change.'

I nudge Lash in the ribs. 'Istan ferkin bull and Bombay, did you hear that?'

'I did, yeah.'

'Remain in your seats. Flight Lieutenant Wentworth will tell you about the political situation in the Far East. Thank you.'

We wait as Flight Lieutenant Wentworth takes centre stage. He consults his watch. 'Good afternoon gentlemen.'

Gentlemen?

'I notice that most of the younger contingent ...'

'Are we a contingent?' whispers Lash.

'Suppose we are, yeah,' I say. 'I know this bloke ... he was at *RAF Wattisham* when we broke in that weekend at *Ganges*. You should have heard what the WRAFs had to say about him.'

Flight Lieutenant Wentworth glares at me and Lash. 'If I can continue uninterrupted ... please,' he coughs into a fisted hand. 'I notice that some of the younger contingent are inappropriately dressed. The current temperature in Singapore is 96 degrees Fahrenheit. In Bombay it will be much the same.'

'That's nice then,' whispers Lash.

Flight Lieutenant Wentworth continues. 'As a part of the planned United Kingdom's withdrawal from its Southeast Asian colonies, the UK is attempting to combine the colonies of North Borneo with the Federation of Malaya. You may remember that the Federation of Malaya became independent from Britain in 1957 and Singapore became self-governing two years later in 1959.' Flight Lieutenant Wentworth consults a piece of paper.

This all sounds complicated: I wonder what all this has to do with the price of beer in Singapore.

Flight Lieutenant Wentworth coughs and continues. 'In May last year the United Kingdom and the Malayan governments proposed a larger federation called Malaysia, encompassing the states of Malaya, North Borneo, Sarawak, Brunei, and Singapore. Initially, Indonesia was supportive of this proposal although the Indonesian Communist Party was strongly opposed to it.' He consults his paper again.

Surely all this isn't going to affect us in any way.

'The Sultan of Brunei is not enthusiastic about joining Malaysia because his vast oil revenues ensure that his country is financially independent.' Flight Lieutenant Wentworth folds his paper and pockets it. 'Any questions?'

Silence. Obviously it isn't just Lash and I who are confused.

'Very good. Enjoy your flight.' Flight Lieutenant Wentworth struts away.

I spend an uneventful night in rather plush RAF surroundings. The mess television is on but I don't pay much attention to it. Tansy, who has been to the Far East before, gives Lash and I his opinions of Singapore and Hong Kong. He says more than once that it's going to be hotter than we imagine, but I don't believe him. I've experienced some really hot West Yorkshire days as a young lad.

In the morning I tuck in to what I think will be my last fried breakfast for some time. We are corralled through passport and boarding formalities and wait in sober anticipation in a bar that is shuttered and closed. Lash and I are sitting alongside a young lad called Charlie from the Communication branch.

'You ever flown before, Pete?' asks Charlie.

'Never.'

'Must be safe though eh? Everybody's doing it these days, aren't they?'

'Suppose so, yeah.'

I'm both apprehensive and excited. My stomach is doing all sorts of gymnastics as I walk across the tarmac to board the waiting aircraft.

'Big aeroplane, isn't it? asks Charlie.

'Tis ... yeah.'

On board the aircraft, we stuff our coats and jackets into lockers above our heads and sit in nervous silence waiting for something to happen. I sit next to a window and Charlie is alongside me.

'What do you think will happen first, Pete?'

'Suppose we'll take off.'

'After that I mean.'

'Don't know. Haven't got a clue.'

'Nor me.'

There is a chattering buzz amongst us. An RAF bloke, with two stripes on his arm, strolls up and down the central aisle. 'Make sure that all your loose equipment such as coats or jackets are correctly stowed in the overhead lockers and that your seat belt is correctly fastened. I will shortly be giving a safety briefing and I want you all to pay attention. Please, no smoking until I say you can.'

Silence.

I clearly hear the words 'safety' and 'safely'.

'Before our first refuelling stop in Istanbul you will be given a pre-packed luncheon ...'

'What's ferkin luncheon?' someone from the back asks.

'My apologies,' says the corporal. 'Din-dins to you Navy lads.'

'Cheers corporal,' says a bloke from the back.

The corporal grins. 'In the event of an emergency you are to remain seated and take instructions from the crew. Your individual lifejackets are stowed under your seat. Thank you for your time.'

'So an RAF luncheon is dinner then?' Charlie asks me.

'Must be.'

Another RAF bloke stands in the centre aisle and shows us how to put a life jacket on. Apparently some of the journey will be over water. I only pay part attention: I've put plenty of life jackets on in my time.

'I need the heads, corporal,' says Lash who is seated behind Charlie.

The RAF bloke with a life jacket round his neck tells Lash that he will have to wait until we are safely airborne.

There's that word 'safely' again.

I sit and stare out of the window as the aircraft slowly trundles its way somewhere. I grip my seat and am dying for a cigarette.

The aircraft comes to a halt. There is a short period of contemplative silence and then the engines roar.

Bloody hell!

I am forced back in my seat as we shoot down what I hope is the runway. Then we leave terra firma behind. RAF Stansted becomes smaller and smaller and ever so small ... then we are enveloped in what I hope is thick, grey cloud.

Charlie says 'Shit!'

'Yeah, shit!' I confirm.

Then we emerge into clear blue sky. I look down and can see bundles of clouds below me and through the gaps I can see the most amazing atlas: roads, fields, houses all laid out like a full colour map. I'm amazed.

'How high do you think we are, Pete?'

'I don't ferkin know, do I?' I'm beginning to realise that everything Charlie has to say ends in a question mark.

The RAF corporal strides up and down the aisle telling us that we can unfasten our seat belts, we can smoke and the toilets are at the back end.

Lash returns from an anxious visit to the heads. 'Heads are crap.'

'Why exactly?' asks Charlie.

'Too small, can't flush the ferkin thing and there's no hot water.'

'No hot water?'

'No.'

'Memories of Bermuda's water rationing then?'

'Exactly.'

Within half an hour we are over the sea.

'Is that the Atlantic do you think, Pete?' asks Charlie.

'English Channel probably.'

'Do you think it will be all right to have a sleep, Pete?'

'I'm sure it will be.'

'There's no women ... air hostesses ... by the look of it then?'

'Doesn't look like it.'

A couple of hours later I step over Charlie and go to the heads. On my way back a lad who is doing press-ups on the back of a seat stops me. 'See you're sitting next to Asker.'

'Is that his name?'

'We call him Asker because he's always asking questions.'

'Yeah ... I've noticed.'

'He'll get on your ferkin nerves eventually.'

'He has already.'

'Just ignore him – he gets the message eventually.'

Once back in my seat I go to sleep.

I am woken by an RAF bloke speaking to us. 'Please take your seats gentlemen. We will shortly be giving out packed Din-dins before landing at Istanbul for a short refuelling stop.'

The packed dinner is OK. For pudding, we have a bun with cream and jam. We have ten minutes to enjoy an after-meal smoke before being told to extinguish our cigarettes and to strap ourselves into our seats for a landing.

The same RAF bloke speaks to us again. 'Unfortunately we are not allowed to leave the aircraft while in Istanbul, so we will all have to remain onboard. Please obey the smoking restrictions while we are on the ground. For those of you with watches who would like to keep track of time, we will be two hours ahead of Greenwich Mean Time. The local time in Istanbul is exactly 12:50 hours.'

I turn my watch two hours forward. The ground below us gets nearer and nearer. There is no cloud. I can see buildings, then roads, then individual cars, then people, then ... thump ... screech! Through the window I see clouds of black smoke. We slow to a sensible speed and trundle our way through fields of broken, brown vegetation, passing a large building flanked by lines of buses.

We stop. After a quarter of an hour a fuel tanker pulls up alongside and stuffs a large fuelling hose into an external orifice. The temperature inside the aircraft is gradually increasing and many of us remove our ties and unbutton our collars.

'Getting hot isn't it, Pete?'

I nod.

'Where is Istanbul exactly?'

'Turkey.'

'Is it really?'

'Yeah.'

'Turkey?'

I nod.

'So we're actually in Turkey then?'

I close my eyes.

Istanbul airport is a no smoking zone so we sit in a metal tube getting hotter and hotter ... without a fag. I open my packet of extra length Duty Free Woodbines and sniff them: it doesn't help.

Just before 14:30 local time, we are fuelled and ready to go.

My second take-off experience is much the same as the first except there is no cloud.

When permitted, I light a cigarette and relax. We fly over large areas of brown, seemingly uninhabited land with the occasional patch of bright blue water. Thankfully, Asker has fallen into a deep, snoring sleep. I purposefully don't wake him when the corporal comes round with a kettle of tea.

I fall asleep as it's getting dark and I'm getting bored with looking down on large tracts of brown land. The small ashtray in the arm of my seat is overflowing. I start to use Asker's.

I awake as the corporal slaps a pre-packed meal on my lap. 'We'll be landing in Bombay in about an hour. Local time is 01:35 hours.'

I mumble a thank you and change the time on my watch.

It's pitch black outside. I haven't moved out of my seat for five hours since my last visit to the heads.

'We'll be on the ground at Bombay for a couple of hours to give you the chance to stretch your sea legs.' He laughs at his joke. There is a grumble of appreciation throughout the plane.

We drop like a stone and hit the ground with a screech of brakes followed by a series of alarming slews. A number of wobbles and squeals follow as flaps on the wing are adjusted. The inner bulkhead linings and the deck vibrate as we come to a stop.

'That was a bit scary wasn't it, Pete?' says Asker.

'Uncomfortable that's for sure.'

'So this is Bombay then?'

I nod.

Our comical Corporal reappears. 'Refreshments will be provided once you leave the aircraft. Make sure that you don't wander outside the confines of the hangar building. Smoking is allowed once you are inside the hangar. Your valuables will be safe onboard the aircraft as the flight crew will remain onboard. The outside temperature is 82 degrees Fahrenheit.'

'That's hot isn't it, Pete?'

'Yeah.'

'It's the middle of the night isn't it?'

One of the doors at the front is opened and I get my first smell of India.

'Pongs a bit don't it, Pete?'

Out of the door and on the top of the steps leading to the ground a wave of hot air hits me. For a moment I think it's the exhaust from the engine but it isn't – it's night-time India. By the time I've walked the short distance to the adjacent hangar, I'm sweating. This is what an Indian 82 degrees Fahrenheit feels like. I'm looking forward to a nice cold beer.

I unfasten two extra shirt buttons: I feel no cooler.

I suppose the RAF have learned from experience not to ply the Royal Navy with free alcohol, so they have organised tea, soft drinks, biccies and not much else. We group around a small table in the centre of a large, dilapidated hangar with filthy walls, and equally grimy windows set high near the ceiling. Impassive uniformed Indians stand around the walls, watching us.

We laugh and joke. Some of the old hands who have visited Bombay before tell stories of erotic females and strange Indian customs.

'Bombay is a great run ashore ... if you know where to go, that is.'

'Not as good as Singers though ...'

'Naah. Until you've spent all night down Bugis Street ... you haven't lived.'

'There's this place near Change Alley where for a couple of Singapore dollars and a smile you can get ...'

'Beware of the beer. Until you get used to Tiger, it will knock your ferkin head off ...'

'Singapore is great ... but save your money for Hong Kong: the women there are unbelievable. Couple of years ago, for a bar of Pears soap ...'

'If we ever get down to North Borneo ... there's a place called Tawau ...'

'Bombay's OK though ...'

'Yeah, downtown Bombay is unbelievable.'

We're eventually ushered back onboard, strapped in, smoking prohibited and ready for the final leg of our journey.

'Our final leg will take approximately seven hours. We should land at Singapore in the mid afternoon local time,' says the RAF corporal, looking increasingly tired.

'We still haven't got any women air hostesses onboard have we, Pete?'

'Doesn't look like it does it?' Asker is really getting on my nerves.

I sleep until my pre packed breakfast is plonked in my lap. I've filled Asker's ashtray as well as my own. I spend the next hours gazing at the Far East laid out below me. I'm fascinated by the canopy of verdant green and the small clearings in which

I can see brown roofed huts. When I see the coast below it's fringed with bright strips of golden sand.

The pre-packed breakfast is disappointing.

We slither onto RAF Changi's sun-soaked runway with barely a thump on Thursday 11 October 1962. Our journey is over. I'm told to put my watch forward another two and a half hours.

'Welcome to RAF Changi, Singapore,' says the corporal. 'Please remain in your seats until instructed to disembark. May your tour of duty in Singapore be a pleasant and rewarding one. Best of luck to you all. Please check that you have got all your personal possessions – this aircraft will be refuelled, checked and back in the air within three hours.'

'So this is Singapore then?' asks Asker.

I ignore him.

I make sure that I'm separated from Asker by at least six people as we disembark.

2

AN AGREEABLE TERROR

My first impression of Singapore is a weird and wonderful mixture of vivid colour and deep, strange smells. The heat is unbelievable. I take deep breaths as my Yorkshire lungs struggle with the humid atmosphere. I remove my jacket and undo the cuffs of my shirt. Everything is so vibrant – the grass is the greenest green I'd ever seen. There is an overpowering smell of rubber and the white airport building we are being ushered towards is the whitest white I'd ever seen. I see my first palm tree up close.

We queue to clear customs. Outside, we are corralled into a reasonable organised bunch and wait under the glaring sun for our transport. A clutch of Petty Officers patrols our periphery. Within minutes my shirt is sticking to my chest and our transport arrives only minutes before I was going to make a bolt for some shade. We load our bags and cases into a series of familiar blue Naval buses. I don't move quickly enough to get a seat and have to stand among the unstable piles of kit bags and suitcases placed down the central aisle. Comfortably astride someone's kitbag, I strain to see out of the windows: we pass groups of strange wooden buildings among the lush green tropical vegetation on both sides of the road. Small, open-fronted wooden shops, roofed with corrugated tin or large leaves, flash by in a psychedelic blur. Surprisingly, everybody – men, women and spindly legged children – is wearing ankle-length, figure-hugging skirts. This colourful, exotic panorama is a living, moving and extremely hot page from one of Mr Parry's *National Geographic* magazines.

Eventually we arrive at *HMS Terror*, the Royal Naval barracks for Singapore. My shirt is like a wet rag and my limp John Collier's suit has lost its Yorkshire constitution. We are ushered into a large room with a number of rotating fans hanging from the deckhead: it's surprisingly cool. The Senior Rates occupy the front row of chairs, leaving the benches for the rest of us.

Eventually a bronzed Lieutenant dressed in a white shirt, shorts, long white stockings and white shoes appears in front of us. There are creases down the front and back of his perfectly laundered knee-length shorts.

One of the Petty Officers calls us to attention. We fold our arms and sit up straight until told to 'Carry On.'

The Lieutenant slowly scans our faces. 'Good afternoon everybody. I know that you have had a long flight so I won't keep you long. My name is Lieutenant Lamin: I want to give you some simple information about Singapore and what *HMS Lincoln*'s projected programme will be ... as we currently understand it. Geographically the Island of Singapore is located sixty miles north of the equator. Give or take a few minutes, it has twelve hours of daylight each day ... and therefore twelve hours of darkness. Every day the sun rises at approximately 06:00 and sets at about 18:00. Although at certain times of the year Singapore experiences periods of wet weather known as monsoons, her days are mostly hot, dry and extremely humid.' He points to one of the windows. 'This weather is what you will experience most days so you need to get used to it and acclimatise yourselves. Paludrine tablets are available in the dining hall at meal times – you are required to take one each day to prevent catching malaria. Any questions so far?'

A few coughs but no questions.

'There must be some questions.' Lieutenant Lamin scans everybody.

Asker puts his hand up.

'Yes, lad.'

'What is the average temperature in Singapore, sir?'

Lieutenant Lamin stares at Asker and shakes his head. 'I don't know the exact figure off the top of my head. I should imagine it's well over 80 degrees during the day and not that much cooler at night.'

Asker still has his hand up. 'What about in the wet weather, sir?'

Lieutenant Lamin makes the mistake of asking Asker a question. 'What about the wet weather?'

'Is it cooler then, sir – when it's wet?'

'No,' replies Lieutenant Lamin. 'What is your name, lad ... and who is your Divisional Officer?'

'Radio Operator third class Atkins, sir. I don't know who my Divisional Officer is. Can you let me know, sir?'

'I'll make sure that the Communications Officer has a word with you, RO Atkins. Now if there are no further questions I'll continue with a subject that you will all be interested in – the ship's programme.'

There is a mumble of agreement from the floor. The Petty Officer who had called us to attention at the start of the talk stands and glares at us. 'Silence!'

Lieutenant Lamin nods towards the Petty Officer. 'Thank you Petty Officer, I can deal with this.' He coughs into a fist. 'Lincoln's programme. She is currently in the dockyard undergoing planned maintenance that is scheduled to be complete after Christmas. During this period you will all be accommodated in HMS Terror. The watch and Station bill, detailing individual jobs and duties, will be posted on the Dining Hall notice board tomorrow morning. In Singapore we work tropical routine, 07:00 until 13:00. There is a 24 hour shuttle bus service that runs between the dockyard and HMS Terror's main gate. Any questions?'

Asker's hand shoots up like a missile. 'Do we finish for the day at one-o-clock in the afternoon then, sir?'

'Yes you do unless you are duty Radio Operator ... third class ... Atkins.'

'Thank you, sir,' mumbles Asker as he reluctantly lowers his arm.

A Petty Officer turns in his chair, his neck straining as he searches for Asker.

Lieutenant Lamin continues. 'Now a few words of warning. I know that some of you have been to Singapore before and I expect you to look after those who are new to this part of the world. Beware the local Tiger beer: it's refreshingly good but takes a bit of getting used to. Do not sit in this sun in the hope of getting an instant suntan. The Singapore sun will burn you in minutes and it is a punishable offence to purposefully inflict damage upon yourselves. My suggestion is to stay in barracks for the first week or so to acclimatise yourselves. There is a well-equipped Canteen here, called the Armada Club, where the Tiger beer is a good deal cheaper than you will find outside the dockyard area. Once again, I expect those of you who have been here before to look after the others. Rig of the day if you are going ashore is smart civilian clothing for Able Rates and above. Number 10As for Junior and Ordinary rates before 18:00 and 6As, white uniform trousers and a clean white front, for leave after 18:00. Remember that going ashore in civilian clothing is a privilege that can be withdrawn. Any questions?'

Silence. The bloke sitting next to Asker drapes an arm over Asker's shoulder, preventing him from raising his hand.

'Members of the Advance Party will show you where your accommodation is. Thank you.'

A Petty Officer calls us to attention as Lieutenant Lamin takes his leave.

An elderly Petty Officer takes to the floor to tell us that both watches will muster tomorrow onboard *HMS Lincoln* at 07:00. Anybody not onboard at that time will be in the rattle. The last shuttle bus to get us onboard on time in the morning will leave *Terror*'s main gate at exactly 06:30. He asks if there are any questions.

Askers hand shoots up.

The Petty Officer is prepared. He points at Asker. 'If you're going to ask me to confirm something I've already explained, then don't waste your breath. You'll find me a lot less understanding than Lieutenant Lamin.'

Asker rotates his raised hand.

'Go on then, lad. Ask away,' says a glaring Petty Officer.

'Err … I've forgotten, sir.'

The Petty Officer waves an arm towards a bloke sitting on the front row.

He sits down as a Chief Petty Officer stands up and tells us once again about the importance of taking the daily Paludrine tablet. 'Don't take more than one each day. Don't stock-pile tablets – there are plenty to go around. Any questions?' He glares at Asker. The bloke sitting next to Asker has him in a Full Nelson. Asker is burgundy with frustration.

We collect our kit bags and suitcases and carry them over to our ground floor accommodation in one of the three Junior Rates' Blocks bordering the Parade Ground. The messes are refreshingly different: long white and spacious, with large bladed fans set at intervals in the high deckhead. Down each side are doubled tiered bunks, each pair separated by a pale blue painted louvered door that opens to the outside. Alongside each pair of bunks are a couple of large wooden lockers the size of a walk-in wardrobe: luxury.

I grab a top bunk and look around to make sure that Asker isn't anywhere near me. The bloke who settles himself on the bed below mine is an Able Seaman gunner.

'What's yewer name?'

'Pete Broadbent.'

'Known as?'

'Err ... Pete.'

'You an AB?'

'No – Ordinary Seaman.'

'Right then. I'm Able Seaman Frank Kidd. Known as Gringo.'

'Gringo, right,' I say.

'So what do I call yew?' Gringo asks.

'Pete will be OK.'

'Pete it is then. Don't suppose yewer old enough to 'ave bin out to this part of t'world before are ya?

'Nope.'

'Nor me. My last ship was Eagle – we never got this far east. What was your last ship?

'Bermuda, then we got transferred onto Belfast for her last trip.'

'She was a bastard, so I heard.'

'Aaah, it wasn't that bad once you got used to it.'

'Are you from Yorkshire?'

'Yeah ... Pudsey.'

'I'm from Ull.'

'Hull?'I ask.

'Aye.' He looks at my arm. 'You're a ferkin Radar Plotter?'

'Yeah.'

'Come on then, Peter the Plotter, let's 'ave a wander – see what we can find.'

So we have a quick wander to get our bearings. Our block runs the full length of one side of the Parade ground. Paths snake away between areas of vibrant, large-leafed grassed areas and colourful flowerbeds. It's overbearingly hot and there is a continual buzzing and chirping sound everywhere.

HMS Terror accommodation

Back in the mess I spot a lizard on the wall above my locker. It's about six inches long, nose to tail, and it's staring directly at me.

'There's a ferkin lizard on the ferkin wall,' I exclaim to Gringo. I point to the intruder as it scuttles away and disappears through the louvers of the adjacent door.

'It isn't a lizard. It's probably a Chit-Chat. On t'Eagle we spent some time int Seychelles, the place was crawling with Chit-Chats. They're harmless. We had a few who lived int mess curled up int damp mess cloths.'

'Chit-chats eh?'

'Their official Latin name is Gecko but they're known throughout t'mob as Chit-Chats.'

As I'm packing my kit in my wonderfully spacious wardrobe locker, I'm slapped on the shoulder.

'Hi there, young 'un.' It's Skid Marks. We were in the same mess onboard Bermuda. 'I've found Lash and Tansy. We're going down the Armada Club for a beer. Fancy it?'

'You're not onboard Lincoln are ya?'

'Cav' ... Cavalier. Been here for a month. Our mess is the next floor up. Coming then?'

'Yep.'

'Best to get acquainted with the delightful Tiger as soon as possible,' explains a serious-looking Skid. He points at Gringo. 'Bring your mate with you.'

Gringo and I join Skid and we collect a few other *Lincoln* lads who are already strolling down a flower-bordered pathway towards the Armada Club.

The Armada Club

The Armada Club is a large open-fronted white building furnished with bamboo chairs and bamboo-legged tables. Large-bladed deckhead fans rotate slowly. Immediately opposite the Club is a football pitch that has tiered seating on two sides and floodlight pylons on each corner. I join Skid at the bar and he orders five pints and one 'top'. The beer is squirted into robust ribbed pint glasses from a hand-held gun. The top of the bar is awash with puddles of beer. The beer smells strange. The barman adds a splash of something to one of the pints. Skid pays for them with what I reckon is Singapore money. Around the table everybody is introduced. There is a bloke called Popeye who has been on a previous ship with Skid who has been out here for two weeks as a member of *Lincoln*'s Advance Party. Tansy, Lash, Gringo and myself make up the remainder of the group.

My first taste of Tiger is disappointing. It's cold and tastes like nothing I'd ever experienced before.

'You'll get used to it, young 'un,' says Skid.

'What's the top you ordered at the bar?' I ask.

'A splash of lemonade. That's for Popeye, who can't take his drink.'

'I ferkin can,' replies Popeye.

I understand why Popeye is called Popeye: he looks exactly like his cartoon namesake even down to the tattooed anchor on his forearm.

'Only joking, mate.' Skid looks around. 'You'll have to excuse Popeye, he's a Janner.'

'Aaaah from Guzz then?'

'Yep.'

By the end of my second pint I'm beginning to appreciate the numbing qualities of Tiger beer.

Skid is about to get the third round in when a Petty Officer wearing his cap appears at our table.

'HMS Lincoln new commission?' he asks Tansy, who is the oldest looking because he has less hair than the rest of us.

'Yes, PO.'

'Have you all unpacked your kit, ready for tomorrow?' He looks at each of us in turn.

Nobody says yes.

'If I were you I'd get back to the mess and sort yourselves out before you start throwing Tigers down your necks. I've got your names,' and he storms away.

'He hasn't got our names,' says Tansy.

I sleep well despite the heat and wake up with my very first Tiger hangover. Everybody else appears bright-eyed and bushy-tailed and ready for breakfast.

Working rig is a number 8 shirt, dark blue shorts and sandals. Pusser's shorts are totally impractical; neither short nor long and made from an inflexible material that chafes the inside of my legs and rubs violently against the back of my knees. This, however, is a relatively insignificant problem when compared to the pain of Pusser's sandals – a strange 'unbending' type of footwear manufactured from some extremely abrasive material that's 100% guaranteed to cut and blister the toughest of feet. One of the lads at the bottom of the mess puts his socks on under his sandals but is quickly told to take them off.

'Where do you think you are … ferkin Blackpool?' says someone with an authoritative voice.

Breakfast in the spacious, cool-white dining hall is wonderful, despite the water, tea, cornflakes and milk all tasting different. For the first time in my life I have a choice of flavoured milk: chocolate, banana, strawberry and so on. An exotic array of chilled, clean fruit is available. Local staff, dressed in immaculate white uniforms, pour ice-cold fresh fruit juices for us. I ignore the option of a full English breakfast and remember to take my Paludrine tablet from the bowl on the end of the serving counter.

I catch the crowded 06:30 bus: I don't get a seat and have to stand. *HMS Lincoln* is a sorry sight. Part-way through a dockyard refit, she looks like a floating scrapyard. Electric cables, air lines and flexible ventilation pipes snake under and around items of machinery that litter every available part of the upper deck. Even at 07:00 in the morning, the noise of pneumatic hammers, chisels and grinders is deafening. Deckhead and bulkhead panels have been removed, exposing the 'spaghetti' of pipes, trunks and wiring. Everything is filthy. Toolboxes, portable pumps, fans, rags and a hundred and one other items of equipment clutter the passageways. There is no natural ventilation: *Lincoln* is hot, sticky and smelling of oil. The perspiring bodies of hundreds of dockyard workers mingle with the tang of *Lincoln*'s new and confused crew. I see a number of monster cockroaches. Apparently Singapore cockies are different from their European cousins: they are longer, wider, taller, have Oriental eyes and are rumoured to be far more intelligent than the average Ordinary Seaman. According to Tansy, they hunt in large, intimidating gangs.

HMS Lincoln

We muster to be told what our duties are. Many are given jobs in *HMS Terror* and are stood to one side. I'm given the job of Bosun's Mate and join a small group mustered at the top of the gangway under a small canvas awning. The morning sun is already hot. I'm the younger part of a two-man team responsible to the Officer-of-the-Day for the security of the ship's gangway. Along with the Quartermaster, I am also responsible for broadcasting the ship's routine throughout the day. There are eight of us in the main watch-keeping team: four Quartermasters and four Bosun's Mates split down the middle into Port and Starboard watches. Between us we will work a system called '24 about'. This means that during each 24-hour period, the port or starboard watch will do alternate watches. One day a Quartermaster and his Bosun's Mate will keep the Afternoon (12:00-16:00), Last Dog (18:00-20:00) Middle (24:00-04:00) and Forenoon (08:00-12:00) then they have twenty four hours off. The following day the same team will do the First dog (16:00-18:00), First (20:00-24:00) and Morning Watch (04:00-08:00). It sounds complicated, but it's a brilliant system: it means that I get every other day completely free. My Quartermaster is Leading Seaman Parker, nicknamed 'Fez'. He's been to Singapore before and by the sound of him comes from Newcastle way. He is my boss and I do all the running around. He calls me 'lad' which upsets me: after all, I'm 18 years old.

'My name is Leading Seaman Parker. Yours is?'

'Broadbent Pete, Ordinary Seaman.'

'From where?'

'Pudsey.'

'Where's that?'

'Yorkshire.'

'I'm from Sunderland. Which football team do you support?'

'Leeds United.'

'My team is Sunderland. I hope that we'll be able to work together despite that.'

I nod. I know that Leeds United and Sunderland are both challenging for promotion from Division 2 this season.

Our first watch today is the Afternoon watch. Fez and I have a quick hand-over from the Quartermaster and Bosun's Mate of the old commission who are currently on watch. They aren't that serious about anything, as they are flying home to the UK in a couple of days. Fez appears satisfied with what he's told: he's done the Quartermaster's job on previous ships.

He gives me a run-down on my duties. 'You are to stay around the area of the Gangway unless told otherwise by me or any of the duty Officers or Senior Rates. It's your job to learn the ship's routine as shown on the board and make broadcasts where indicated.' He shows me how to use the ship's microphone. 'Everything else, you'll learn as we go along. Divent let anyone hear you call me Fez. While on duty I'm Quartermaster, Hooky, Leading Hand or Leading Seaman Parker. I will call you whatever I like.' He cracks a wide smile. 'But mostly I'll call you Ordinary Seaman Broadbent, Bosun's Mate, or if I can't remember your name I'll call you 'lad' – is that OK?'

'Yes.'

'Yes what?'

'Yes, Hooky.'

'That's better,' he smiles. 'Let's get ourselves organised then, shall we?'

As the rest of the crew pile into buses to take them back to *Terror* at 13:00, our dinner arrives. Fez and I have been on watch for an hour. An Indian gentleman, in a skirt, emerges from a blue Naval Tilly carrying a couple of silver drum buckets. He smiles as he comes to attention on the inboard end of the gangway.

'Dinner for gentlemen's. Welcome sirs to HMS Lincoln new crew. I am Sadiq, I bring food for watch-keepers in Dockyard every day except Christ-maas.' He opens each of the circular clipped compartments of the drums: one contain a steaming main course and the other a crispy slab of crumble swimming in piping hot custard. He hands them to us. 'You like curry?' He looks inquiringly from Fez to me.

I shrug my shoulders.

Fez says an enthusiastic 'Yes.' He turns to me. 'You don't like curry?'

'Never had one.'

'Never had a ferkin curry?'

'No ... sorry.'

'Don't know what you're missing.' He turns to Sadiq. 'Sadiq my friend, in four days' time, when we are next doing the afternoon watch, we'll both have a curry – OK?'

'I will ensure. Tell me names please.'

'Leading Seaman Parker and Ordinary Seaman Broadbent.'

Sadiq tapped his temple. 'I remember. What you wan' for supper?'

'What's on the menu?' asks Fez.

'Don't know exact ... sorry Mister Parker sir.'

'We'll have two what-evers then.'

'Two what-evers for Lincoln.' He taps his temple. 'I remember.'

As Sadiq steps onto the gangway, Fez asks 'What are our names then, Mister Sadiq?'

'Misters Parker and Mister Broad-something,' he replies without turning.

'That's close enough.'

We watch as Sadiq drives away.

'Do we have any knives and forks, Hooky?' I ask.

'Bugger!' exclaims Fez.

Fez manages to eat his dinner using his seaman's knife. I find a six-inch wooden ruler in the Quartermaster's desk and I use that.

We aren't officially allowed off the ship during our twenty-four period of duty, so when Leading Seaman 'Charlie' Chaplin and Gringo relieve us at 16:00 Fez decides that we should spend the next couple of hours finding somewhere to sleep. 'Let's start down aft in the officers' cabins. None of them will be in use, mebiz we'll find a couple that are in a fit state for us to use. Have a look around the galley for some eating irons.'

The cabins are stripped bare, no bunks or mattresses. I find some knives and forks in the Wardroom Pantry.

As we start the Last Dog Watch at 18:00, a little Malayan guy arrives with four bunk-sized maroon containers. Each contains a thin mattress, a navy counterpane. a sheet, a pillow and a clean starched pillow case. 'Mister Parker and Mister Broad-something, this is bedding for you individually. Sleeping mess is Forward Seamen's Mess starboard side where are eight bunks for use. I bring extra four tomorrow.'

Fez shrugs and points towards the forward screen door. 'Take 'em down for us then.'

'Natural sure Mister Parker sir.'

 And away he goes.

Before we go off watch, Sadiq arrives with supper. It's hot and is rice with something. There is also a slice of fruitcake with pink and white icing sugar and a cold Mars bar.

I take a bite of my Mars bar ... and it cracks. I become an instant fan of refrigerated chocolate.

'Never had chocolate straight from the fridge before?' asks Fez.

'No, never.'

'You don't have chocolate in Yorkshire?'

'Of course.'

'Fridges?'

'Of course.'

'Of course ... what?'

'Of course, Hooky.'

'That's better. Now I'll call you Pete when off-duty.'

'Thanks.'

'Were there any spoons in the Wardroom pantry?'

'Think so, yes.'

'Nip doon and get a couple then, there's a good lad.'

Already our working relationship is becoming a little more relaxed.

I find where the Malayan bloke has put our beds and as we have nothing else to do, both Fez and I get our heads down for a couple of hours before starting the Middle Watch at midnight.

I enjoy my first Singapore Middle: It's warm, quiet and strangely subdued. Our gangway light attracts all sorts of flying insects and there are unidentified sounds everywhere. Fez and I take it in turns to wander around the ship, finding our way around. I walk up and down the jetty because Fez tells me to check the berthing ropes. I watch as a trio of large brown rats help each other to negotiate their way over our circular metal rat-guards. I sit on a 50-gallon oil drum and watch a couple of ginormous cockroaches doing their bit to guarantee the next generation – at least, I think that's what they're doing. I find a crate full of Frazer & Neave bottled orange juice and take a couple of them onboard.

Fez tells me all sorts of stories about the delights of Singapore town. The girls, a tribe of strange girly-boys called Kie-ties and places called Sembawang, Neesoon, The Britannia Club and Raffles. By the time it's time to shake Charlie and Gringo at 03:45 I've learnt a lot about the attractions of 'Singers'.

Surprisingly I sleep soundly until Sadiq gives me a gentle shake a little after 06:00 with the promise of 'Full English breakfarst Mister Broad-whatever. I have cleared area of mess table.'

After breakfast, I wipe my greasy fingers on my shorts. 'How do we wash, Hooky?'

'I divvent kna'. Go find a bathroom with runnin' water.'

I discover one bathroom that has cold running grey water. The brown overalled Dockyard staff start shuffling onboard at 06:30 and the crew start to arrive shortly after. I read the ship's routine and made my first Tannoy broadcast at 06:55. I hold the microphone close to my mouth and depress the silver bar as demonstrated by Leading Seaman Parker ...

'OUT PIPES ... BOTH WATCHES OF THE HANDS MUSTER BY THEIR PARTS OF SHIP AT 07:00.'

An irate Petty Officer comes strutting up to the gangway and hands Fez a slip of paper. 'Pipe for this lad to come to the gangway, QM.'

Fez hands me the slip. 'There you are, Bosun's Mate – pipe that.'

Then I made my second broadcast ... or pipe.

'JUNIOR STORES ASSISTANT WAKEFIELD REPORT TO THE GANGWAY.'

The Petty Officer taps my shoulder. 'Pipe it again and say immediately.'

'IMMEDIATELY JUNIOR STORES ASSISTANT WAKEFIELD REPORT TO THE GANGWAY.'

Fez grabs the microphone.

'JUNIOR STORES ASSISTANT WAKEFIELD REPORT TO THE GANGWAY ... IMMEDIATELY.'

I nod: another lesson learned.

For the remainder of the Forenoon Watch I stand around at the top of the gangway and speak to loads of people. Fez answers a pack of questions and I make lots of broadcasts. I becomes really good at it and I'm quite proud to know that everybody onboard can hear me. I particularly enjoy it when I have to pipe for a Petty Officer, a Chief or an Officer to report to somewhere or other.

To my knowledge, Junior Stores Assistant Wakefield never does report to the gangway.

Fez asks the Officer-of-the-Day why our wooden dado that runs around the edge of our upper deck is painted red. The Officer promises to find out for us.

'It's normally painted grey on every other ship,' Fez explains to me.

At 12:00 we are relieved and my first twenty-four hour period of duty is over. I'm not required back onboard until the First Dog (16:00) tomorrow.

After dinner, Fez takes me on a tour of *HMS Terror*, a collection of perfectly proportioned white-painted buildings with red-tiled roofs, all set among beautifully trimmed emerald green lawns and multi-coloured flowerbeds. Sweet-smelling tropical flowers, called orchids, grow everywhere in well-manicured clusters. A group of local men dressed in full-length skirts and wide-brimmed hats busy themselves sweeping and cutting. They all have a ready, friendly smile and amazingly white teeth. Fez explains that the constant chirping sound is crickets; it is already becoming nothing more than a pleasant background noise. He also explains that the full-length skirts are called sarongs and the strappy things on their feet are called flip-flops.

We have a pint of Tiger in the Armada Club at dinnertime. Then we wander back to the mess. We pass the camp laundry with its acres of clothing hanging from rows of parallel washing lines. It's my first close-up of oriental women dressed in tight figure-hugging sarongs: very, very nice. Alongside the laundry are shops selling oriental artefacts, porcelain dinner services, sets of bamboo cups on bamboo trays, clocks, brightly coloured shirts and sarongs, camphor wood chests, jewellery, tropical footwear and sensible male underwear. Fez tells me that I can buy locally made No 8 shirts and shorts for a couple of Singapore dollars. They are thinner than the Pusser's ones and easier to wash and dry. The local sandals are also better than the Pusser's ones and suggests that my first Singapore purchase should be a pair of flip-flops. I pay 65 cents for a pair of grey ones. I'd never seen or worn flip-flops before. I can't wait to get back to the mess and try them on: my Pusser's sandals are gouging painful shapes into my delicate Yorkshire feet.

Fez explains to me that the ditches that run everywhere are monsoon drains, designed to carry the rainwater away during the monsoon season. I look up at a cloudless blue sky and can't imagine it ever raining. The drains are about two feet wide and three feet deep spanned at regular intervals by narrow concrete bridges.

'You've never seen rain like a Singapore monsoon.' He points to a pile of green-waxed rolls, each with a bamboo handle. 'You'll need one of those when the monsoon starts ... a Wan Chai Burbs.'

'A what?'

'A Wan Chai Burbs.' He grabs one that is hanging from the roof and after a few attempts manages to open it.

It's a green, waxed umbrella with Chinese painted patterns on the upper surface and it smells of long dead fish – awful.

'An ordinary umbrella will be ripped to shreds in the monsoon. These will keep you dry.'

'How much?' I ask.

'Dollar.'

'I'll have one.'

'The monsoons don't normally start until late November.'

'I'll leave it till then ... then.'

We have a slow, appreciative walk back to the mess. We slow down to a crawl as we pass the stretching and bending laundry women in their tight sarongs. Tired from our stroll, we lounge on the sundrenched wicker chairs to absorb some well-earned sun. The rest of the ship's company are arriving back from the dockyard as we scramble onto our bunks and get our heads down. I'm glad that I have a top bunk: I can feel a whisper of tepid, wafted air from the closest deckhead fan.

Fez gives me a black marker and tells me to write WATCHKEEPER on the bulkhead next to my bunk with an arrow pointing to my pillow. This will ensure that I won't be disturbed in the morning.

In the evening Lash and I find a corner table in the Armada Club and decide to give the Tiger beer a proper appraisal. As the evening wears on, the Armada Club fills up and we are joined by Skid and Tansy. I buy my first round of Tigers and carry them back to the table like everybody else does, with my fingers hooked over the rim of the glasses and dangling in the beer. Nobody seems to bother where my fingers have been. A pint of this golden liquid is 45 cents which Tansy calculates is equivalent to one shilling and tuppence in proper money. I try a pint with a splash of lemonade, a Tiger-Tops, but I don't like it, preferring my beer undiluted.

Tiger's unusual taste disappears after pint number three. We are all interpreting the Medical Officer's advice to 'Drink plenty of liquids.' in our own individual ways. Consequently, before turning-in that night I carry out my first personal inspection of the monsoon drain running alongside the mess block. I'm not the only one who 'calls for Hughie' in the first week. According to those who know about such things, it's due to a combination of heat, change of water and jet lag. Thankfully, it has nothing whatsoever to do with the fact that I'm drinking significant amounts of deceptively strong Tiger.

I'm not prepared for my early morning shake by a bloke in a peaked cap. He comes storming through the mess, banging the bunk frames with a wooden stick.

'Gerrup, Gerrup, Gerrup. Show A Hairy Leg. The Sun Is Burning Your Eye-Balls Out. It's 05:00 And The Weather Forecast For Today Is Singapore Hot. Everybody GERRUP.'

It's still dark.

The second time he passes my bed I manage to say 'I'm a Watchkeeper, PO.'

He bangs his heels together and glares at me. 'Glad to meet you, Watchkeeper. I'm the Duty Petty Officer and I've been up all night dealing with drunken little sods like you who haven't yet learned how much beer their pink little bodies can deal with. Now Gerrout Of Your Stinkin' Pit And Put Your Manky Little Feet On The Deck NOW.'

'But Leading Seaman Parker says that if I ...'

'Get out of your stinking pit, LAD.'

So I do. After a quick shower I shuffle over to the Dining Hall for breakfast and Paludrine. Then, as the rest of the crew trudge over the parade ground to catch the dockyard bus, I go back to bed.

Later, Fez assures me that he will sort out the early morning shake problem.

Today I decide that my white West Yorkshire Y-fronts are not designed for tropical comfort. In this climate they are chafing the most sensitive of areas, so I decide unilaterally to ditch them in favour of some locally made boxer shorts. I opt for a couple of delicately striped pairs with elasticated waistband and one with a rather outrageous black and red flower design. It's my first ever underwear purchase and I feel surprisingly pleased with myself. I dhobi my Y-fronts and hang them over the frame of my bunk to dry. An hour later they have disappeared ... into the mess scran bag no doubt.

The following day Fez and I have the First Dog Watch onboard *Lincoln*. As soon as we have settled ourselves, an Officer dressed in immaculate whites explains to Fez all about the red-painted dado. Apparently, we are the only ship in the Royal Navy allowed to paint it red. It's a tradition dating back to the seventeenth century when the first *HMS Lincoln* claimed the right to mount its guns on 'Lincoln Scarlet' in memory of Robin Hood who had a fondness for the colour. Personally I don't believe a word of it.

After a week in Singapore, I consider myself completely acclimatised and decide to tackle the business of getting myself a proper suntan. My sallow Pudsey complexion identifies me as a new arrival and it's important not to be seen as such. Despite what we have been told, I decide to spend at least a quarter of an hour each day in the full glare of the sun with my shirt off and my lower parts clad only in my skimpy, locally made underpants. Between watches I find myself a quiet spot up behind the funnel. I lie on a pile of wooden pallets and do battle with the Singapore sun.

In *HMS Terror* I discover the Junior Rates pool and spend some of my spare time sunbathing and swimming. There are diving boards, poolside showers, loungers, chairs, a few small tables and a couple of saronged gentlemen wielding brooms and nets who keep the place tidy and the pool water sparkling clean. Surprisingly, given the lecture about over-exposure to the sun, there is no canopy shade. The nearest shade is from a bunch of palm trees fifty yards away across a grass patch that sounds as though it's alive with rampaging crickets. The only thing wrong with the pool is the lack of girls. According to Fez, those who are permanently shore-based in Singapore and have their families with them have a separate swimming facility a good distance away from us on the other side of the dockyard complex.

Within days, hitherto concealed parts of my West Yorkshire body turn a frighteningly vivid scarlet. The surface of my upper shoulders, that has been a part of me for as long as I can remember, flakes away to reveal terrified-looking skin underneath. The difference between the colour of my forearm and the strip of white skin beneath my watchstrap gradually increases. Some of my messmates are turning golden brown without much effort: obviously not of pallid grey, West Yorkshire stock.

I have a wristwatch that cost Mum a reasonable amount of money some months ago. Unfortunately little flecks of water appear on the inside of the glass. When I ask Fez about it, he explains that watches that aren't tropicalised suffer because of the humidity and temperature. He says that a bloke down by the laundry sells small circular green plastic stickers that he claims are guaranteed to deflect the sun and solve the condensation problem when placed on the watch glass. Fez wears an expensive waterproof watch he bought in Hong Kong yonks ago.

Until today I had absolutely no idea exactly how far the sun is from the earth. Judging by the temperature it's a lot closer to Singapore than it is to Pudsey.

Tansy is spread-eagled on one of the rattan loungers when I find him. I stand by his feet, purposefully placing him in cooling shadow.

He slowly opens one eye and looks at me. 'What the ferk are you doing, young 'un?'

'Nothing really, I wanted to ...'

'93 million miles those rays have travelled ... 93 million ferkin miles ... and you cut them off in the last few feet.'

'Sorry.' I step aside.

Once again bathed in Singapore sun, Tansy relaxes and closes his eyes. 'Thank you – now what is it you want?'

'You coming down the Armada Club for a pint?'

Tansy bounces up onto his feet and punches me playfully on the shoulder. 'Why didn't you say earlier?'

On the way to the Armada Club I ask, 'Is the sun really 93 million miles away?'

'Give or take a couple ... yeah.'

Brilliant. I've learnt something important today. The next person to stand between me and the sun will receive the same information ... without the expletives perhaps.

Gringo and I almost convince Lash to come for a swim. Lash doesn't like water much and when it comes time to get into our swimming costume he bottles out and decides to have a wander around the shops instead. When Lash joined the Navy he couldn't swim. It took him months to pass the standard swimming test and I clearly recall the look of triumph on his face when he walked into the mess at *HMS Ganges* the morning he had officially passed his Royal Naval swimming test.

'Suppose most have either got their heads down, gone down the village or are in the Armada Club,' says Gringo, as he drapes a towel over the back of one of the pool loungers. We have the pool to ourselves.

I can't wait to get into the water. Gringo and I splash around for ten minutes or so. I mastered the highest diving board at Pudsey's Municipal Baths when I was thirteen and consider myself to be something of a high-board diving specialist. After three attempts I manage to do a couple of dives from the platform that is about ten feet below the top one. Gringo is impressed.

'You got any sisters?' asks Gringo.

'No. Only a brother. Tony, four years younger than me. You got any?'

'Two.'

'Two?'

'One's mi twin and t'other is eighteen months older. Good-looking girls if I say so misen. I've gorra photo int mess somewhere. I'll show yew later.'

'Right then, thanks.'

I dive into the empty waters of the pool. Gringo does a 'bomb' that splays water everywhere.

Back in the mess, Gringo finds the picture of his two sisters.

I pull an appreciative face. 'They're good-looking girls.'

'The one wearing the shorts is mi twin. The ancient one with her hand on her hip is the oldest – works in a bank. Mi twin is a bit of a lass, she wants to be a singer.'

'Wha' ... a real singer?'

'Yeah.'

Lash crawls out of his bunk to have a look. 'They got boyfriends?'

'Dunno,' says Gringo. 'Boyfriends change regularly. I'll ask 'em in mi next letter and let ya know.'

Lash plonks himself on a spare lounger and removes his shirt. 'The weather at home is terrible apparently.'

'Really,' says Gringo. 'Pass me mi flip-fops and shorts.'

'Snow apparently,' says Lash. 'Lots of it.'

'Shame,' I add.

The following morning my scarlet skin is drum tight and crackles whenever I move. The prospect of wearing shorts and a short-sleeved shirt that will further expose parts of my body to the sun doesn't seem sensible to me, but I can't figure out a way to avoid it.

By the time I go on watch the first signs of crazed red skin appears on my forearms.

Fez is unsympathetic. 'Been out in the sun then. You know what they say about mad dogs and Englishmen who go out in the midday sun.'

'No.'

'They're ferkin idiots.'

'Right then.'

'The Singapore sun doesn't give you a good tan anyway. It's got a yellowish tinge to it.'

'Is there anything that I can put on my skin to stop it from peeling?'

'Not as far as I know ... no.'

'It's ferkin uncomfortable.'

'We've all gone through it. Takes years of practice to get it right. Us English are not designed to go brown.'

'There's a bloke in the mess who works on the Quarterdeck who's going brown. He's darker each time I see him.'

'That's Able Seaman Brick Wall. There's a touch of the tar-brush about him.'

'What do you mean, tar-brush?'

'Not one hundred per-cent English.' Fez looks at his watch. 'Two minutes to Stand-easy.'

I grab the microphone and watch as a couple of Dockies manhandle a large piece of complicated-looking machinery over the brow. They're an attractive brown colour.

After I pipe Stand-easy, I slope off around the starboard side, away from the brow, for a cigarette. My back and my chest are actively throbbing. The fag helps a little.

Down the mess, off-watch, Fez and I play Crib. He tosses his cards on the deck after I get home with a 'two for a pair'.

'You're a jammy little bugger,' he says.

'Got good cards.' I scratch the front of my chest.

'Go down to the Terror shops tomorrow morning and ask the bloke who sells Tiger Balm if he can recommend something for your skin. Even if he hasn't got anything he'll try and sell you something.'

'What's Tiger Balm then?'

'Little jar of paste like stuff. Apparently, it cures almost everything. The locals love it but the rumour is that it contains opium. There's also Tiger Oil. Both are illegal in the UK.'

I awake the following morning leaving sheets of dead, scarlet skin on my sheets.

I stroll down to the shops and find the place that sells Tiger Balm. The shop owner sells me a small glass jar with a gold coloured top after offering me a good sniff at the contents. It's relatively expensive; the equivalent of five or six pints of Tiger. He also sells me something in a plastic bottle for my flaking red skin. He shows me how to massage the stuff into one of my forearms.

'It goo,' he says, displaying a mouth full of gold teeth.

'Thanks.'

'This ferkin sun hoh ... eh?'

'Wha?'

'Hoh ... ferkin sun hoh.'

'Hot ... certainly is. Thanks.'

After payday I solve my sandal problem. I pay a visit to the local 'shoe-shoe' who measures my feet and sells me a pair of comfortable and flexible handmade sandals. Fez explains that shoe-shoe is probably the only person alive who has any respect for Pusser's sandals: their impractical design keeps him in business.

The green plastic sticker hasn't yet solved my watch's condensation problem. I decide to give it another week.

Lash and I, along with Gringo, agree to join Tansy and Skid on a trip to Sembawang village. Having mastered the Singapore Dockyard area and the Armada Club, it's with a mixture of excitement and trepidation that I take my first trip outside the dockyard gate. Outside *Terror*, we catch the bus that takes us on a tour of the dockyard, passing *HMS Lincoln* and many other ships and down a long, straight road to what I assume is the main dockyard gate. Immediately outside is Sembawang Village, a collection of rattan-roofed open-fronted shops and bars set back from the road. Litter-filled monsoon drains run alongside both sides of the main road. The village shops sell bicycles, watches, embroidered Chinese silk clothes, camphor wood chests, porcelain, electrical stuff, bamboo artefacts and a million other things. Nothing is priced and can be purchased for whatever the stallholder thinks he can get away with. We are lambs to the slaughter when it comes to bartering. I pay 10 dollars for an attractive-looking wristwatch with a 100% genuine leather strap.

'How much did ya pay?' enquires Gringo.

'Eight dollars,' I lie.

He whistles through his teeth. 'Going price for a cheap cocky watch in the village is five dollar, seven if it has a metal strap.'

'I can afford it. What did you call them?'

'Cocky watches.'

'Why?'

'If you take the back off you won't find a normal watch movement, you'll find a little spring wound up by a cockroach who spends his days stomping around inside the back of your watch.'

'Naah.'

'Unless you feed it regularly it won't last a week.'

'Naah.'

It's within the open-fronted retail establishments of Sembawang that I am to practise – and never master – the delicate skill of bartering. The most popular local cigarettes are 'Lucky 7's' so I buy myself a packet to commemorate my arrival. A persistent shop owner almost convinces me that I can't live without a camphor-wood chest priced at about three months' pay. I'm briefly tempted because I like boxes and I do like the smell.

We have a number of bars to choose from and it seems appropriate that we try the Sembawang Bar first. I quickly discover that entering a moderately well air-conditioned bar from the heat and humidity of outside is probably one of the most refreshing feelings in the world. We find a table and Skid immediately gives us the benefit of his experience.

'The bar girls will join us before we order our drinks. They'll sit down next to you and try to entice you to buy them a drink. They know all the tricks and if they see that you're not sure and that you haven't been out here long enough to get a Singapore tan they'll start to work on you. If you're lucky you can ...'

From the back appear four smiling ladies. One is wearing an eye-patch. One is smoking a clay pipe, one has extraordinarily wide shoulders and the fourth is tottering on a pair of very high-heeled shoes. They are all wearing Chinese dresses. The girls each grab a chair and sit among us. The one smoking the pipe settles herself down alongside an unsure Gringo. Between Lash and I sits the lady with tremendous shoulders and a large plastic flower jammed in her cleavage: she has a large red gemstone on the side of each nostril and smells of something unusual. The girl on the high-heeled shoes hovers expectantly at the head of the table. 'Dinks?' she asks without smiling.

'Four bottles of Tiger, love,' says Skid.

The girl on the high-heeled shoes suddenly jabs a pointed finger directly at Skid. 'Yew on Aircwaft Cawiya two an half year ago. Yew drunken, thievin bastar! Yew owe bar twelve dollar twenty cent. Yew ferkin Skid Man!'

Skid jumps up, opens his arms and yells, 'Rosie ... you've grown. You used to work in Teddy's ...'

'Change name. Now call Sally. Twelve dollar an twenty cent you Skid Man,' she replies as she is enveloped in a strange Skid-type hug.

'They never forget, these girls,' Skid says to Lash who is staring glassy eyed at the ceiling. The girl with the shoulders has her hand under the table and is doing something. 'You buy me dink?'

'Don't say yes, Lash ... not yet,' says Skid. 'You need to know how these girls operate before buying them drinks.' Skid waves all the girls away and they obediently file away to greet a group of recent arrivals from *HMS Loch Lomond.*

'I was enjoying that,' says Lash.

'These girls get you to buy them drinks that are nothing but coloured water ... at a dollar a glass. They will stay with you as long as you keep buying them drinks. They only earn anything if they entice you into the back room.' He turns in his chair. 'Do you see the little old lady sitting at the corner of the bar? She's the Mama-San – she's in charge of the girls. If you want to take one of them into the back you have to see her – she'll take the money and arrange everything.'

'I want to go now!' says Lash. 'I want the one with the big shoulders.'

'They're hard-working girls these in Sembawang.' Skid looks at his watch. 'It's almost 17:00, they've probably been hard at it since dinner. They should be well oiled by now.'

'You mean, they've been,' Lash points to the darkened area beside the bar, 'at work behind there?'

'They've got to earn,' states Skid.

'I'm not too sure about it any longer.'

I've smoked a few of my Lucky 7's and my throat is screaming sore.

Night-time descends on Singapore in dramatic fashion. There is no dusk. At 17:55 it's eye-scorching sunshine and at 18:05 it's dark.

Once it's dark, Sembawang Village is transformed from a shopping area with bars into an eating area with shops and bars. Portable wooden 'Makan' stalls appear between the bars/shops and the roadway. Each stall is constructed around a central charcoal-fired wok tended by sweaty, vested Malays. The small kerosene or gas lanterns strung under the canopy of each stall light up the Sembawang evening. Skid introduces us to the delights of magnificent fried rice dishes, knocked up in no time, priced at one dollar. The raw-meat constituents suspended around the canopy attract all manner of flying objects. I become an instant fan of Nasi Goreng, a fried rice and vegetable dish topped with scrambled egg. Served piping hot and washed down with bottles of ice-cold Tiger, a 'Nasi' is a brilliant way to round off an evening in Sembawang. After our first Makan meal, Skid tells us that in all the time he has spent in Sembawang village he has never seen a cat or a rat. Gringo, Lash and I laugh because we have consumed loads of Tiger ... and we don't get the point. Lash becomes a fan of Mami Soup, but it contains too much of something called garlic for my taste. It's anti-social: I can smell it on Lash for days afterwards.

I'm on the ship's Tannoy ...

'STAND EASY'

An Officer hands Fez a slip of paper. 'Pipe that.'
Fez hands me the slip of paper. 'Pipe that.'

'DO YOU HEAR THERE ...'

I like that bit.

'DO YOU HEAR THERE. CLEAR LOWER DECK. SHIP'S COMPANY IS TO ASSEMBLE IN THE TERROR CANTEEN AT 14:00 THIS AFTERNOON.'

After dinner, Fez and I join the rest of *Lincoln*'s crew in the Armada Club. The usual dinnertime staff behind the bar can't cope with the unexpectedly large number of customers and a long, thirsty queue has formed. We eventually get ourselves drinks and wait for something to happen. Nothing does, so we order ourselves more Tigers ... and wait.

We are halfway through our second pint when the Buffer, Petty Officer Annie Oakley, appears looking flustered. 'What are you all doing here?'

Someone replies, 'Mustering in the Canteen as instructed.'

'Who said muster in the Canteen?' asks a bouncing Buffer.

Fez raises his hand. 'We were given a piece of paper that said muster in the Canteen at 14:00.'

'Who are you?'

'Quartermaster of the Forenoon Watch, PO.'

'And on this piece of paper did it actually say muster in the Canteen?'

'Yes, PO. Muster in the Terror Canteen at 14:00.'

'Are you positive about that?'

'Yes, PO,' he turns to me. 'Tell him, Ordinary Seaman Broadbent.'

I clear my throat: I didn't expect to be called as a witness. 'That's correct, PO ... Canteen at 14:00.'

Annie scans the tables, mentally calculating the number of empty Tiger bottles. He turns, says 'Shit!' and stomps away.

We drift back to the mess for a well-earned lie-down.

Fez wakes me from peaceful slumber sometime later.

'I bet I know what's happened. They wanted us to muster in the Dining Hall, but they made a mistake and said the Canteen ... otherwise known as the Armada Club.'

A few hours later Annie Oakley stomps through the mess. 'Muster in the Dining Hall at 16:30; everybody muster in the junior rates Dining Hall at 16:30.'

In the Dining Hall we sit and wait in contemplative silence. I tap my watch – it's stopped. The cocky has passed away.

'Cocky dead then?' inquires Popeye who notices me banging the watch on the underside of my chair.

'I expected it to last more than six ferkin days.'

'Could have been an elderly cocky when you bought it.'

'Lincoln ship's company attention,' bellows Petty Officer Oakley.

We sit up straight as Lieutenant Lamin appears. His crisp white shorts still have a razor-sharp crease down both the front and back. Annie Oakley stands rigidly to one side.

'Lincoln ship's company sit easy.' Lieutenant Lamin removes his cap and places it on the table behind him. I give my watch a final bang. The second hand moves for five seconds and then stops.

Lieutenant Lamin begins. 'There have been a number of avoidable problems reported to me from HMS Terror's Sick Bay. I expected those of you who have experience of life in Singapore to look after those who are here for the first time. In this climate, it's most important that you pay particular attention to certain aspects of your personal hygiene. After showering, remember to dry between your toes – failure to do so can result in a severe inflammation known as Chinky-toe-rot. Make sure that you rinse yourselves thoroughly after showering to avoid the irritating dhobi-itch. Dry the inside of your ears well: there is a parasite in the local water that likes to burrow itself inside European ears – this is known locally as Singapore Ear and can be acutely painful. Salt tablets will be made available for those of you who are not sweating as much as others. They will be made available alongside the Paludrine tablets in the Cant ... Dining Hall. Finally, I know that you are all keen to get a suntan. Over-exposure to the Singapore sun can be particularly harmful. That's all.' He turns smartly to Annie Oakley. 'Carry on, PO.'

Sembawang village becomes a habit. Lash and I normally have a few pints in the Armada Club before strolling the mile or so to the village where we drink until midnight. To end our evenings I usually have a 'Nasi', Lash has a 'Mami' and we zigzag back to *Terror*. Some nights, depending on the money situation, we get a 'fast-black' for the final leg of the journey. The girls in the Sembawang Bar now welcome us as regulars but the Mama San keeps her distance. 'Silly' Sally is getting to grips with her high-heeled shoes. She is an enthusiastic 'sticky green' earner because she has what fascinates the men of the Royal Navy ... a pair of prominent nipples. The barman, a young Malay we call Charlie, is in the habit of bouncing each bottle of Tiger off his forearm before opening it. One night some lads from *HMS Cavalier*, who have been in Singapore longer than us, tell us about a group of girls working out of the next village called Nee Soon who are an entertaining bunch. Apparently, there is a distinctive red-white-and-blue mobile food stall by the side of the main road where they all congregate. Collectively they are known as the 'Nee Soon Virgins'. Apparently, one of these Virgins is ridiculously inexpensive because she has no noticeable nose. Although none of the *Cavalier* lads admit to having seen No-nose in the flesh, it makes a good sea-story. Anyone who is really hard-up and missing for more than ten minutes in Nee Soon is normally accused of being 'away with No-nose'.

The following week I'm sitting in the Armada Club having my first Tiger of the afternoon when someone grasps my shoulder from behind.

'Well if it isn't the second-best heaving line thrower on the Quarterdeck,' says a familiar voice.

I turned to face a grinning Able Seaman Kayne. 'Sugar!'

'Young Broadbent. Fancy seeing you here.'

'What are you on?'

'A pile of junk called *Loch Lomond*. Flew in yesterday. We're in the mess directly above yours.'

'Nice to see ya,' I say.

'If you've got nothing else to do, I've got some business to conduct in the Village. We can meet up later for a few drinks.'

'Right then. What time and where?'

'About three in Lakki's.'

'Where?'

'Next to Teddy's, two or three up from the Sembawang Bar. You can't miss it.'

The air-conditioning in Lakki's Bar is brilliant: much more efficient than in the Sembawang Bar. The peanuts on each table are shelled, unlike those in the Sembawang Bar that are left whole: it's a small, but important difference. Lash and I sit down; there is no sign of Sugar. The girls are more attractive and flit around quicker. They smile more often and are more talkative. A couple of girls – one wearing a green cardigan over a bright yellow cheongsam and the other wearing unattractive baggy black trousers, white ankle socks, plimsolls and a floppy top – leave the table to our right and join us. The one in the green cardie introduces herself to Lash as Lilly. The one sitting next to me has a perfectly round face and muscular arms. She introduces herself as Glenda from Ulan Bator.

Lash is the first to spot Sugar: he enters the main bar from somewhere in the back, his arm wrapped around the shoulder of a little old lady with a small nose and a face like a knurled walnut.

'Hello lads. Let me introduce the best Mama-San in the Far East. She's in charge of discipline and entertainment in this bar.'

She looks like the Mama San in the Sembawang Bar except she has a dark brown growth in the front of her left ear lobe from which sprouts a lengthy cluster of wispy grey hairs.

Lilly sits up straight and removes her hand from Lash's thigh.

Lash blinks and stares straight ahead.

Glenda places a strong hand on my lap. I'm shocked but respond in the expected fashion. She winks and smiles at me.

Mama-San waves a hand and Lilly skips away to the bar. Mama-San looks up at Sugar, cracks a smile and says. 'Sugar an me gooda fren many year now.'

'I knew her when she was on the game.'

'You didn't?' I ask.

'Course I didn't. She's old enough to be my Gran.'

'What you been doing in the back then, Shug?' asks Lash.

'Renewing old acquaintances Lash, renewing a couple of old acquaintances and paying off some debts.'

Lilly reappears with a tray of bottled Tiger and some small glasses of green liquid.

'On House,' explains a smiling Mama-San. 'Firs welcome dink on house all roun.'

I tell Sugar that we'd been in the village with Skid recently.

'Is he on Lincoln?'

'Cavalier. One of the girls in the Sembawang Bar remembered that he owed her twelve dollars from a couple of years ago.'

'They don't forget if you owe them money. A couple of years ago twelve bucks was the going rate, so somehow Skid once got his leg-over on tick ... which is not an easy thing to do, believe me ... unless you know the Mama San very well.'

As Sugar leans over to grab a beer, Mama-San taps his backside, smiles a knowing walnut-type smile and shuffles away.

'Keep on the right side of her, lads – the benefits are well worth it.' As he sits down, Lilly downs her green drink and leaves. A lady wearing a tight white Cheongsam with a slit up to the waist stands behind Sugar's chair. She taps him on the shoulder and as he turns around she pouts.

'Sugar man ... yewwa butterfry man.'

Sugar composes himself quickly. 'Gentlemen, let me introduce Suzie Right. She originally called herself Suzie Wong but when I explained to her that there was nothing wrong with her she changed her name to Right.'

Suzie Right smiles, winks at us all in turn and says in flawless English, 'Nice to meet you,' then reverts to Bargirl English. 'Any fren' Sugar Man's is fren' o mine.'

'Number one girl in Lakki's Bar,' says Sugar. 'Best bar in the village. Whose round is it?'

It's my turn. Instead of waiting at the table I walk to the bar where the lady from Ulan Bator looks down at me and smiles, exposing a number of intimidating grey-black teeth.

'Yew ly some more company. You a fren' of Sugar Mans?'

'Yes, Sugar man is a friend … and err sorry no thanks.' She is much taller than I am and she scares me.

Sugar comes over and whispers to me.

'She's known as 'Piano' – her teeth look like a piano keyboard. I think it's B flat that's missing.'

He disappears into the back again and Lash and I tot up our money and call it a day, as we are fast running out of dollars.

The toilets are in the back. I search for Sugar but can't find him. The lady from Ulan Bator waves sweetly at me as Lash and I take our leave.

'Did you see the size of her hands?' I ask as we skip over the nearest monsoon drain.

Lash exhales. 'I'm not one hundred percent sure it's a woman.'

'Sugar says she is.'

'Must be then. Sugar would know, wouldn't he?'

Apparently her working name is Piano … because of her teeth.'

Lash splutters and almost loses his balance.

Lakki's Bar becomes my village local. On a very personal level I have taken an instant liking to the cleaning lady. According to someone from *Cavalier*, she comes from Burma and has an unpronounceable name. She is tall and slim with a strangely long neck and a beautiful face. Unfortunately, she doesn't speak a word of English. I find her permanently smiling face extremely attractive and make a point of always smiling at her whenever I can catch her looking in my direction. I call her Burma, as does everyone else.

I rarely spend a evening in the mess. Even when I am short of money, there is always someone willing to lend me enough for a couple of Tigers and a Nasi Goreng. As a Watchkeeper, I have time to write my letters during the peace and quiet of the Middle or Morning watch, although I am not a natural letter writer. I promised Mum that I would write every month or so and I dropped her a note shortly after I arrived to let her know that I was safe. Able Seaman Jeremy Wall – known as 'Brick' – has a great tan, but he has a noticeable letter-writing problem. His girlfriend Polly, from Cork in Ireland, promised to write every day while he was away. In return, he pledged to do the same. The letters stream in from Polly and Brick is duty-bound to scribble a daily reply. I'm glad that I don't have a pushy girlfriend in the UK as I doubt if I could find enough news to fill a daily letter. When the rest of us are drifting off to the Armada Club or the village, Brick stays behind.

'Fancy a pint in Sembawang Brick?' we occasionally ask, although we know what his answer will be.

'No thanks. I'll just drop Polly a quick letter,' he says, sorrowfully.

One particular evening in Lakki's, Lash brings up the subject of Polly.

'I saw a picture of Polly this dinnertime. It fell out of Brick's letter.'

'And?' I ask.

'How can I put this politely?' says Lash, rolling his cold bottle of Tiger over his forehead.

'Put what politely?'

'Polly.'

'Don't get ya.'

'She's a real dog.'

'Doggo?'

'You said it, not me.' Lash smiles and takes a long swig.

'Tell me.'

'Let me put it this way,' he says leaning over the table towards me. 'Think of the girl that you would definitely throw out of bed – the ugliest girl you can think of.'

'Right then,' I thought of Norma, the elder sister of my best school friend in Pudsey.

'Got a picture of someone in your mind?'

'Yep.' I pull a disgusted face.

'Well she's rather attractive if you compare her to Polly.'

'Impossible.'

'Believe me, mate. Polly is certainly not worth a letter a ferkin day.'

'You'd kick her out of bed then?'

'She'd never get through mi garden gate, mate.'

'You've got a ferkin garden?'

3

BARTERING ... A BEGINNER'S GUIDE

Life without a working wristwatch is difficult and that narrow strip of skin normally covered by the strap is now glowing pink and itching.

In the village one evening, after a couple of Tigers, I excuse myself, saying that I'm going to buy myself a new watch.

Despite Lash having no interest in wristwatches, he is a mate and offers to come with me, knowing that a degree of barter will be necessary.

'I can deal with it,' I say with only a smidgen of confidence.

I leave Lash draped over a bowl of Mami soup and skip over the adjacent monsoon drain. I hear something scuttle below me: it isn't a cat – I can recognise a running cat.

A severe-looking Indian gentleman wearing a scarlet turban owns the village shop with the best selection of wristwatches. I take my time scanning the hundreds of watches on display beneath a glass-topped counter.

The proprietor flicks a switch that lights up the display cabinet.

'You looking for new timepiece, young sir?'

'Might be.' I play it cool, not wanting to appear too keen.

'Very good selection sir.' He twirls the end of his waxed moustache. He unhitches a wooden cage containing two birds and places it on the counter away to my right. The birds sit shoulder to shoulder on a thin bamboo stick. They are feathered bright green and grey with yellow beaks and purple, staring eyes. They scuttle from one end of their bamboo perch to the other and back again.

I spot a watch with a date window on the face: I'd always fancied a watch with a date window.

'Can I have a look at that one please?' I waggle a finger.

He gently extracts the watch and shows it to his birds before placing it on a square of blue material on the counter top. He breaths on the watch and gives the watch face a polish. 'First class wristwatch, young sir, fully waterproof and anti magnetic. I can adjust the time and date for you.'

'How much?'

He looks heavenwards with his mouth set in a thinking pose. 'This is special watch with date which I would like to sell to you. I am concerned however young sir, that the price may be beyond your reach.'

'How much?'

'To you, young sir – let me see.' He turns and scribbles on a sheet of paper. He crosses it all out and writes more figures. 'How much do you have to spend, young sir?'

I'm not prepared for this. 'Nine dollars ... and,' I count my change, 'fifty five cents.'

'I have plenty of wristwatches that I am prepared to sell to you for exactly that price, young sir ... but regrettably not this one.' He pulls a sorrowful expression.

The birds look at me. One could be sniggering.

'I can't have that watch for nine dollars fifty five cents then?' I blurt without looking directly at him.

'Unfortunately not, young sir. I make a living from profit and there is no profit at that price level – only a loss.' He waves an arm over his counter top. 'Select another model and let us come to an amicable agreement.'

I stand firm. 'No thank you. I'm only interested in that one.'

'Very good, young sir. At least we now know where we both stand now.'

'How much then?'

'Fifteen dollars to you, young sir. I can tell that you know something about time pieces.'

'I haven't got fifteen dollars.'

'I can keep this watch for you until payday, young sir. That is not a problem. I will even put your name on it to ensure that it will remain safely here for you when you return with the required amount.'

'I'm not sure.' I adopt a thinking pose and stroke my chin. The birds are giving me the evil purple eye.

I turn and leave.

Lash has bought me a John Collins.

I imagine the watch on my wrist. As I finish my drink I ask Lash to lend me five dollars and forty-five cents which he does without question.

Back in the wristwatch stall, the bloke in the scarlet turban welcomes me like a long-lost friend. The birds are suspended from the roof and follow my every move.

'I've only managed to borrow four dollars which gives me a total of thirteen dollars and fifty five cents. Can I have the watch for that price?'

'Unfortunately not, young sir. It has been an unusually bad day for watch sales and I have a wife and a number of fast growing children to cater for ...'

'I'll have to leave it then ... sorry.'

He extracts the watch from under the counter top and gives it a blow and a polish.

I light a cigarette and he notices my Ronson Varaflame lighter with the tortoiseshell sides.

'That's a fine cigarette lighter, young sir. If I am not mistaken that is made by the English Ronson cigarette lighter factory.'

'Is it?'

'I believe so yes, sir. May I have a look please?' he holds his hand out.

I'm a little reluctant to hand over my lighter, but he smiles in an honest, reassuring way. He rolls the lighter between his fingers before placing it on the glass counter top. He makes a noise as he inhales through tight lips.

'This is a fine cigarette lighter, young sir – despite obvious signs of wear on the tortoiseshell banding. Very nice.' He looks at his birds. They look from me to him and back again. 'Young sir. I will exchange the wristwatch you require for your Ronson Varaflame cigarette lighter.'

'You wha?'

'I will exchange the wristwatch you require for your Ronson Varaflame cigarette lighter.'

'You're joking. The lighter is worth much more than 15 dollars.'

He grabs a silver-cased lighter from a display cabinet behind him. He holds it so that it reflects the light. 'I will also give you a brand new Zippo cigarette lighter as well as the watch in exchange for your Ronson Varaflame.'

'No money will change hands?'

'None whatsoever, young sir.'

He flips the top of the Zippo lighter and lights it. He holds it up for me to see. 'The perfect cigarette lighter for the discerning young mariner, sir. Guaranteed to light every time even in the worst of storms.'

That convinces me: the Ronson Varaflame doesn't light well in a strong, upper deck wind. I hand my Varaflame over in exchange for the watch and the Zippo lighter. I convince myself that I've done a great bit of business.

Back at our favourite Makan stall, Lash is tucking in to a plate full of steaming fried rice. I buy two bottles of Tiger and show Lash my Zippo and the watch.

'How much?'

'Nowt.'

'What does nowt mean?'

'Nothing.'

'So nowt is Yorkshire for nothing?'

'Yep.' I return his five dollars and forty-five cents. 'I did a deal and exchanged my Varaflame for this watch and a lighter called a Zippo. No money involved,' I light my new lighter. The yellow blue flame is steady and undisturbed by the heat from the adjacent Wok. 'Apparently it's guaranteed to light every time even in a typhoon.'

'That's impressive,' says Lash, as he shovels another forkful of fried rice into his mouth. He isn't interested in watches and as a non-smoker isn't interested in cigarette lighters either.

I am lounging, with Lash and Gringo, on our rattan loungers on the sunny side of the mess block. Lash is watching Gringo roll himself a 'tickler'. He does it well enough.

'Pete can roll a tickler with one hand,' says Lash.

Gringo rolls the end of his cigarette into a point, tosses it into his mouth – a trick he is rather proud of – and lights it. Through a cloud of exhaled smoke he says. 'What?'

'Pete can roll a tickler with one hand,' repeats Lash.

'Can ya?' He looks at me.

'Yeah. An old bloke in a Felixstowe café taught me when I was at Ganges.'

Gringo tosses his cigarette papers and his tobacco at me. 'Show me.'

So I roll a cigarette, lick the end of the gummed paper, give it a twist and toss a perfectly formed tickler onto the table. 'Can I smoke that then?' I ask.

Gringo nods and watches me light it. 'That's ferkin brilliant. Show me again.'

'I've never seen anybody else do it except for Pete and Tug at Ganges,' says Lash.

'You need a strong index finger and a flexible thumb,' I explain.

After multiple attempts, the scattering of much tobacco and torn cigarette papers, it's apparent that Gringo has neither a flexible thumb, a straight index finger or the co-ordination necessary to master it.

'Ferk it,' yells a frustrated Gringo.

On the first day of November, a small dog takes up residence in our part of the mess. Popeye Barrett, who has a dog at home, declares it to be a man dog and suggests that we check him out for any noticeable problems. We don't find anything that looks dangerous or infectious, so as a group we declare him fit and healthy. For some unknown reason we call him 'Tweekers'. Secretly, a few of us give him food we remove from the dining hall. Goodness knows where he sleeps: he wanders away as we are getting ready for bed and we don't see him again until morning. He is a quick learner and responds well to English commands like 'sit', 'come here' and 'ferk off you manky little bastard'.

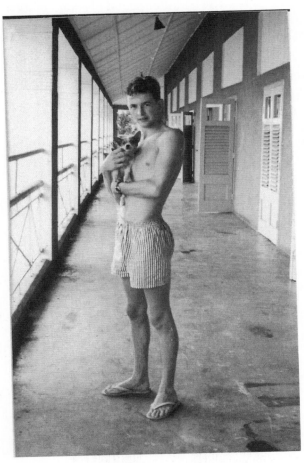

HMS Terror, *November 1962. There are a number of firsts in this picture: I am wearing my first flip-flops, I'm holding my first dog, 'Tweekers', and it's the first time I've been photographed in my underwear*

On Saturday, Lash and I agree to accompany Sugar into Singapore City to celebrate Bonfire Night. We feel it's a good enough reason to extend our horizons now that we have come to terms with what Sembawang Village has to offer us.

I learn why Singapore taxis are referred to as 'fast-blacks': all the taxis queuing up outside the dockyard gate are post-war black Mercedes Benz diesels. They all have leather seats, a small dashboard fan to cool the interior and are driven flat out all the way to town. We flit through Nee-Soon village without noticing it.

Somewhere the other side of Nee-Soon we screech to a halt and pick up an elderly Chinese man dressed in his pyjamas and pink plastic flip-flops. Lash and I move over as our new passenger squeezes on to the back seat. He stacks two twig-and-twine boxes on his lap, each containing a cowering white-feathered bird. When he is comfortable he taps the driver on the shoulder and we take off again. Lash and I look quizzically at each other. Our Chinese fellow traveller stares straight ahead, expressionless. One of the birds shits on the gentleman's pyjama trousers. Lash and I pretend not to notice.

The driver zig-zags through narrow streets in what we assume to be Singapore City. He pulls up outside a tumbledown building on a street full of tumbledown buildings. Our Chinese guest grunts something in Chinese; our driver responds. The old man slides out of the taxi, and with a bird cage in each hand shuffles away towards a partially open door.

We watch him shoulder the door open and disappear inside.

'What was he then?' Sugar asks the driver.

'Fatha,' replies the driver. 'Fatha of fren of wife who need today lift.'

We all nod in silence.

'He didn't pay then?' asks Sugar.

'Give me bird tomorrow sure.'

The driver pulls away from the kerb, narrowly missing an elderly wandering goat with a long grey beard and bright red eyes.

Sugar gets the taxi to drop us off in the centre of town and we walk. Singapore City is everything I could imagine a large oriental City to be: noisy, crowded, full of life, a different smell around each corner, run-down, dirty, potentially dangerous, entertaining and absolutely wonderful. The Singapore streets are an experience: we do battle with shopkeepers and hawkers trying to sell us things that we don't want. It's hot and sticky – there is no cooling breeze. We take refuge in a canopy bar where we enjoy a tepid Tiger. We refuse noodles. The streets and alleys are packed with people, rickshaws and old men riding pre-war black bicycles. Women in brightly coloured dresses, sarongs, or wraps that cover them from head to toe, peer from around partially open doors and coyly divert their eyes when we look at them.

Despite the fact that Singapore is awash with small bars and places serving food, Sugar is taking us to the city's main watering hole, the Britannia Club – a large NAAFI facility on Beach Road that, for some unknown reason, is located almost opposite the very exclusive Raffles Hotel. These two establishments couldn't be further apart socially. The Brit' Club is the main watering hole for Her Majesty's serving junior ranks. Raffles is exclusively for those with money or influence. It's impossible to get into Raffles wearing a 'lower-deck' uniform. As an Ordinary Seaman I'm required to wear my uniform ashore, so Raffles is most definitely out of bounds to me.

On the ground floor of the Britannia Club is a large, music-filled room. Alongside there is a spacious, well-ventilated Bar and a full-sized swimming pool. On the upper floor are further bars and a restaurant. Tonight is dance night: a scattering of young daughters of the Service community are being danced off their feet by a string of smooth-talking servicemen. Sugar knows some of the white-coated staff by name, but surprisingly none of the young girl dancers. True to form, Sugar manages a series of dances with a willowy blonde-haired beauty who hasn't yet grown out of, or discarded, her white ankle-socks. She is genuinely disappointed when her barrel-chested father arrives to take her home.

'Win some, lose some,' is Sugar's response. Not for the first time I wonder what he has that the rest of us don't.

There is something in the Singapore atmosphere that dislikes our UK clothing. A local form of humid mildew contaminates everything that isn't washed regularly. Inevitably Singapore has a solution. *HMS Terror*'s solution to the 'galloping green fungus' is Peanuts – a rotund, good-humoured Singapore Malay who owns a dry-cleaning business and has an exclusive contract with the Royal Navy. Every day he strolls down the centre of each mess followed by a couple of frantic assistants dragging large bags full of collected items of clothing.

'Hello Ingliss: anything for dry-clean?' Peanuts will chant. 'Excellent dry-clean or just cheap wishy-washy. You tell me.'

Peanuts always departs with a truck full of clothing and delivers freshly laundered or dry-cleaned items back to the mess within 48 hours. It's an extremely efficient business and I have no doubt that Peanuts will eventually retire a very wealthy man. He also lends money at a reasonable rate of interest during blank weeks. If you gave a false name and mess number it is possible to avoid repaying the loan that is never much more than 20 Singapore dollars. My grey John Collier's suit with the scarlet lining is definitely not suited to Singapore: during my eighteen months in the Far East I never wear it, yet Peanuts removes the 'galloping green fungus' for me half a dozen times.

By the middle of November, watch-keeping is becoming a way of life. I know most of the crew either by name or by sight and I'm very well acquainted with the layout of *HMS Lincoln*.

I find an old bike in the dockyard and with the help of a young Chinese guy called John, who has a cycle shop in Sembawang Village, Fez and I manage to get it dockyard-worthy. We trade export Woodbines for new spokes, chain, saddle and sets of brake blocks. Fez and I do timed races around a prescribed dockyard course when we are off-watch and in a competitive mood. Fez has cyclist's legs and normally beats me. My legs are swimmer's legs.

My suntan is coming along fine as I spend some of my off-duty time at the pool. Lash doesn't bother with the pool and instead does his sunbathing on a patch of grass outside the mess. He has told me many times that he lives in Lincolnshire, miles from the coast, and had never been in the water before joining the Navy. However, he is an enthusiastic sunbather and is a couple of shades darker than me: I suppose Lincolnshire is that much further south than Pudsey.

The Singapore monsoon arrives on the third Thursday of November. Fez and I, who have just started the First Dog watch, watch the clouds approaching from somewhere aft. At exactly 16:15 a warm wind picks up and snaps at our small protective awning. At 16:30 it starts to rain – gently at first but quickly increasing in intensity. Within minutes the rain is thundering down. Fez and I huddle under our awning. I can't see anything beyond *Lincoln*'s guardrails that are only four feet away. We slope the awning and the water pours off like a waterfall.

'Stay under the awning. That rain will hurt you if you step outside,' bellows Fez.

The rain hammers down. Our decks are awash and water is streaming out of the scuppers. The surface of the jetty is covered with bouncing water. Water is cascading from the top of the buildings opposite. The nearest monsoon drain is already full to overflowing. The noise makes conversations difficult – we have to shout.

'It'll last about an hour,' says Fez.

'It's amazing.'

'Now you know what the monsoon drains are for.'

'I thought they were for spewing up in.'

'That as well. Did you get yourself a Wan Chai burbs?'

'No.'

'This will happen at more or less the same time each day for the next six weeks or so.'

'Really?'

'So the next time we have the First Dog we'll slope the awning on the other side and we can have a monsoon shower.'

'Seriously?'

'The best shower you'll ever have.'

Back in *Terror*, Tweekers does a runner and we never see him again. Maybe he has other things to do during the monsoon season.

The Diving Officer places a notice on the main noticeboard asking for volunteers to train as Shallow Water Divers. Apparently *HMS Lincoln* only has one qualified diver and she should have at least five. 'Sooty' Stacks and I have a brief talk about it and decide to volunteer for the course that is held in *HMS Terror*. We are both good swimmers, tempted by the status, the badge and the extra money.

Immediately after my request is approved, someone is detailed off to do my Bosun's Mate job and on a Monday morning Sooty and I, along with half a dozen others, find ourselves in a small classroom in *HMS Terror*'s Diving School. Our Instructor is a bloke called Petty Officer McMurdo, hereinafter referred to as 'Deeps'.

The first day of the six-week course is concerned with safety and learning all about the equipment and the language of shallow water diving.

On the second day we dress ourselves as divers. The diving equipment is typical Ministry of Defence stuff: heavy, durable, uncomfortable and black. It's also always damp and never dries completely during the monsoon season. Next to our skin we wear a knitted wool dry-suit – an all-in-one affair which zips up the front. On top of this, we wear a wet-suit made of heavy-duty neoprene with tight elasticated cuffs at wrist, ankles and neck. It's relatively easy to get into the legs, but the upper half is impossible to pull on by yourself. Working in pairs, we pull and twist first one arm then the other, followed by more manoeuvring to get the metal neck-ring in place. A rubber hood is placed over our head followed by a chest-mounted canister, associated strapping and an oxygen bottle. Wearing all this, and carrying a pair of huge flippers, we make our way down to the jetty and jump into the waters of the Singapore Straits. While flapping around to get the feel of our equipment, we are tested on how well we can swim. Because all the ships in the dockyard are short of divers, we all pass this first assessment. The course is to be a combination of classroom diving theory, physically testing runs and a prescribed number of day and night dives.

On the third day we are given weights and, with all our kit on, we tread water while adding or removing weights to establish our individual buoyancy characteristic. It takes a while for Deeps to issue us all with the correct weights. Then, for the first time, we dive under water. This is a strange experience – to be totally submerged in water and breathing.

Shallow Water Diving in the Royal Navy is 'tended'. This means that every Shallow Water Diver is permanently linked to a shoreside handler by means of a lifeline which is also used as a communication tool. There is a code of 'pulls' and 'bells' that cover most diving contingencies and which have to be memorised.

The first dive is uneventful enough. With all the weight we carry, we do exactly what we are equipped to do: sink like a stone to a point 10-12 feet below the surface. Once on the muddy bottom we have to slow-count to a hundred, then make the required signal to our handler who hauls us back to the surface.

After my first dive, I'm questioning if I have done the right thing. Although I'm comfortable in the water, this diving business is hard work and not that enjoyable.

'Do you think we've made a cock-up, Sooty?' I ask that evening in the Armada Club.

'Dunno.'

We are drinking orange juice, as Deeps has warned us not to drink alcohol while on the course. We have a morning dive tomorrow.

'There's more stuff that I expected to this diving,' I complain.
'You're ferkin right there.'
'Is it worth it for four and six a week?'
'Not yet it isn't.'

Next morning we get kitted up again. With a pair of long black flippers over my shoulder I double down to the foreshore and out onto the dive jetty. I'm knackered by the time I flop into the water. One of the class spews up inside his facemask and is pulled out immediately.

'Didn't I tell you not to drink alcohol before a dive?' bellows Deeps.

The guy, with a face mask full of carrots and an unidentified green vegetable, nods.

'You're off the course. Get yourself cleaned up. Clean your kit, return it to the Dive Store and report to the Ship's Office.'

It's a lesson to us all: no alcohol means ... no alcohol.

On day five, we are set to work underwater. We are each given a hacksaw and told to remove a six-link length of chain from a pile tied around one of the underwater pier support stanchions. I make myself comfortable on the bottom. I'm immediately engulfed in a cloud of brown stuff. Eventually it settles and I identify my pile of chain and get to work. We can all see each other, so it's a competition to see who can saw through their link the fastest. Sooty, whose dad has a fishing boat in Great Yarmouth and who is used to dealing with chains, is the first to finish. He gives the signal and is hoisted to the surface. I'm not second ... but neither am I the last.

Back in the classroom the reason for the red light positioned above the blackboard is explained. Whenever this light comes on, we have to drop everything, rush outside, get dressed in full equipment and run down to the diving pier. So, instead of concentrating fully on the classroom blackboard, we spend our time watching the red light that is switched on at least once a day.

Another member of the class decides that Shallow Water Diving is not for him and leaves us.

On Friday afternoon, as we are packing our kit away and looking forward to a weekend of no diving, we are told to report back to the school at 18:30 for a night dive. Rumour has it that this is the most terrifying part of the course.

At 20:45 we are fully kitted out and standing on the unlit pier. The only light is from the instructor's torch. The waters of Singapore Straits look ink-black and uninviting. We are once again issued with a small hacksaw. Deeps explains that our task is the same as last time: to cut another length of links from a chain, but this time by feel only!

Under water there are millions of dots of electric blue and bright green lights darting everywhere in the dark waters. Deeps had warned us about the phosphorescence and it had taken me a while to come to terms with it, despite it being weirdly attractive. As I sit on the bottom cuddled up to my pier stanchion and groping for a chain that I can't see, a large pulsating electric-blue jellyfish joins me. I panic and wave my hacksaw at it. It takes no notice and just stays, pulsating and silent with its long tentacles waving an arm's length from my facemask. I grope for the chain while keeping one eye on my pulsating companion. It takes me ages but I cut my link, make the signal and am hoisted up to the surface, flicking my electric-blue companion with my flippers as I pass it on my way upwards.

Sitting on the jetty, still trembling, I remove my mask. 'I've just seen the biggest ferkin jelly-fish ... monstrous bastard ... hovering inches from me while I was working.'

'That would be Gordon,' says Deeps. 'He always comes along for the first night dive just to give one of you a bit of a scare. He's a baby really. Out there are really big bastards, six or seven feet across with tentacles as thick as your leg.'

'You're kidding.'

'You're kidding WHAT?'

'You're kidding, PO.'

'That's better. Not a bit lad, not a bit. Get out of the water, hang your equipment up and off you go back to your mess. Give the Armada Club a wide berth. Check your swimming costumes.'

My swimming costume requires a seriously good 'crashing out' and an overnight soak in hot water.

Boy, do I sleep. I have a dream starring Gordon.

In the morning I have a dreadful earache. Following Lieutenant Lamin's talk about the dangers of Chinky Toe Rot and Dhobi Rash, I habitually dump loads of foo-foo on my feet and my groin area, but I overlook my ears. I show Deeps my aching and inflamed ear and he confirms that I have contracted the dreaded Singapore Ear. He removes me from the course immediately. I'm devastated but he tells me that I can re-apply at a future date. Of course I will have to start at the very beginning again.

The following day I'm back watch-keeping. I tell Fez all about the diving, the Singapore Ear and Gordon.

'It ferkin hurts,' I complain.

'It goes after a few days if you keep your ears dry. Don't swim and don't get your ears wet in the shower.'

'Sooty' is also bumped off the course for contracting Singapore Ear.

During the First Dog watch, Fez and I prepare ourselves for the rain. As the dark clouds approach, I slope the awning on the starboard side. As an ex-quarterdeck member on a Battle Cruiser I'm good at sloping awnings. Fez and I take it in turns to strip down to our underwear and shower. I have fully soaped myself and am preparing to rinse myself off when the rains abruptly stops.

I present myself to Fez covered in soap. 'Somebody switched the ferkin monsoon off!'

He laughs. We attach a dockyard hose to a fire hydrant on the jetty and Fez hoses me down. Fortunately there is nobody in authority about.

The sun comes out and soon everything begins to dry. The smell of a wet dockyard combined with the aroma of freshly watered vegetation is tremendous. Within an hour most of the water has drained or evaporated away.

The following day, I go down the 'stalls' and buy myself a waxed bamboo umbrella designed to withstand the monsoon rains. My Wan Chai Burbs costs me one dollar and fifty cents. Almost everybody in the mess has bought one. Individually they stink of fish glue. In large numbers, drying on the balcony of the mess, it smells like Bridlington harbour on a good fish-landing day. It makes sense to carry a Wan Chai Burbs if you are liable to be outside between 16:00 and 18:00 and I get into the habit of always carrying mine with me. I wonder what Mum would say if she knew I carried an umbrella around with me. I write her an amusing letter and explain all about the monsoon weather and the Wan Chai Burbs. I don't tell her about the Singapore Ear or the failed diving course.

During the First watch, because I have nothing better to do, I read a copy of the English-language *Singapore Straits Times*. Apparently on 8 December, 4,000 men of the North Kalimantan National Army attempted to capture the Sultan of Brunei, seize his oil fields, and take European hostages. British forces in Singapore responded promptly and within 30 hours Gurkha troops had secured the town of Brunei, thereby ensuring the Sultan's safety. In early December the British Far East Command claimed that all major rebel centres were now occupied. British forces, composed of five UK battalions plus a Gurkha infantry battalion, are now deployed in Singapore, Malaya and Hong Kong. The rebel TNKU still have significant support in Kuching and Tawau in Sarawak.

I receive a letter from Mum telling me all the Pudsey news and that the weather forecast is for a severely cold winter. My brother Tony, who is almost 14, has been caught by the local copper playing 'you show me yours and I'll show you mine' with the ginger-haired girl over the road. I write him a letter and tell him what I know about ginger-haired girls in general and the one who lives over the road in particular.

I also receive a letter from Wilco that contains lots of explicit sexual stuff. Her handwriting is beautifully feminine but her spelling could be better, particularly when she's writing about bodily bits and pieces. I read her letter over and over again ... and come over all unnecessary.

In mid-December we are told to prepare ourselves for Ships' Company Divisions on the Parade Ground at *HMS Terror*. Panic. Immediately, almost everybody tries to find a way of avoiding them. Some of the more experienced manage to get themselves excused ... but not me, despite it being my scheduled 24 hours off-watch. Ships' Company Divisions are arranged purely so that we can meet the Captains of *HMS Lincoln* and *HMS Terror* and they, and our Divisional Officers, have the privilege of meeting us face-to-face. It's also to make sure that we all have a smart white tropical uniform.

There are a number of yellowed suits on parade and I'm thankful that I took mine home during my last UK leave to be washed and altered. It's almost impossible to avoid scuffing my white canvas shoes.

There is a failure in communication somewhere down the line and we are kept waiting, stood at ease in the hot sun facing the Parade Ground mast waiting for the Captain of *HMS Terror* to appear.

By the time he arrives, accompanied by our Captain, we are glowing red hot. While the Seaman Division are stood to attention, waiting to be is inspected, our Divisional Officer leans over my shoulder from behind. 'Name?'

'Err – Broadbent, sir.'

'Rank?'

'Ordinary Seaman sir.'

'Who advised you, Ordinary Seaman Broadbent, to wear black-and-red flowered underpants under your uniform trousers on today of all days?'

'Nobody sir.' I look down. Through my well-fitting, sweat-soaked trousers I can clearly see the outline of red orchids and green foliage on a black background. Oh shit!

Lincoln's Captain passes me without comment, as does the Captain of *HMS Terror*. A Lieutenant, one of the skippers' retinue, stops and smirks at me. 'Not a sensible choice of underwear, Ordinary Seaman Broadbent.'

'No, sir.'

'How are you coping with life onboard *HMS Lincoln*?'

'Very well sir, thank you.'

'Now pass that ruddy starring exam.'

'Yes, sir. Will do, sir.'

'And wear neutral-coloured underwear under your white uniform in future.'

'Yes, sir.'

We march past the saluting dais to the tannoyed tune of 'The Lincolnshire Poacher'.

I write to Mum. Then, not having any experience in writing sexual stuff, I have to decide how to respond effectively to Wilco.

I notice 'Brick' Wall lying on his bunk, writing. He has a pile of letters tucked under his pillow. 'Have you got to reply to all those, Brick?'

'Yeah. We're going to get engaged when I get home.'

'And is she writing every single day?'

'Yep.'

'Crikey ... so you're having to write every day as well then?'

'Every other day.' He pushes Polly's letters further under his pillow.

'How about postcards instead of letters ... they're quicker.'

'Never thought of that.'

'And she'll get a picture.'

'Good thinking, Pete. Cheers mate – I'll give it a try.'

'Does ... err Polly ever write anything ... you know ... of an explicit sexual nature?' I ask.

Brick stares wide-eyed at me. 'Good God no, mate.'

'Never?'

'Never.'

'Forget I asked.'

Leading Radio Operator George Wild and Fez are good friends. George gets UK news almost as soon as it happens as he is working in the Communication Centre in *Terror*.

Fez has an uncharacteristic grin on his face as we begin the Afternoon Watch on the Sunday before Christmas.

'Another hot day then, Pete lad?'

'Yeah.'

'Apparently the UK is in the middle of a big freeze.'

'Is it really?'

'Don't suppose you heard the football results this morning?'

'No.'

'We were playing you.'

'At Elland Road?' I ask.

'No. Roker Park.'

'And?'

He smiles. 'Sunderland 2 ... Leeds 1.'

'It's only a game,' I shrug.

'You wouldn't say that if you'd won.'

My first Christmas away from home. Santa hasn't brought me any presents so, along with some friends, I drink Tiger

Christmas 1962 is the first one I have ever spent away from home. We have a terrific dinner in the Dining Hall served by our Officers and Senior Rates. It's a naval tradition for them to serve us Christmas dinner and to make sure that our glasses are kept topped up.

A large group of us slip down to Sembawang for a couple on our way to Singapore town and The Brit' Club, where we get 'well- oiled'. It's our way of forgetting that Santa didn't bring us any presents this year!

Between Christmas and the end of the year *Lincoln* is awash with Dockyard workers carrying, lifting, fixing, hoisting, lowering, bolting and welding. All our machinery is reinstalled and *Lincoln's* transformation from floating scrapyard to operational warship is complete according to schedule. On the last day of 1962, *HMS Lincoln* officially emerges from refit.

George Wild has assumed the role of the bloke who keeps us informed of local events. He posts his first Crisis Report, giving us some background information.

Malayan Crisis Report #1

Last year the island of Borneo was divided into four separate states. Kalimantan, comprising four Indonesian provinces, is located in the south of the island. In the north, separated from Kalimantan by a 1,000 mile-long border, are the Sultanate of Brunei (a British protectorate) and two colonies of the United Kingdom, British North Borneo (now renamed Sabah) and Sarawak.

The three UK territories total some 1.5 million people, about half of whom are Dayaks who are spread throughout the country in village longhouses and are not politically organised. About 25% of the population are Chinese and the remaining 25% are Malays.

The creation of Malaysia means that Malaysian Army units are deployed in Borneo (now East Malaysia). RN guardships make a seaborne attack unlikely, but the myriad creeks and rivers around Tawau, Cowie Harbour and Wallace Bay are a challenge.

The enemy are opposite Tawau on the Indonesian half of Sebatik Island. This force consists of five companies.

On 17 October this year six insurgents dressed in civilian clothes crossed into Sabah and burnt down a village. In late December, an insurgent force of approximately 200 crossed into Sabah and remained in the swampland undetected for eight days. The mission was to capture Kalabakan and then move on Tawau with Indonesian expatriates rising to join them. At 11:00 on 29 December, an allied position was taken by surprise, with eight killed, including the commander, and 19 wounded. An attack on the police station shortly after failed. The attackers moved north instead of east to take Tawau. Gurkhas have been flown in, and the fighting was over after a month. Two-thirds of the insurgents were killed or captured and admitted that they expected the population to rise and greet them as liberators.

I will publish more information as it becomes available.

LRO George Wild.

New Year's day is a holiday and most of our crew and that of HMS Loch Lomond spend it in the Armada Club: we don't make it as far as the Village. Skid and Sugar join me and Lash, and as a group of ex-Bermuda's we have a great time drinking over old times. Sugar is particularly edgy most of the afternoon. Eventually he takes his leave, telling us that he has a date with the fair-haired offspring of a sergeant in the Parachute Regiment.

'That has the hallmarks of a potential problem,' says Skid.

'I know, but she's a one hundred percent natural blonde and you don't find many of those in this part of the world,' grins Sugar.

'But her old man is in the Paras.'

'Some things are worth the risk,' he declares, smirking.

We watch him strut away to his mess to get changed..

'A natural blonde ... does that mean her hair is naturally blond?' asks Lash.

'Yes, Lash lad,' says Skid.

The following day *Lincoln* is cleaned, fixed and ready to do her duty. With everything in its correct place, *Lincoln* looks like what she is: a Type 61 Salisbury Class Aircraft Direction Frigate, displacement 2,190 tons driven by eight ASRI Diesel engines connected to controllable pitch propellers. To defend herself from air or surface attack she is armed with a twin 4.5" turret and an anti-submarine Squid mortar on the Quarterdeck down aft. I don't yet know what type of radar she uses.

Our red wooden gunwale rail that runs around the entire upper deck was given an additional coat of Admiralty-approved scarlet yesterday by the men under punishment. Now we are reclassified as a seagoing ship, I'm very proud of our distinctive red edge – it makes us stand out from the crowd.

HMS Lincoln is officially commissioned on Saturday 5 January. The section of the jetty alongside the ship is clear of dockyard rubbish, swept and hosed down by an army of dockyard workers.

Dressed in my full white uniform for the second time, and with neutral-coloured underpants firmly in place, I muster on the jetty with the rest of the Ship's Company at 11:15. Many of us stand in hung-over silence as the Commissioning Warrant is read, followed by the National Anthem. The Ensign, Jack and the commissioning pennant is hoisted and the Captain addresses the crew ...

'Brethren ...'

Brethren! All of a sudden we are brethren.

'Brethren, seeing that in the course of our duty we are set in the midst of many and great dangers, and that we cannot be faithful to the high trust placed in us without the help of almighty

God, let us unite our prayers in seeking His blessing upon this ship and all that serve here now and in the days to come.'

We sing the first hymn: 'Lead us, heavenly Father, lead us, o'er the world's tempestuous sea ...'

One of the three Chaplains in attendance prays for us. *HMS Lincoln* is formally blessed and we sing 'For those in peril on the sea', at the end of which the Chaplain, with arms raised, encourages us to 'To go forth into the world in peace and be of good courage ...'

'Go forth into the world and multiply would be more fun,' whispers someone behind me.

HMS Lincoln is now a fully paid up, albeit apprenticed, member of the Far East Fleet's 8th Destroyer Squadron – despite the fact we are very much a Frigate.

Our messes were allocated on the noticeboard in *HMS Terror* some weeks ago. Along with eight others I'm in 15 mess, that is a partitioned section of a large messdeck area located below and a bit aft of the forecastle. Each section is separated from its neighbour by a two-tier bank of lockers. On the ship's side of each section are two bunks that fold down to form a long-backed seat. Down the centre of the mess section is a single Formica-topped table flanked by two burgundy-cushioned benches. Leading Seaman Tansy Lee is in charge of our mess and he has one of the bunks; the other is given to Popeye, who is the senior Able Seaman in the mess. 'Tommy' Steel is disappointed when he is identified as the second most senior Able Seaman. The rest of us are issued with hammocks. Thanks to Tansy, I'm allocated one of the three slinging points above the mess table. The remaining two mess members have to find slinging points in the main mess passage.

The others in the mess are Able Seamen 'Apple' Pye, 'Brick' Wall, 'Lash' Trainer and 'Gringo' Kidd. I'm the only Ordinary Seamen in the mess – although I have passed professionally for Able Seaman, I'm unrated because of the ruddy starring exam. Lash is a few months younger than me but outranks me because he is more interested in the Radar Plotting stuff than I am. The messing is the same as on my previous ship. We collect food from the main Galley in trays and eat it in the mess. Tansy draws up a roster of 'cook of the mess' and mess cleaning duties etc.

He gathers us all in the mess and lays down the rules. 'No gambling openly for money. You can play for matchsticks or cigarettes that represent money but no money on view. Understand?'

Everyone nods.

Tansy refers to his scrap of paper. 'Cooks of the mess are responsible for collecting the food trays from the galley at meal times. They are responsible for dishing out the food, cleaning and returning the trays to the galley. Individuals are responsible for cleaning their own plates and eating irons. Cooks of the mess can only swap duties with my permission. Clear?'

Everyone nods.

'Cooks of the mess will do messdeck cleaners after both watches the following day. Hammocks are to be lashed and stowed before breakfast. Morning watchmen should arrange to get time off to lash and stow their hammock. Don't leave items of kit loafing around the mess. I'll run a Scran-bag if it starts getting untidy. OK?'

Everyone nods.

'If I ever find a dry towel over a locker door I'll be having a word. No crabs in this mess – OK?'

We all nod.

'Mess dress is to be dress of the day. As we lack any air conditioning I don't mind if we sit around the mess with shirts off, but you will all wear a shirt or a white-front at meal times. Understand? No drying of dhobying on the black heaters – there's a heated drying room down aft.'

Everyone nods.

'I'll issue other instructions as time goes on. You've all lived in messes before so the normal messdeck etiquette applies. Before I forget ... girly magazines are to be stowed away, don't leave them loafing, remember we share this area with members of the Communication branch and others who are capable of removing said magazines, even if they don't understand what it's all about. OK?'

Everyone nods and grins.

Tansy claps his hands and stands. 'Anyone who wants to talk to me about anything ... I'm always here.'

We all nod again and disperse.

To celebrate *Lincoln's* commissioning, Lash, Gringo and I go down the Village, buy some of the girls 'sticky greens', enjoy their company and get staggeringly drunk.

The food onboard *Lincoln* is much better than I expected. We have uniformed local Chinese Cooks and Stewards onboard, plus a small number of Chinese 'unofficials'. There is a Wardroom messboy, four laundry crew managed by a bloke called No1 Laundry Man, and a tailor called Sew-sew who has a small compartment up forward. In a tiny compartment on 01 deck aft is a cobbler called Shoe-shoe who has a noisy caged parrot for company.

Most of us trundle to *HMS Terror's* Armada Club on Saturday evening to watch our football team play *HMS Caesar* in the final of the 'Small Ships Cup'. Conveniently the pitch is directly opposite the club, so we don't have far to go to keep ourselves hydrated. We outnumber *Caesar's* crew on the terraces as we have all been given a token for two pints of free Tiger from the ship's tombola fund. PTI 'Gunga' Dyne has been telling us for some weeks that he has put together a particularly good football team considering our size. Although we haven't played many matches, we have yet to be beaten. Tonight *Lincoln's* first eleven, resplendent in a brand new strip of Lincoln green, soundly beat the team from *HMS Caesar* 5-0 to win the Small Ships Cup. We are a noisy, celebratory mob who catch the last couple of buses back to the dockyard.

In the mess, sitting in a tailor-made, marine-ply stowage position on top of the forward bank of lockers along with the rest of the mess-traps, is the sacred mess rum fanny. It's newly issued and it's inside surface hasn't yet developed the required rich amber colour. Apparently, the darker the inner surface, the better the rum tastes. Traditionally the inner surface is rinsed but never, ever seriously cleaned. Those of us younger than twenty years old are told that we will make ourselves scarce at tot-time, which takes place in the mess at noon each day. The daily ceremonial is overseen and controlled by Tansy, with Popeye as the designated Rum Bosun and Tommy as his assistant.

Popeye takes the mess rum fanny to the forward capstan flat at exactly 11:30 each day. There he waits, with all the other mess Rum Bosuns, for the Officer-of-the-Day along with the Duty Petty Officer and the Duty Stores Assistant to arrive. The neat rum is mixed with the specified amount of water (ratio 2:1) in a large brass-hooped half-barrel emblazoned with the words 'GOD SAVE THE QUEEN' in polished brass lettering. The mixture of two parts water mixed with one part of neat rum is issued to those below the rank of Petty Officer: the addition of water causes the mixture to go flat after an hour or so, thus preventing its storage for 'a rainy day'. This dilution process is known as 'Grog'. Under the watchful eye of the Officer-of-the-Day, the identity of each mess and the amount to be issued is called out by the Duty Petty Officer and measured and poured by the Stores Assistant. Each mess is issued with enough rum for each entitled member.

Popeye enjoys his job as Rum Bosun. Having collected the Rum, he takes it down the mess and dishes it out, and is traditionally offered 'sippers' from every recipient's 'tot'. After everybody has been issued their tot there is generally some rum left in the fanny – this is called 'Queen's' and is distributed equally around all the eligible members. The tot is the ultimate marketable messdeck commodity: everything onboard has a tot-percentage attached to it and much business is conducted via the rum fanny. For a full tot you can get someone to do your duty, sling your hammock for a week, ditch an unwanted girlfriend, or swear black is white for you. If you are offered a full tot, tradition dictates that you return at least a quarter of it: to drink all of someone else's tot is considered discourteous. Other mess deck percentages that apply are 'halfers' which is approximately a quarter of a tot; 'gulpers' (approximately half a 'halfer') or a 'wet' (half a gulper). 'Sippers' is roughly half a 'wet' and is considered an acceptable 'thank you'. The least that can officially be offered is a 'snifter', which is when a full tot glass is slowly passed under the nose of the recipient. All these measures are approximate and are mutually agreed before any transfer takes place. It's dangerous to take more than is offered. Occasionally those of us who are under-age get 'sippers' or a 'snifter', but very rarely. In our mess we have one of the few men in the Royal Navy who is officially classed as 'temperance'. Years ago, on reaching the age of twenty, Tommy Steel elected to be credited with 4d a day as financial compensation for not drawing his tot. Tommy explains that it isn't because he doesn't like a drink – he does, but he just doesn't like rum or beer and has decided long ago that working out what to do with his daily tot was more trouble than it was worth.

Popeye makes one final attempt. 'How much does Pusser pay you for not taking your tot, Tommy?'

'Fourpence a day.'

Popeye rubs his hands together. 'I'll pay you a tanner for it ... three and six a week or, if you prefer, fourteen bob a month ... payable in advance of course. I'll even give you a good exchange rate in local Singapore dollars. That's a great deal, isn't it?'

'Can't do it, Pops. Once temperance, always temperance unfortunately. I can't revert.'

'Can't you give it a try?'

'I'll go down the Pay Office and give it a go,' agrees Tommy.

I'm sprawled on one of the mess benches enjoying a fight between two ladies – Poker Alice and Madam Moustache in *Wildcats*, one of J T Edson's well-thumbed paperbacks.

'You like reading, then?' asks Tansy.

'Yep.'

'Ever heard of Dennis Wheatley?'

'Nope.'

'Great writer. I've got a series of his Roger Brook books if you want to read something a bit more stimulating.'

I fancy the idea of something stimulating. 'Yeah, OK then.'

He rifles in his locker and extracts a thick paperback book.

Tansy thuds it on the table in front of me. '*Launching of Roger Brook*. That's the first in the series – great place to start.'

'It'll take me ages to get through that.'

'It won't because you'll get hooked, believe me,' says Tansy as he taps me on the shoulder. 'And don't dog-ear any of my pages.'

'I've got a bookmark.'

He taps me on the shoulder again, 'Good lad.'

Unbeknown to us, a major plumbing operation is being planned by members of the Stokers department. When the daily rum issue is finished each day in the forward capstan flat, the Officer-of-the-Day is responsible for making sure that any leftover rum in the barrel is disposed of correctly. Conveniently, the forward heads is alongside the rum issue area and the spare rum is carefully poured into the only hand washbasin located near the door. The Stokers are working out how to re-route the drainage pipework from the washbasin to somewhere other than the grey water tank.

Tommy reports to Popeye that he can't revert from temperance.

'Who did you ask?' asks Popeye.

'Leading Writer.'

'Can't we approach higher authority?'

'I'll give it a go.'

On Monday 14 January *HMS Lincoln* levers herself away from the jetty and, under her own power, manoeuvres herself out of Sembawang Dockyard for her post-refit trials. Because of current restrictions to the south and east of Singapore, we head up the west coast of Malaya to fine-tune ourselves. The Watch & Station Bill is published and posted. At sea I am still a Bosun's Mate. During Action Stations I'm in the Ops Room and a member of the whaler's crew for Kumpit Stations, whatever that is.

We regularly exercise the inevitable ...

'HANDS TO ACTION STATIONS. ASSUME DAMAGE CONTROL STATE ONE CONDITION ZULU ALPHA. HANDS TO ACTION STATIONS.'

Our designated role as an Aircraft Direction Frigate is to detect aircraft at long range with our sophisticated long-range radar. Given favourable atmospheric conditions we can, in theory, detect high-flying aircraft at a range of 180-200 miles with our type 960 air search radar. In the starboard side of the Operations Room are a couple of large circular horizontal radar screens; I'm the junior member of a team of experienced Radar Plotters who man these screens in almost total darkness plotting and reporting the positions of any surrounding aircraft. The Air Detection team were reasonably efficient during their Pre Commissioning Training at *HMS Dryad*. I had a bit of a struggle to fit in, but Petty Officer Rogers was a great help.

4

TWO INHERENT DESIGN PROBLEMS

It's rumoured that we will visit Penang on the west coast of Malaya, but this is cancelled and we scuttle on past. Those who have been to Penang before say it is a rather pleasant 'run ashore'.

Our fresh-water evaporating equipment is not working as well as it should ...

'DO YOU HEAR THERE, WATER RATIONING. ALL BATHROOMS FORWARD OF SECTION GOLF WILL HAVE WATER BETWEEN 09:00 AND 12:00 EACH ALTERNATIVE DAY STARTING TODAY. BATHROOMS AFT OF SECTION GOLF WILL HAVE WATER BETWEEN 14:00 AND 18:00 EACH ALTERNATE DAY. THE MAIN AND WARDROOM GALLEY ARE EXEMPT FROM WATER RATIONING.'

As we muster for both watches the following morning, The Buffer makes an uncharacteristic appearance.

He calls us to attention and paces up and down in front of the front rank for a while before speaking.

'I will not apportion blame, but someone ...' he draws breath ... 'someone who shall remain nameless forgot to collect the gash chute from its refit position on the dockyard jetty. HMS Lincoln is therefore chuteless. We can expect some repercussions when those on the bridge realise what we have overlooked. I suggest therefore that this information is kept to ourselves and that we exercise some common sense when ditching gash. We shall rig a canvas dodger and something to cover the deck on the Quarterdeck where gash is to be ditched. I know the names of those responsible and their heads will roll, believe me.'

We travel west through the clear blue Andaman Sea.

'DO YOU HERE THERE. THIS IS THE INFORMATION OFFICER SPEAKING. WE ARE CURRENTLY APPROACHING THE NICOBAR ISLANDS: TILLANCHANG, TARISA, CAMORTA, KATCHALL, NANCOWRY, LITTLE NICOBAR AND THE IMPRESSIVE GREAT NICOBAR. WELL KNOWN FOR THEIR ATTRACTIVE FEMALES WHO ARE UNCOMMONLY ATTRACTED TO FAIR SKINNED MEMBERS OF THE SENIOR SERVICE. WE SHALL BE SPENDING SOME TIME AMONGST THE ISLAND BUT WE ARE NOT PROGRAMMED TO VISIT ANY.'

After cavorting around the Nicobar Islands for a few days we head east to Langkawi for a promised Banyan.

'Roughing it' on Lankawi

We anchor off a deserted beach. Those who want to spend a couple of hours on a sun-drenched tropical beach with only palm trees for company are shuttled ashore in the whalers. As no alcohol is allowed to be taken ashore, Lash and I take some bottles of Frazer & Neave orange juice. Onshore the sand is as fine as talcum powder and the water crystal-clear and warm. Sitting on a warm, tropical beach with sand between my toes, staring out across the blue waters to where my floating home is anchored, is what I have been looking forward to ever since I walked into that Leeds Recruiting Office four years ago. The only thing missing is company ... female company. We hide our bottles of orange juice in a small hole dug in the sand below the water surface to keep them cool. We hide them so well that we lose them. Tommy has a camera and he takes some photographs. I decide to buy myself a camera from Sembawang's camera shop when we get back to Singapore.

HMS Lincoln has two inherent problems. Firstly, her evaporation equipment can't make enough fresh water to satisfy the basic needs of the crew in the tropics. Despite sailing with our water tanks full, within ten days our fresh water reserves run so low that we are subjected to the dreaded 'water rationing'. The shower cubicles are roped off and selected bathrooms locked. When our bathroom is open we bathe, shave and crash out our 'smalls' in as little water as possible. Everybody accepts the situation in good spirit.

The second problem is much more inconvenient. *Lincoln* was designed for North European waters and is equipped with lots of efficient black bulkhead-mounted heaters. What she lacks in the tropics is air conditioning.

The forward Seamen's mess is overflowing with practical individuals and it doesn't take long for someone to figure out a way of reducing the temperature in the mess. Tansy, Popeye and George between them arrange for a large canvas tube to be rigged from the forecastle access hatch down a ladder, a short way along a passageway and down through the mess hatch. Weather permitting, this arrangement provides a reasonably refreshing flow of cooling air into the mess.

While at anchor off Lankawi, Tansy arranges with the Engineering Department to run fire-fighting pumps to flow cooling seawater over the forecastle to cool our deckhead down a fraction.

Fortunately, my hammock slinging point is under a ventilation punkah louvre. At least I get a flow of tepid air that lowers my body temperature a little. But I'm 18 years old and physically adaptable: I'm getting used to the high temperatures. Away from the humidity of Singapore, the far eastern sun is very different. I spend much of my off-watch time on the upper deck, exposing myself to the very clearest of solar rays and the contrast between the colour of my upper body and the strip of skin under my watchstrap is increasing significantly. My teenage skin is becoming nicely weather-beaten. Brick is definitely the champion when it comes to colour change – he is a good deal darker in complexion than Shoe-shoe, who is a naturally dark-skinned Chinese.

Down the mess, Popeye hasn't given up on Tommy.

'Tom mate, did you ask someone higher about your tot?' asks Popeye draping a friendly arm around Tom's bared shoulders.

'PO Writer said no chance ... but I'm going higher.'

'Where?'

'Sew sew.'

We all laugh.

Popeye doesn't see the funny side of it. 'Seriously Tommy, what's the latest?'

'No chance mate ... I can't revert.'

'It's shit,' declares Popeye.

'There speaks one who has considered all aspects of the situation ... and made an informed decision,' says Tansy.

'It's shit,' repeats Popeye.

George posts his periodic UK news bulletin on the mess noticeboard. Most of it is boring political stuff. A bloke called Kim Philby has defected to the Soviet Union. We don't know why.

Popeye has taken it upon himself to bond with the ship's cooks. He insists that a good relationship with the cooks always has benefits. He reports that the Chief Cook is called Fu Kuo, which we all decide is rather amusing. One of the UK cooks is called 'Figgy' McDuff, a strapping bloke whose face is covered in combat scars earned as part of a number of Royal Navy rugby teams. Nobody argues with Figgy who has the shoulders of Charles Atlas. As a boy, Figgy had wanted to join the Navy as a Seaman, but because he was called McDuff, his Dad persuaded him to join as a cook where he could probably make a name for himself.

Popeye occasionally appears in the mess with a brown paper bag full of goodies for nine-o'clockers.

Life as a Bosun's Mate is different at sea. The watchkeeping routine is the same as in harbour, except I keep my watches in the wheelhouse, a small compartment containing the ship's wheel, port and starboard engine telegraph repeaters, a gyro compass repeater, a microphone to the bridge, a voice-pipe to the bridge (in case the microphone fails), a ship's Tannoy control panel and a couple of red canvas chairs. It's located three decks down from the bridge just aft of the main Radio Room. It's reasonably well ventilated when the door is fully open and tied back.

There is a series of very specific protocols for communicating with the Officer-of-the-Watch on the bridge. Whenever anybody takes over the wheel he identifies himself to the bridge in the prescribed fashion ...

Click the microphone on. 'Bridge wheelhouse.'

'Bridge,' comes the reply from above.

'Ordinary Seaman Broadbent on the wheel sir, course to steer three five seven, both engine telegraphs showing full ahead.'

'Very good, Ordinary Seaman Broadbent.'

... and then Pete Broadbent, a lad from Pudsey West Yorkshire, is driving *HMS Lincoln* and everyone onboard ... be they asleep or awake!

There is a basic hand/eye co-ordination skill involved in keeping *Lincoln* on course. The gyro repeater is mounted high on the forward bulkhead in front of the wheel and constant adjustment of the wheel is necessary to keep the lubbers line within a few degrees of the designated course. Inevitably, due to boredom, inattentiveness or just skylarking around, there are times when everybody drifts off course. If you can get it back on course before the Officer-of-the-Watch on the bridge notices then nobody is the wiser. But sometimes...

'Who is on the wheel?'

'Ordinary Seaman Broadbent, sir.'

'What course are you supposed to be steering?'

'Three five seven, sir.'

'Not three four zero?'

'No, sir.'

'Then get back on course ... and pay attention.'

'Aye aye, sir.'

As quickly as possible I'd rectify my error.

Click the microphone on: 'Bridge wheelhouse.'

'Bridge.'

'Course three five seven, sir.'

'Very good, Broadbent. Now pay attention.'

'Aye aye sir.'

When you hand the wheel over to someone else you click the microphone on: 'Bridge wheelhouse.'

'Bridge.'

'Permission for Junior Seaman Curd to take the wheel, sir.'

'Does Junior Seaman ... err ... who?'

Click the microphone on: 'Curd, sir. Junior Seaman Curd, sir.'

'Has Junior Seaman Curd had experience on the wheel?'

'No, sir. This will be his first time on the wheel, sir.'

'Who is the Quartermaster in charge?'

'Leading Seaman Parker, sir.'

'Is Leading Seaman Parker on the wheel now?'

'No, sir. It's Ordinary Seaman Broadbent, sir.'

'Junior Seaman Curd can take the wheel if he is continually supervised by Leading Seaman Parker.'

Click the microphone on: 'Aye aye, sir.'

Click the microphone on: 'Junior Seaman Curd on the wheel, sir. Course to steer ... err ... three five seven, both engine telegraphs showing full ahead.'

'Very good, Junior Seaman Curd. Concentrate and listen to the instructions from Leading Seaman Parker.'

'Aye aye, sir.'

We make sure the microphone is clicked off.

'I'm going for a piss,' says Fez.

With the departure of Fez, a couple of inexperienced Seamen are in total control of the entire ship!

In addition to steering the ship we have to make all the daily routine Tannoy broadcasts. One rather pleasant duty we have to perform is waking everybody up during the Morning Watch. In the Radio Room we rifle through the stacks of old 78 rpm records and find something to play that will really irritate everybody first thing in the morning. The 1812 Overture, or anything by Max Bygraves, always goes down badly. We take the wheelhouse telephone off the hook and close our door for a while afterwards.

Petty Officer 'Roy' Rogers, the senior Radar Plotter onboard, is an understanding type and arranges for me to spend half an hour with him each evening. He guides me gently through the basic principles of Radar Plotting *Lincoln* style. I apply myself to the hitherto perplexing world of radar and slowly begin to make sense of things.

Early in February, Captain 'D' and his staff carry out a post work-up inspection, which *Lincoln* passes. We are now officially allowed to play our part in the large International Naval Exercise, Jet 63. Joining us are warships from the Australian and New Zealand Navy along with Royal Naval Aircraft Carriers, Cruisers, Destroyers, Frigates and Submarines.

During the two-week exercise *Lincoln* gains a reputation for accurate anti-aircraft shooting: better than some of the custom-built Anti-Aircraft Frigates. For much of the time *Lincoln* is stationed a long way ahead of the main convoy to provide long-range early-warning air cover for the Aircraft Carrier *HMS Albion*. *HMS Loch Lomond*, *HMS Loch Alvie* and *HMS Cavalier* are skitting around defending the convoy from 'enemy' submarines. The remainder of the fleet, which includes four Royal Fleet Auxiliaries, are formed up in convoy formation some hundred miles astern of us. In the distance is the verdant coast of Sumatra.

We exercise towing other ships of the convoy and they tow us. We replenish ourselves with fuel and food from the Royal Fleet Auxiliaries and we regularly transfer concrete sinkers from one ship to another. Occasionally we have to transfer individuals. For some strange reason whenever we transfer an Officer we are unable to keep the jackstay transfer line taut enough to prevent his lower body getting wet.

Tansy is the Coxswain of the motor-whaler and I'm his chosen bowman. Whenever the boat is called away, Tansy and I – along with a Stoker and a young Seaman to act as stern sheetsman – scuttle up to the starboard waist. We do a lot of man-overboard exercises and on at least two occasions are called away to recover floatable bits of lifesaving equipment that have been tossed overboard.

During the final week, when nobody is looking, we slide away quietly into the South China Sea. We are getting used to our system of water rationing and the fact that our only air conditioning is a canvas tube. When water isn't coming over the forecastle we rig the chute from the forward hatch. Any change in the ship's course requires some of us to scramble up to the forecastle to check on the weather: the last thing we want is water coming down our chute. The chute is beginning to show signs of wear and we fear that it won't last long unless we carry out some running repairs. Along with Gringo, I'm initiated into the art of canvas repair. It isn't long before I become rather skilled at reinforcing or repairing canvas using a sail-maker's needle and palm.

I don't know if the any of the ships exercising Jet 63 noticed our disappearance but we appear to have escaped successfully.

Unusually we don't have a mess comedian, but Apple's cousin, Judith, regularly sends him jokes in her letters. Apparently it's her way of helping her favourite cousin keep his pecker up when he is so far away from home.

Apple slaps his letter. 'Got a good joke from our Judith.'

'Go on then,' instructs Tansy.

Apple coughs and focuses on his letter. 'A senior representative of Wimpy Burgers goes to see the Pope. He has a proposition. "My organisation is willing to donate five million pounds to your church, your Holiness." "Very generous of you, my son," replies the Pope.

"However," says the bloke from Wimpy. "We are a business, and there is one small condition attached. We would like you to change a line of the Lord's Prayer from 'Give us this day our daily bread' to 'Give us this day our daily burger.'" "I am sorry my son," replies the Pope, "We can't alter the holy text." "OK," says the bloke from Wimpy. "Ten million quid then." The Pope considers for a while. "I'll consult with my Cardinals." Some days later, the Pope addresses his assembled Cardinals. "I have some good news and some bad news." The Cardinals nod in unison. "The good news is, I have found a way of earning the church ten million smackeroonies." The Cardinals smile. "The bad news is – we'll have to terminate our contract with Hovis."'

Apple laughs. So do the rest of us apart from Brick who is busy putting his latest batch of letters from Polly into date order.

*

I spend my nineteenth birthday somewhere in The Andaman Sea, a good distance from any licensed premises. To celebrate,

Fez comes round to my mess with his tot to give me 'gulpers'. Fez is a Sunderland supporter, of course, and right now there is more than a hint of rivalry between us, as Sunderland and Leeds United are both battling for promotion from the second Division. In exchange for my 'gulpers' I give Fez both my bottles of Tiger.

The card game Euchre is becoming a problem. Every mess in the Royal Navy has its own rules. Because the Wardroom has decreed that inter-mess competitions should take place, a Euchre Standardisation Team is established and one person from each mess is elected to the team. Popeye is our chosen member because he wasn't paying attention when a show of hands was called for and fails to understand what is going on.

We rejoin the Jet 63 fleet as the International Naval Exercise is abruptly declared a success. An Admiral onboard one of the capital ships declares that he has a previous appointment. Pleasantries between all the participating ships are exchanged and gradually we disperse.

The rumour down the mess is that we are dispersing directly to Hong Kong.

'Hope you've saved some money for Honky Fid,' says Popeye.

'For all that Wan Chai has to offer,' adds Tansy.

'The place is crawling with women.'

'Good-looking women.'

I do a mental fiscal calculation. 'I've got money.'

'Spend it wisely, young 'un,' says Tansy.

Brick pauses in his letter writing. 'What's that?'

We all understand that when Brick is writing to Polly, he's oblivious to most things going on around him.

'Talking about the Hong Kong girls, Brick. Not that you will be interested,' says a smiling Popeye. 'What will Polly say if she knew you were gallivanting down the Wanch?'

'The where?' asks a perplexed-looking Brick.

'Back to your letter.' Popeye slaps Brick's writing pad.

Brick does exactly what he's told. He sticks the end of his pen in his mouth and ponders.

I'm all ears. Wan Chai ... Wan Chai: it sounds very Chinese ... and very inviting.

Seeing the mountainous mainland of China for the first time is a strange experience. Even the word China conjures up exotic thoughts – a mysterious land, about which I know little. There is an air of mystery about the name. I have heard about Mao Tse Tung, his Little Red Book and the Communist Red Army ... and, as an ex-philatelist, I can tell the difference between a Japanese and a Chinese postage stamp.

I sit alone on my favourite upper deck locker and glare at the Chinese mainland away on the port side ... until I run out of cigarettes.

Tansy volunteers Lash and I to act as Security Sentry for a short ceremony to be held in the forward capstan flat after supper.

I am instructed to close and clip the hatch leading to the Forecastle and then Lash and I are told to station ourselves on the aft side of both access doors to prevent anybody entering.

Standing outside the forward heads are two large Stokers: both are dressed in night clothing, one brandishing a polished wheel spanner. The one with a beard is wearing a large non-uniform cap. Tansy and George Wild are in conversation with the Stokers.

Another Stoker with a large oil-smeared face and wearing a pair of badly stained overalls emerges from the hatch that leads to the compartment below. 'All ready,' he says before disappearing through the hatch once again.

The bearded Stoker removes a bottle of Tiger beer from an adjacent cleaning-gear locker. 'Gentlemen,' he says. 'Today the

Mechanical Engineering branch are proud to announce a crucial modification to HMS Lincoln'vs waste water system.' He holds the bottle aloft. 'In this bottle is a 'tot' graciously provided by ME2 Glennister tae celebrate his 27th birthday. Tae demonstrate that the modifications work I shall now pour this into the sink.'

His partner takes over. 'The waste pipe from the sink has been modified and lined so that anything poured down can be collected in a glass container in another place. The object of this exercise is to collect the waste rum that is normally poured into this sink each day.'

The contents of the Tiger bottle are poured gently into the sink. Both Stokers take a deep breath and silently wait.

The overalled Stoker emerges from the hatch holding a single tot glass, being careful not to spill any of the contents.

The glass is ceremoniously handed to the bearded Stoker. He nods in thanks, closes his eyes and takes a mouthful. His eyes bulge. He nods, satisfied and hands the glass to his colleague who hands it to Tansy.

When all five of the party have had 'gulpers' and the glass is empty, the bearded Stoker officially declares the operation a success.

'The Stokers branch will ensure the continued cleanliness of the modified pipework and will correctly divert drainage flow at 11:00 each day. It has been agreed that the Stokers will be entitled to two thirds of the collected rum. The Seaman and Communicator's mess will split the remaining one third in whatever way they choose.' He sniffs the empty glass. 'Thank you for attending, gentlemen. Remember that we are the only ones who know about this. Shtum is most definitely the word.'

Popeye resigns after the first 'Euchre Standardisation Team' meeting as he doesn't understand a word that is said. He admits to us all that his card expertise begins and ends with 'Snap', and he's not so good at that when it speeds up.

Someone pins a notice on the mess noticeboard ... it's the agreed *Lincoln* rules for playing Euchre. I remember onboard *Bermuda* the playing of Euchre caused more arguments and physical violence than any other messdeck game.

I read and re-read the published rules, but can't understand them. I decide never to play.

The following morning, bright and early ...

'DO YOU HEAR THERE. THIS IS THE INFORMATION OFFICER SPEAKING. WE SHALL SHORTLY BE ENTERING HONG KONG AND BERTHING ALONGSIDE ADJACENT TO HMS TAMAR. THE NAME HONG KONG MEANS FRAGRANT HARBOUR IN CHINESE. HOWEVER YOU WILL NOTICE THAT THE WORD FRAGRANT HAS A TOTALLY DIFFERENT MEANING IN CHINESE THAN IT DOES IN ENGLISH. HONG KONG HAS ITS OWN WATER SHORTAGE PROBLEMS AND IS UNABLE TO SUPPLY US WITH FRESH WATER DURING OUR VISIT, WE WILL THEREFORE CONTINUE WITH OUR WATER RATIONING SCHEDULE. THE SHIPS COMPANY ARE WARNED OF THE INHERENT DANGERS OF VISITING AREAS ON THE ISLAND AND THE NEW TERRITORIES THAT ARE LISTED ON THE MAIN NOTICEBOARD AS OUT OF BOUNDS. PTI DYNE REPORT TO THE BRIDGE.'

Lincoln's Physical Training Instructor PTI Dyne, who is in the adjacent mess, stops in mid press-up. 'Wonder what they want now?' He wriggles into his tight white singlet and bounds up the mess ladder and away.

We all look on in silence.

'Brick,' says Tommy. 'You've got a pen. Go and copy the out-of-bounds list from the main noticeboard.'

Five minutes later Brick returns.

Reading from his slip of paper he says, 'The Shacks on Hong Kong Island. The Walled or Forbidden City in Kowloon. Any unlit alleys or backstreets. Any border areas with mainland China, Aberdeen's floating village and doubtful looking accommodation on Hong Kong island. There was something on the bottom I couldn't read because the paper was folded.'

'Good lad,' says Tommy. 'Now back to your letter writing.'

'Thanks,' says Brick.

The shacks

The 'fragrance' of Hong Kong hits us long before we enter harbour.

'That's the Hong Kong aroma,' says Tansy as he stands on the upper deck staring out towards an undulating green coastline.

I sniff and can smell something and fish …

'CLEAR LOWER DECK FOR ENTERING HARBOUR PROCEDURE ALPHA. CLOSE UP SPECIAL SEA DUTYMEN. ASSUME DAMAGE CONTROL STATE ONE CONDITION ZULU ALPHA. CLOSE ALL UPPER DECK SCREEN DOORS AND HATCHES. RIG OF THE DAY FOR ENTERING HARBOUR IS AS PUBLISHED ON DAILY

ORDERS. HANDS OUT OF THE RIG OF THE DAY CLEAR OFF THE UPPER DECK.'

In white fronts, white shorts, long blue socks, shoes and cap with chin-stay down we fall-in for entering harbour. It's a damp and misty morning. Hong Kong appears to have very little flat surface: the densely overgrown mountains explode skywards more or less directly from the shoreline. Finger-like grey mist strands swirl among the tall, slender glass and concrete buildings crammed along the waterfront. I suppose they are skyscrapers: tall buildings topped with signs advertising things in Chinese. Against the dark green backdrop of the slopes it all appears out of focus – surreal. Hong Kong looks as though she has drawn a silken veil over herself. Alluringly suggestive, it adds to her mystery. Hong Kong beguiles and intimidates me immediately. The Hong Kong aroma is a mixture of fish, oriental sewage and lots of Oriental people. My nostrils twitch: fragrant harbour indeed.

'One of the most densely populated places on earth apparently,' whispers Popeye who is standing next to me.

'Silence In The Ranks!' yells Petty Officer Oakley.

We berth on the outboard side of the jetty alongside *HMS Tamar*, the Hong Kong Royal Naval Barracks. An efficient battalion of little men wearing floppy pale-blue uniforms and rattan hats receive our berthing ropes.

The first person to bound over our gangway is the local salesman from Bernards, the Naval tailor's, dressed in a smart pinstripe suit. A line of other individuals with cases and boxes at their feet wait patiently to be given permission to come onboard.

As we tidy up all our berthing equipment, selected local traders are allowed onboard. Tailors, jewellers and junk sellers swamp the ship, moving quickly from mess to mess trying to drum up as much business as possible before we have the chance to find the same stuff better and cheaper ashore.

Already at home in our mess is a bloke offering to transpose our favourite photographs onto plates or pillows. It's good fun doing business in the mess – it feels as though we have the upper hand as we haggle on our home territory. Many of the traders set up shop on the upper deck adjacent to the gangway.

I've heard so much about Hong Kong: it has a tremendous reputation to live up to. If only half the stories I have heard are true, this is going to be one hell of a good run ashore.

As it's our first day in Hong Kong, *Lincoln* is visited by a host of local dignitaries. The Captain spends much of his time welcoming people onboard before being whisked away in a long, black limousine. Once the number of visitors is reduced to a trickle, leave is granted and simultaneously Hong Kong's veil is swept aside as the sun dips behind the darkening silhouette of the mountain backdrop. Hong Kong's lights reveal her sparkling splendour. The waterfront becomes a magnificent neon display: a kaleidoscope of electric colours. Skyscrapers become large multi-coloured light shows, dazzling against the black of her slopes. Large neon advertising hoardings ornament the tops and sides of the tallest buildings that I have ever seen, boldly tempting us in English and Chinese to buy San Miguel Beer, Mido wristwatches and a 101 other things. The place buzzes and pulsates with an overwhelming energy. Popeye, Lash and I skip through the dockyard and under the large, three-legged yellow crane. Once through the Dockyard gate, Popeye shows us the way to The China Fleet Club, a large building conveniently situated on the harbour waterfront. On its lower floor is a reception area leading to a large bar and a restaurant. The top two floors are accommodation units. The main bar is of typical Canteen décor: tough, semi-comfortable chairs and Formica-topped tables. The local beer is bottled San Miguel. According to Popeye the China Fleet Club's main bar is always crowded as it's used as a starting point for those heading around the corner to Lockhart Road and Wan Chai. We order beer ... and more beer.

Wan Chai is a neon-lit paradise – a confusion of bars, more bars and the occasional eating place. Between the bars there are long thin shops, but they go unnoticed. Lockhart Road is a multi-coloured enticing chasm. A blinding profusion of neon signs blink, flash and rotate: music gushes out of partially opened bar doors. Green double-decked, bow-fronted tramcars sporting

The China Fleet Club

Chinese adverts rumble sedately down the centre of the street, ploughing a furrow between rickshaws and taxis and what appears to be a million frantic Chinese. The roads and pavements are packed with hawkers, beggars and groups of staggering matelots intent on nothing more complicated than finding the next bar. Popeye is determined to take us to his favourite place.

Inside the dimly lit Old Toby Bar, the air-conditioning, the full blast of the jukebox, the smoke, the smell of excessively applied perfume, sky high testosterone levels and spilt beer hits me simultaneously. As soon as we are seated the girls arrive. They are certainly a lot more attractive than those in Sembawang, but they clearly have the same objective. The 'tight' Yorkshire part of me says not to waste my hard-earned cash on 'sticky greens'. The other, more masculine and spindrift part of me says go for it ... whatever the cost.

One of the girls punches Popeye gently on his shoulder 'I rememba yew! Yew come back to see me ... yew cheeky han-sum bastar.'

Popeye smiles and invites her to sit next to him. She is stunning, with long blue-black hair and is wearing a brightly coloured cheongsam that leaves little to the imagination.

Not much to tempt us here, then ...

My mouth is hanging, limply open. She organises a couple of her colleagues to join us. We do what we had rarely done in Sembawang: we buy the girls a drink, a small glass of two-dollar green liquid.

'Wha sheep yew on?' asks the girl next to me as she grabs my hat and gazes at the cap tally. 'Ah drinkin' Lincoln. We member last year wi Lincoln sheep.'

Popeye establishes the tone for the remainder of the session and refuses to buy his girl the next 'sticky green'. We follow suit, so they all leave us.

Popeye explains the Hong Kong system to us. By paying the Mama San a 'take-out' fee you can depart with the lady of your choice and then the rest is up to you: find and pay for a room and pay the girl her required fee. If you want to spend the day with a girl it will cost a packet to take her out of the bar during the afternoon. It gets progressively less expensive as the evening wears on. The cheapest 'take-out' rate applies after midnight but the girls' fees are increased as the evening's alcohol consumption makes it a sellers' market. 'They're all available. Pay the Mama-San at the bar and you can be whisked away into the back alleyways of Wan Chai for a session of oriental fun and frolics.'

'Are they clean?' Lash asks.

'VD, you mean?'

'Yeah.'

'Ferk knows,' replies Popeye. 'They'll always tell you that they are ... and they will show you a paper in Chinese which they say is a certificate.'

'Right then.'

'But it could be nothing more than a restaurant menu.'

Another gang of girls tries to relieve us of money for green water. We let them stroke our legs and tell us how handsome we are before refusing to buy them anything. Eventually Mama-San gets the measure of our table and stops sending girls over. We get on with the business of drinking and smoking ... relatively undisturbed. Every table is full and the girls are working hard. There is a variety of under-the-table stuff going on. There is a resounding farewell cheer as an occasional lad departs the bar in the company of a cheongsamed lady. Mama-San doesn't like the cheering and tries unsuccessfully to discourage it by waving her skinny little arms.

We have a drink or two in some other bars as we make our way back to the dockyard. All are similar. Those with well-maintained exteriors generally contain the more attractive girls. The run-down bars contain somewhat run-down girls. After my first night out in Hong Kong I think I have a little bit of it figured out. Hong Kong has an atmosphere which is difficult to define. At street level, it's much more than just another run-ashore: there is an intensity and a passion about the place. There is an unseen force somewhere beyond the neon facade of Wan Chai. In the back streets away from the bright lights, you sense the unknown and the inscrutable. I can feel it when walking the streets. The overwhelming number of Chinese makes me feel unusually vulnerable. According to Popeye, the Chinese will gladly sell you anything, smile and appear friendly, but will put a knife in your ribs for the contents of your wallet.

Fez and I are hanging about the gangway the next morning when a couple of elderly green open-backed trucks judder to a halt on the jetty at the bottom of our brow. A troop of tall, broad-shouldered ladies wearing well-washed blue jackets and paint-spattered, tight blue trousers stomp up the brow and march forward. Surprisingly, they appear to know exactly where they are going. I look on, open-mouthed. Apart from the shock of seeing thirty or so pyjama-clad ladies march onboard I'm impressed by their assuredness and transfixed by their appearance: there are a number of very shapely bottoms amongst them.

My hangover is forgotten. When the last of the backsides undulates away up the port forward ladder, I asks Fez. 'Who are they then?'

'Jenny's side party. Jenny has a contract with the Navy to work on the ship's exterior structure.'

'Doing what?'

'Chipping, painting. Whatever the Buffer requires.'

'So they're going to be working onboard then?'

'Depends what they've been contracted to do.'

'Some great arses.'

He waved a dismissive hand at me. 'You young 'uns are all the same. One run ashore in Hong Kong and you're experts. They're tough women. They'd have you for breakfast.'

Once the morning Stand Easy is finished the ship explodes with noise. It's the clatter of what I imagine a hundred machine guns sounds like.

'What the ...?' someone shouts.

'That'll be Jenny and her girls,' Fez says.

'Doing what?'

'Chipping. Sounds like windy hammers.'

The pneumatic paint-chipping hammers rattle continuously. Access to both sides of the forecastle is roped off. I easily step over the barrier up forward and look up at the forecastle. About twenty squatting ladies, all in a line and each wielding a noisy hammer are removing the green deck paint. There is a cloud of paint and rust forming at ankle level. Black compressed-air lines snake everywhere. The noise is deafening. For a while, I stand and admire Chinese backsides under tightly stretched blue trousers. I sigh and leave them to it.

'DO YOU HEAR THERE, THIS IS THE ENGINEERING OFFICER SPEAKING. I WILL LIKE TO SHARE WITH YOU THE GLORIES OF A DOUBLE REVERSIBLE FUNICULAR TRAM SYSTEM THAT CAN TRANSPORT YOU BEYOND THE POPULAR DELIGHTS OF WAN CHAI AND KOWLOON TO THE WONDERFUL PANORAMA OF HONG KONG'S PEAK 1,300 FEET ABOVE SEA LEVEL. I RECOMMEND IT TO EVERYBODY.'

Down the mess Tansy explains that Jenny, an elderly Chinese lady, works on every Royal Naval ship that visits Hong Kong. Apparently she is more efficient than the Seaman branch when it comes to stripping and applying upper deck paint. It's surprising how quickly our inbuilt noise-filter masks the sound of windy hammers. It eventually becomes nothing more than a background noise. Jenny's ladies don't stop for dinner.

A couple of Jenny's ladies are stationed outside the main galley as I collect our mess trays. They're a fine-looking pair with ruddy round faces and well-developed upper bodies. They don't look at me as I smile a friendly greeting. One of them has a long diagonal line of dried red paint splattered across her frontage. They are both wearing distressed straw hats.

'Two of Jenny's girls are hanging about the galley,' I say as I plonk the tray of fish steaks, mashed potato and carrots on the end of the mess table.

'They get food as part payment,' explains Tansy. 'Particularly when fish is on the menu.'

'Do you know what year 1963 is in the Chinese Calendar?' asks Tommy.

'Nope.'

'It's the year of the black water rabbit.'

'What?'

'The year of the black water rabbit.'

'What's a ferkin black water rabbit?'

My Hong Kong 'going ashore' routine is falling into place. On my days off I tie a chit to my hammock that identifies me as a Watchkeeper and grab a few hours' sleep and wait for Lash to get himself ready. We have already discovered that excessive dinnertime and afternoon drinking screws up the evening session so, after 'one-for-the-road' in the China Fleet Club, we head for Victoria where, among other things, we enjoy hailing a couple of rickshaws to have noisy sightseeing journeys through the crowded streets.

The Engineering Officer was right – the double reversible funicular tram system is an eye-opener. At the top of Hong Kong Island, above the pollution line, the air is crystal clear. The view is staggering. The greyish water of Hong Kong harbour, dotted with ships and junks of every size, is laid out far below. On the opposite side of the harbour is Kowloon and further in the distance the mountainous mainland of Red China and the New Territories. It's the most amazing bird's-eye view I have ever seen. Lash and I 'drink it in' while lounging in a convenient bar. To exercise we take a slow wander down the myriad of narrow paths, admiring properties belonging to those wealthy enough to afford them at this altitude.

During the first week we spend every other afternoon in cultural pursuits. After our first visit to The Peak, we go to Repulse Bay where I enjoy a swim while Lash sits on the beach looking after my clothes. Overlooking the bay is the Repulse Bay Hotel which is designed with a large hole in its centre. Apparently this is so that the dragon, that lives in the mountains behind the hotel, retains its unrestricted sea view. I don't know whether to believe it or not. The weirdest place we visit is Aberdeen and the floating village. Having slowly got used to the smell of the main harbour, neither of us are prepared for the nasal onslaught that is Aberdeen harbour. Tansy, who is with us, explains that it's a floating city of rattan-topped boats where children grow up, become adults, and die – all without apparently ever setting foot on dry land. The boats are moored hard up against each other in what is the safest place to be in Hong Kong during the typhoon season.

Aberdeen's floating village

'Typhoon season!'

The water I glimpse between the boats doesn't move despite the fresh offshore breeze.

Tansy also shows us the ornate slab-sided Floating Restaurant: a large black-red-and-gold pagoda sitting on top of a large green barge. Renowned for its food, it's one of the many places in Hong Kong where you can select your fish from an aquarium and have it cooked for you. It's moored far enough from land to provide a good living for the operators of the small 'bum boat' ferries that scurry back and forth.

In the evening Lash and I 'invest' our hard-earned money in the bars of Wan Chai. Some of the many bars we try are The

Cherry, The Suzie Wong, Kowloon Nights, The Mermaid, The Neptune, The 4 Sisters, The Blue Heaven, The Ocean, The Pussycat, The Playboy, The Pink Lady, The 4 Aces, and the Horse Shoe on Cameron Road.

We regularly end up in The Old Toby on Lockhart Road. Tonight Popeye and Brick are already there, occupying the best table; the one in a darkened corner between the bar and the heads. They are playing host to a couple of girls. Brick is glaring at the ceiling – something is happening under the table-top.

Popeye ushers his female companion away.

'Join us, lads. Brick here has an itch that needs scratching. It's the second time in three hours.'

We look at Brick at the exact time his itch is well and truly scratched. He exhales, closes his eyes and lowers his forehead to the table. We wait.

Brick's companion snakes her way back to the bar.

'What would Polly say?' whispers Tansy.

Brick raises a silencing hand. His nose is dripping with spilt beer.

'Si down plea,' says a lady in a partially unbuttoned black cheongsam who gently pushes me onto a chair. 'You flom drinkin' Lincoln?' she asks.

Lash already has an arm draped over the shoulder of an extremely attractive lady with bright red hair.

'Careful, Lash,' says Popeye. 'That one in particular will take you for all the money you have.'

'That'll be nine dollars and eleven cents then,' replies Lash.

Brick raises his dripping cheek. 'That was worth every penny.' He cups his chin in his hands and stares at the table-top.

'Dollars,' corrects Popeye.

'How much?' asks Lash.

'Can't remember,' mumbles Brick.

'Yew buy me dlink hand sum?' A red-cheongsamed lady drapes her arm around my shoulder.

I look at Popeye.

He shakes his head.

'No thanks,' I say somewhat reluctantly. She's absolutely gorgeous.

'Got enough for a round, Pete?' asks Popeye.

'Yeah.'

'Get 'em in then.'

'Can we have five San Migs, please,' I ask the departing lady in red.

She undulates away. Cheongsams do an awful lot for women. Tight with perfectly positioned slits – they're brilliant.

'Annie' Oakley eyes me closely when I pass him in a passageway the following morning. 'I didn't know that you'd put in a request to discontinue shaving, lad.'

I stroke my chin. 'I haven't.'

'You haven't WHAT.'

'I haven't, PO.'

'But I can see stubble, lad. Stubble.'

I stroke my chin again. There is a slight resistance.

'When did you last shave?'

'Yesterday, PO.'

'I think you have reached the age, young man, when you need to shave each and every day.'

I smirk. 'Thanks PO.' I'm growing up.

Down the mess, we have mail.

A picture of a very attractive lady accidently falls out of Apple's letter.

'Who's that then, Apple?'

'Mi mother.'

'Never.'

'Tis.'

'But she's beautiful ... and you're so ferkin ugly.'

'Maybe he's adopted,' says Tommy.

'That's a possibility,' agrees Lash.

'I wasn't adopted,' says a suddenly flustered Apple. 'That's my mum.'

'You must have inherited your dad's ugly features then,' says Tommy.

'My dad's a good-looking bloke I'll have you know.'

'It doesn't make sense,' declares Popeye.

'There's sometimes a glitch ...'

'A mystery,' whispers Lash.

'Look,' says Apple as he stands up and jabs a finger at the picture. 'That's a picture of my mother, OK? And my dad is a good looking fella ... right?'

'You're definitely a glitch then,' says Popeye.

'Confirmed,' confirms Tommy.

'Piss off,' says Apple as puts the photograph back in the envelope and stomps away up the mess ladder.

'Let that be a lesson to you all,' says Tansy. 'Be careful what drops out of your envelopes.'

When it comes to my being cross-examined about all things Radar Plotting I have an extremely bad record and it has been officially recorded on my RP history sheet. However, on Thursday 21 March 1963, I sail through an examination by Petty Officer 'Roy' Rogers, the Senior Radar Plotter onboard. I know all I need to know about 293 and 982 radars and I can read and write upsidedown.

I'm awarded my RP star badges with little ceremony.

'Better late than never,' says Petty Officer Rogers.

'Thanks, PO.'

'Make out your request form to be officially promoted to Able Seaman. Do it now. Get your Divisional Officer to sign it and give it to RPO Warden to be included in First Lieutenant's Requests tomorrow.'

On my Radar History document the following has been noted ...

'Finally starred. Not over bright, but may improve with time.'

I make out my request form just before dinner. The details of my belated promotion have been leaked and a few of the guys, who draw their tot, give me celebratory 'sippers' down the mess. Popeye gives me 'snifters', the tight-arsed bastard.

I'm a little light-headed as I make my way to the Officers' cabin flat.

Lieutenant Conway opens his cabin door looking like he has been disturbed. 'Yes?'

'Can you sign a request form, please sir.'

'Err, all request forms should be signed before lunchtime, lad.'

'I didn't know I needed a request form until an hour ago, sir.'

'What's it for?'

'To be rated Able Seaman, sir.'

'You must be Ordinary Seaman Broadbent.'

'I am, sir.'

'I've read your service history sheet, Broadbent. You've failed to pass your RP Starring exam three times.'

'Yes sir, onboard HMS Bermuda. But I passed this morning.'

'Right then. I also understand that you come from Pudsey and that you knew Sir Len Hutton and played for HMS Bermuda's first eleven.'

'Only once sir.'

'And how did you do?'

'Scored 12 batting at four, sir.'

'Can you bowl?'

'Yes, sir.'

'Have you got any whites ... cricketing whites?'

'No, sir.'

He holds his hand out. 'Give me your request form.'

I hand it to him. I turn round as instructed and he uses my back to support the form while he signs it.

'I'll let you know when we arrange our next match. We had a match organised in Hong Kong but our hosts cancelled at the last minute.'

'Thank you, sir.'

'Congratulations on passing your exam ... at long last.'

'Thank you, sir.'

'Can I smell rum? Are you old enough to draw your tot?'

'No, sir.' I turn away quickly.

At the First Lieutenant's Table the following day, I'm reminded of my new responsibilities. Lieutenant Lamin, the guy who had lectured us on personal hygiene in *Terror*, is a tall, rangy individual who is growing a beard. There are fine red lines on both sides of his hawkish nose. 'As an Able Seaman, Broadbent, you now have to set an example to the younger members of the crew who will look up to you for guidance and as an Able Sea ...'

He goes on and on.

I wait for those immortal words 'Request granted. Rated Able Seaman effective 22 March 1963.'

RPO Warden repeats: 'Request granted. Rated Able Seaman effective 22 March 1963. Right Tin ... Quick March.'

And that's it. I don't concern myself much about all that 'setting an example' rubbish. All I'm interested in is that I now have all-night leave, I can go ashore in civilian clothes and my basic pay is increased to £5-19-0 a week, about 50 Singapore dollars or approximately 100 Hong Kong dollars.

Unfortunately I'm duty and can't go ashore to celebrate this momentous day.

I'm clear eyed and bushy-tailed the following morning and make a point of commenting on the greasiness of the morning's bacon and sausages. Tommy, who staggers back onboard minutes before leave expires at 06:15, is particularly unimpressed with what's on offer. Tommy, who doesn't drink beer but has a liking for gin in all its forms, spent yesterday taking photographs of Hong Kong and last night in the arms of a member of staff from The Pink Pussycat Bar & Grill on Hennessey Road.

'The woman that he spent the night with was a real dog,' explains Popeye.

'Really. You do surprise me,' says Apple.

'She wasn't that bad,' states Tommy.

'She was the only one left in the bar,' says Popeye. 'Nobody else had the guts to take her out.'

'She wasn't that bad,' restates Tommy.

'She was a dog,' says a confident Popeye.

'What was her name, Tommy?' someone asks.

'I don't ferkin know, do I?' he replies, red-faced, and pulls himself up the mess ladder.

On the last Sunday in March 1963 I don a pair of narrow blue trousers and my white Rael-Brook poplin shirt, that I never have to iron, and go ashore in civilian clothes with 'Sooty' Stacks, Lash and Brick. It's one of those runs ashore when the drink takes advantage of us all. We have a few drinks in a bar that Sooty found a few days ago. The girls are a little on the aggressive side. Four of them sit down next to us as soon as we sit down. Without any introductions, they each slap a fidgety hand on our respective groins and demand 'dinks'. Brick's uninvited companion is wearing a pink bobbly cardigan over a yellow cheongsam and – unusually – is wearing spectacles. The hand on Brick's groin must have been something special. He buys his spectacled companion a couple of 'dinks', goes and has a chat with the Mama-San and we don't see him again. Lash and I along with Sooty relocate to the Old Toby Bar where the ladies have a little more style and are a little less aggressive at tables.

Despite having the prospect of all night leave before me, I sit at the bar talking to a nice young lady called Ruby and stagger back onboard alone in the early hours. Lash and Sooty stay for a while longer. I know that neither of them have sufficient funds to pay for anything ... but they probably haven't told their companions that.

We are due to sail at lunchtime on Monday and nobody has seen Brick. We tell Clink where we last saw him and give him a reasonably good description of the girl wearing the pink, bobbly cardigan and spectacles. Clink and Tansy are partway through emptying Brick's locker when a bearded Stoker pokes his head down the mess ladder. 'We've found a black bloke called Able Seaman Wall in one of our shower cubicles. The Sick Berth Attendant is examining him.'

'Why didn't you discover him earlier?' asks Clink as he throws a pile of socks and underwear back into Brick's locker. 'I know you Stokers are not fond of showers but ...'

'The ferkin water's switched off down aft,' replies the Stoker. 'Any excuse.'

'Stokes' disappears in a huff.

We 'single up' and without the aid of tugs detach *Lincoln* from 'Honky Fid'. Everybody is feeling a bit low until the Captain broadcasts that we will be back. It gives us something to look forward to. We slip graciously down the 'fragrant harbour' on our way back to Singapore for a two-week dockyard maintenance period, designed to sort out any of our niggling post-refit problems. Jenny and her girls have done a brilliant job on the Forecastle, the Quarterdeck and the bridge top as well as repainting our red gunwale. I'm particularly sad that my first visit to Hong Kong is over: I had formed a friendship with the luscious Ruby who says she is trainee management at The Old Toby Bar. We've exchanged photographs, so it could be a relationship that is going somewhere.

Once we depart the fragrant harbour, Brick begins to string a few sensible words together.

So what happened to you then, Brick?' asks Gringo.

'A clue haven't got.'

'You don't remember anything?'

'Nothing.'

'You were found curled up in the foetal position in the Stokers' showers,' says Tommy.

'I know ... what's a foetal position?'

'Have you got your ID Card and wallet?'

'Dunno.'

'What will Polly say?' asks Gringo.

Brick collapses. He bounces his head on the mess table ashtray and covers his head with his arms.

As an Able Seamen I'm taken off watchkeeping duties and now work on the Top part-of-ship. It's the area around the funnel and includes the port and starboard waste where the sea boats are stowed. As an Able Seaman I don't get the really crap jobs anymore and I spend the journey back to Singapore removing clips from each of our watertight doors, greasing and replacing them. Those of us who work on the upper deck are distinguished by our tan and I'm turning a very acceptable shade of mahogany.

After dinner each day a group of sun worshipers, from those parts of the ship where the sun never shines, appear on the upper deck with their towels. For an hour or so, they fry themselves.

5

THE GASH CHUTE'S CEREMONIAL RETURN

On the first Tuesday in April we berth in Sembawang dockyard. The following day *Lincoln* is re-classified and we become a member of the 24th Frigate Squadron. The numbers on the side of our funnel are changed. We are once again swamped by busy little men in brown overalls and the noise of serious work envelopes the ship.

I happen to be on the brow handing my Bosun's Mate duties over to an Ordinary Seaman when the Buffer arrives with an unofficial Side-Party to man the brow with Bosun's Calls at the ready. He does a few practise runs to make sure that the ceremonial is perfect. Lash is one of those selected and he is panicking because he isn't that good with his Bosun's Call.

Normally, a ceremonial Side Party dressed in whites and mustered at the brow, welcomes high-ranking guests or those of senior service rank onboard. Today's Side Party is dressed in working clothes and sandals: a relaxation of Queen's Regulations and Admiralty Instructions, according to Fez.

Fez is the first to spot what is going on. From around the side of a building opposite, a couple of lads from the Buffer's Party carrying our freshly painted gash chute on their shoulders, zigzag around piles of jetty rubbish and stop at the bottom of the brow.

The Buffer calls his assembled Side Party to attention: 'Side Party ... Side Party ... Har ... Ten ... Shun.'

Lash and I exchange a glance. I have a vague idea of what is going on and Lash is nervous about the piping bit.

The gash chute, stable on the shoulders of two of the Buffer's Party, is slowly carried up the brow.

As it approaches the top the Buffer yells, 'Side Party ... Side Party ... Pipe Ah The Side.'

As practised, an official 'Pipe-the-side' is trilled.

The gash chute and its two supporters stand motionless at the top of the brow.

The Buffer and Fez salute. I don't know what to do, so I do nothing.

Tommy takes a photograph.

A flustered Officer-of-the-Day, having heard the 'Piping of the side', appears from nowhere, does a jump and wags a hand at a departing Tommy. 'You, lad ... you, lad – come back here.'

Tommy disappears through a screen door.

'Who was that? the Officer-of-the-Day asks a grinning Fez.

'Don't know, sir.'

He turns on me, 'Who was that individual with the camera?'

Lower deck solidarity kicks in. 'Never seen him before, sir. Could be a Stoker, sir.'

The Officer-of-the-Day watches as the gash chute disappears down the ladder leading to the Quarterdeck. He glares at the Buffer and scans the Side Party. 'Someone must know who that man was.'

Fez stares at me.

Silence.

The Officer-of-the-Day slaps the top of the Quartermaster's desk, stuffs his telescope under his arm and stomps away.

'Who's he?' I ask Fez.

Fez looks at today's Daily Orders. 'Officer-of-the-Day today is Sub Lieutenant Sergeant.'

'Never seen him before.'

'I think he's the one who joined us the day we left Hong Kong.'

The official return of the gash chute is complete. The Side Party is dismissed.

The Buffer hands Fez a slip of paper. He reads it and hands it to his new Bosun's Mate. 'Pipe that, young 'un.'

I show my relief how to operate the microphone. He takes a deep, nervous breath.

'DO YOU HEAR THERE. DESPITE OUR MISSING GASH CHUTE BEING RETURNED ONBOARD, GASH IS TO BE DITCHED ON THE JETTY IN THE BINS PROVIDED. THE GASH CHUTE HAS BEEN CROSS EXAMINED ...

He suddenly realises this isn't serious, but has to check with Fez. He covers the microphone with the palm of his hand. 'It's a joke ... right?'

'Yeah, the Buffer cleared it with the First Lieutenant. Carry on,' says Fez.

'THE GASH CHUTE HAS BEEN CROSS EXAMINED ... AND THE CAPTAIN IS SATISFIED THAT ITS LENGTHY ABSENCE WAS UNINTENTIONAL. IT HAS BEEN SEVERELY REPRIMANDED AND ITS LEAVE CANCELLED WHILE WE ARE ALONGSIDE IN SINGAPORE.'

'That's the funny side of the Buffer,' explains Fez.

'Is it really?' I ask.

Down the mess Tommy is sitting cradling his camera.

'The Officer-of-the-Day isn't happy about you taking the photographs.'

'Sod 'im.'

'He's only been onboard since the last day in Hong Kong.'

'He doesn't realise that I'm the official lower deck photographer then.'

'Probably not,' I reply.

Brick is staring at a pile of unopened letters on his lap.

'How many, Brick?' asks Lash.

'Sixteen.'

'All from Polly?'

'Fifteen of 'em ... and one from mi mum.'

I have a letter from my Mum who hopes that I'm enjoying myself and thanking me for the postcard I sent from Singapore when I first arrived. The Forces Postal Service is cheap but it isn't that quick to and from West Yorkshire. I also have a rather vulgar letter from Wilco full of smutty, suggestive stuff. She is progressing her transfer to Singapore NAAFI. There are loads and loads of kisses and smudged lipstick on the bottom.

'You'd better get down to some writing then, Brick,' says Lash. 'Polly ...'

'I know,' replies an unsmiling Brick.

Lash leans over and whispers in my ear. 'Must be difficult when Polly looks like the inside of a ship's gash shute.'

We both giggle.

Brick gathers all his letters and his writing pad, and stomps up the mess ladder.

I've eventually finished *The Launching Of Roger Brook*. Dennis Wheatley is a long-winded writer, but he tells a good yarn. I hand the book back to Tansy.

'Hope you haven't dog-eared any of the corners, young 'un.'

'No ... I used a Leeds United bookmark.'

'Want the next one in the series?'

'Please.'

It's another monster of a book, *The Shadow of Tyburn Tree*. I reorganise the upper shelf of my locker and stow it away.

After a number of Tigers in the Armada Club and a round or two in Lakki's, Popeye agrees to take me and Lash to Bugis Street to celebrate his forthcoming birthday.

We forego a drink in Sembawang as, according to Popeye, time is marching on and we want to get to Bugis Street before the action starts and early enough to get a table.

At the dockyard gate we grab a fast-black. Popeye sits in the front passenger seat, Lash and I sit in the back.

'Where you go, sir?' the driver asks Popeye. 'You wanna womens ... or maybe mens ... you tell me, I have contact all place in Singapore.'

'Bugis Street, John,' says Popeye.

Lash and I understand that Popeye calls every male Singapore resident 'John'.

'Bugis Street very popular place with Navy,' says the driver as he puts the Mercedes in gear and, without checking the traffic, pulls out into the main road. 'Do you know history of Victoria Street and Queen's Street, sir?'

'Not really John,' says a surprised Popeye.

John coughs. 'Race of pirate from Sulawesi province of Indonesia called Buginese came to Singapore to trade many, many year ago ... long before we born, sir. They settle in Tanjong Pagar area of Singapore and a violent and ferocious community is begin.'

'Is that so, John?' asks Popeye craning his neck as we pass through Nee Soon village.

'Accurate history, sir. At the beginning of the second World War Tanjong Pagar area become popular as Hawker Market to sell goods and food.'

'Can you switch the fan on, John?' I ask. It's getting hot.

John switches the fan on that takes a little time to reach full speed. A paper ticket with a picture of an elephant on it swirls and a string of beads wrapped around the rear view mirror rattles.

Lash and I make sure the back windows are open enough to give us a breath of air.

'You're very knowledgeable, John,' says Popeye.

'I have degree in tourism.'

'A degree? So what you doing driving a cab then?' asks Lash.

'Earn money, sir,' says John turning slightly to answer a question from the back seats.

'So what were those streets you mentioned?' I ask. 'Victoria Street and the other one?'

'Victoria Street and Queen's Street,' says John. 'They are two street that change from normal street into Bugis Street every night.'

'OK.'

'But still rat infest and filthy. Never been clean up like centre of town.'

Lash and I nod. Popeye gives the noisy fan a nudge, which quietens it down.

'So there are rats in Bugis Street?' I ask.

'Oh yes. Make fine meal when stir fry.'

'Whaa?'

'Only joke ... sorry, sir.' says John quickly.

'What do you know about the Kai-ties, John?' asks Popeye.

'Big community in Jalan Geylang area.'

'Where's that then?'

'Not far from Bugis Street. Government working out way to send them to Kuala Lumpur to clean area up.'

'Why?' I ask.

'Lee Kuan Yew not like them. Not suit new Singapore image for Prime Minister. He no like Buginese or Bugis Street reputation ... or lady boys.'

'But it's a popular place for tourists, John,' says Popeye. 'When I was last down there about three years ago there were loads of tourists.'

'Lee Kuan Yew wanna knock whole area down and replace with new shopping area all glass and up market.

'What about the rats then?' asks Lash.

Bugis Street

'Rat a speciality in Tanjong Pagar area. Prime Minister no wanna stop eating place business.'

We arrive and John pulls up in front of a series of yellow-painted metal road barriers. We all contribute a third of the fare and give John a dollar each as a tip. I think it's the first time I have knowingly tipped anyone.

'Thank yew, sirs. Have a nice evening. Careful of lady boy with patch over one eye, it on bail waiting trial for man slaughtering.'

'Thanks, John' we say as we scale the barrier, watched by a pair of seriously armed Singapore Policemen.

Bars and food stalls down both sides of the street have spread their tables across the street leaving a narrow walkway down the centre. Hundreds of gas lanterns and wood-fired woks are lit and the whole place smokes, smells wonderful and pulsates with life.

Popeye switches to table-hunting mode. Lash and I are gazing, trying to drink it all in. The hundreds and hundreds of tables topped with bottles, glasses and overflowing ashtrays are all occupied, with barely enough room between them to walk. There is a continual cacophony of orders being shouted and excited, exaggerated conversations.

'Quick ... quick,' yells Popeye. 'Over there by the far end of that prop supporting the end of that ragged corrugated iron roof.' He waves an arm in the general direction. Lash and I try to follow Popeye who almost climbs over tables in his haste.

We reach a table as it's being vacated by four blokes each sporting a moustache.

'RAF eh?' asks Popeye.

One of the departees nods.

'Always knew you lot couldn't last the night.'

'The Kai-ties are coming and we want to be outside the toilets as they come through,' says one of the departees.

'Takes all sorts,' says Popeye as he plonks himself in one of the vacated seats and looks around for someone who is waiting tables. 'Six Tigers here, John.' he shouts.

'Sex Tyga,' the waiter confirms.

'Those as well,' says a smiling Popeye.

Once we are settled and have a couple of ice cold beers each at our disposal, I ask Popeye about the Kai-ties.

Popeye takes a long swig of his Tiger and belches. 'When I was last here they were mostly Asian transsexuals but I've heard recently that a number of Caucasians have swelled their numbers ...'

'What are Caucasians?' I ask.

'Us.' He waves an arm at Lash and I. 'We're ferkin Caucasians.'

'Are we really?'

'Yeah.'

'Right then.'

'The Navy reckon the white Kai-ties are all ex-RAF, conversely the RAF are convinced that they are all ex-matelots.'

'If they were RAF they'd have to shave their moustaches off, wouldn't they?' says Lash.

'Suppose so.'

'If you can't distinguish the real women from the Kai-ties you revert to the tried and trusted rule of thumb – the 'Kai-ties' are drop-dead gorgeous while the rest ... are just plain women,' explains a serious Popeye. 'They'll be here before midnight. Once they are here, avoid the toilet block over at the junction there,' he points, 'like the plague.'

'Why?' I ask.

'It's the focal point of the street,' says Popeye. 'Traditionally it's the street's stage. A variety of ritual stuff is regularly performed on the roof. God knows what goes on inside.'

The cacophony of wolf whistles and a barrage of lewd

comments from somewhere to our right signals the entry of some of the Kai-ties.

I light a cigarette and look around me. We are surrounded by smoking, eating and drinking individuals, mainly male. A couple of tables have been put together to our right and are occupied by a reasonably young bloke, a woman and a couple of grey-haired pensioners.

'Army?' asks the reasonably young bloke.

'Navy,' I reply.

'What ship?'

'Lincoln.'

'Never heard of it. What kind is it?'

'Frigate.'

He points to the pensioner with grey hair. 'My father was in the Navy between the wars.'

The grey-haired gentleman sucks his teeth. 'It was hard then, lad … bloody hard.'

A series of high-pitched whistles start some way to our right.

'They're coming, mother,' the reasonably young bloke says to the grey-haired lady.

A young boy, aged about ten, has engaged Lash in a game of noughts-and-crosses. Lash loses three games in quick succession and the boy asks him for three dollars.

'Tell him to piss off,' says Popeye. 'These kids do it for a living – you'll never beat 'em.'

My Dad had taught me how not to lose at noughts-and-crosses and I beckon the boy over. He flips his pad to a clean page and quickly inscribes the playing grid. I pour the last of my first bottle of Tiger into a not-too-clean plastic tumbler.

Three drawn games later the boy is beginning to understand he is up against an expert. He loses concentration during the fourth game and I get him with an uninterrupted line of crosses.

I hold my hand out. 'Dollar.'

The lad points to Lash. 'He owe mi thri dolla. He pay yew.' He holds his hand out to Lash who sniffs and reluctantly gives him a couple of dollars. I hold my hand out and Lash refuses.

Lash tosses the coin. 'Heads or tails?' he asks the boy.

'Head.'

Lash uncovers the coin and with a grimace hands the boy his dollar.

The grey-haired gentleman on the adjoining table is on his feet and beckoning towards a pair of very attractive-looking ladies who have stopped opposite us. They are both wearing very short skirts and low-cut blouses. In the background I notice the one wearing an eye-patch.

'Sit down, father,' says the reasonably young bloke.

'I want your mother to meet some of these...'

'Kai-ties, father ... Kai-ties.'

'I want your mother to meet them up close.'

'Sit down, will you, Ernest,' says mother.

'I only wan ...'

'Sit down. You're showing us up.'

'Beware of the one with the eye-patch. Apparently she's on bail awaiting trial for manslaughtering,' I say.

I watch as the low-cut blouses and eye-patch sashay away to a table full of excitable lads on the opposite side of the street.

Lash squeals.

A 'girl' with long brown curly hair has placed a muscular arm around his neck and is kissing him firmly on his cheek. Lash looks to Popeye for guidance.

Popeye points at the front of his neck. He had told us in the taxi that pukka ladies don't have a noticeable Adam's Apple.

'You're a very good looking young man,' says Lash's assailant in perfectly modulated English. 'Would you like me to join you? My name is Ruth and I can afford to buy my own drinks.' Lash looks around for a spare chair.

I can't see Ruth's neck as it's obscured by a colourful scarf wrapped high under her chin.

Ernest, from the next table, offers Ruth his chair. Mother looks on open-mouthed as Ernest graciously carries his chair around and places it perfectly between me and Lash. Ruth gives her enormous breasts a push-up. Popeye looks skywards.

'Any foo?' asks a grease-encrusted old bloke with a blackened spatula stuffed in the waistband of his sarong. He has appeared at my shoulder from nowhere.

I look inquiringly at Lash and Popeye. They nod.

'Two Nasis and a Mami soup please.'

'Make that three Nasis,' says Ruth who is gently stroking Lash's cheek.

Then I spot it – the brief bobbing of an Adam's Apple.

The grey-haired gentleman on the next table is explaining to his wife. 'It's just surgery, my love. Anybody can have a good pair of tits if they want them these days ... even me. It's the groin area that's difficult.'

The reasonably young bloke leans over towards his mother. 'Don't take any notice of him, mother. He's had too much to drink.'

Mother nods. 'Where's the Ladies?'

'Ladies?'

'Toilets,' says a desperate-looking Mother.

All us blokes have nothing to say. A Kai-tie from the next table readjusts herself and offers to accompany her. They walk off arm in arm. The grey-haired gentleman looks on, open-mouthed. 'Quick,' he says to the reasonably young bloke, 'take a picture of your mother and her ... her ... err ... friend.'

The reasonably young bloke scuttles after his mother waving his camera.

The Nasi isn't as good as those in Sembawang. The opening refrain of the 'Oggie Song' drifts over from the other side of the street where one of the low-cut blouses is walking away with one of the lads. There is much high-waving of glasses ...

'And we'll all go back to Oggie land,
To Oggie Land, to Oggie Land,
And we'll all go back to Oggie land,
Where they can't tell sugar from tissue paper,
tissue paper ... marmalade and jam.'

Then everybody yells 'Oggie, Oggie, Oggie!'

Memories of Invergordon Canteen come flooding back.

Ruth leans over to stub her cigarette out and I get an eyeful of manufactured cleavage that, to be perfectly honest, isn't that unattractive.

She kisses Lash on the cheek and whispers something in his ear. Popeye looks on ready to intervene. I politely divert my eyes. Ruth licks her lips and gives Lash's knee a squeeze.

Lash ponders a while and firmly shakes his head. Waiting in the wings is the young lad with his noughts-and-crosses paper at the ready.

Popeye breaths a sigh of relief.

As Ruth stands up to take her leave, the grey-haired gentleman offers to buy her a drink. The reasonably young bloke looks disgusted.

'And we'll all go back to Oggie land,
Where they can't tell sugar from tissue paper,
tissue paper ... marmalade and jam.'

Something raucous is taking place down by the toilet block: full-bodied cheers fill the air. A table full of RAF lads launch a rattan chair over the street to where a couple of Kai-ties are busy negotiating with a table full of lads from *HMS Albion*.

A green plastic chair crashes into an RAF table somewhere behind us.

'Want to join in? asks Popeye.

'Not really,' says Lash.

I shake my head.

'Let's get out of here then. This has started early tonight.'

We wait until Ernest's wife makes it safely back to her table. There is a brief ceasefire while mother and her family group grab their belongings. Then the chairs and the inter-service insults began to fly again.

We grab our bottles of Tiger and climb the barriers at the end of the street. Behind us, the central walkway is awash with overturned chairs, tables, smashed bottles, ashtrays, and drunken individuals not quite knowing what to do or how. I shove one of the barriers to the side to allow the reasonably young bloke and his parents to squeeze through. Half-a-dozen armed and dangerous-looking Singapore policemen look on as though they've seen it all before.

We finish our Tigers in the back of the taxi.

We stop off in Sembawang for a final John Collins. All the girls in Lakki's are working. The Mama San sits by herself at the end of the bar and ignores us. I give Burma a lopsided smile as we leave.

Popeye is slurring his words but we manage to understand him when he tells us that it's his ambition to see the sun come up over Bugis Street before he goes back to the UK. Immediately it becomes one of my ambitions.

The following morning I have the hangover of all hangovers: I can hardly move, I can't talk or eat very well. Thank goodness I have the forenoon and afternoon off: I'm not on watch until the First Dog.

Fez has heard all about our Bugis Street visit and Lash's brush with Ruth. In his own strange way, he is gentle with me throughout the First Dog and doesn't have me running around all over the place doing unnecessary things. By 18:00 I'm feeling a little better.

In the mess, Brick is hunched over the mess table frantically scribbling away with a pile of Pollys' letters at his elbow.

'How many have you replied to then, Brick?' asks a not-very-interested Gringo.

'Six done. I'm on my seventh,' replies Brick without looking up.

'When do you reckon you'll have the time for a run ashore?'

'Day after tomorrow if you let me get on with it.'

'Want to see a picture of my sisters?' asks Gringo.

'Piss off,' says Brick.

Lash holds his hand out. 'I'll have a look.'

Gringo slowly extracts a photograph from the back pocket of his shorts. It's a bit crumpled.

Lash examines it. Turns it over and back again. 'That's the same photograph you showed us before.'

'I know.'

'Why do you keep it in your back pocket?'

'Safety reasons.'

My first contact with our Australian naval cousins is an unfortunate one. A few Royal Australian Navy ships are in Singapore on what is loosely termed a 'cultural visit'. Lakki's Bar is full, every table piled dangerously high with glasses and bottles. It's my round, and as I walk back to the table carrying four pints of Tiger, I trip. I hit the corner of a table, occupied by half a dozen monster Aussies, and send everything crashing to the deck. A couple of the Aussies grab me, one each side, and frog-march me to the outside where they toss me headlong into the nearest monsoon drain. Without a word or a backward glance, they leave me.

Lash appears and helps me out of the drain that is thankfully dry. 'You're manky – fancy a beer?'

'Not at Lakki's though.'

'Armada Club then.'

'What if there are Aussies in there?'

'Give 'em a wide berth.'

We decide to stroll back to Terror, but unfortunately the Club is awash with Aussies.

I am determined to buy myself a decent camera. When I was at school I had a Box Brownie that I took on a trip to Switzerland. Because my father bought rolls of cut-price films from a bloke in a Leeds back street, all my developed pictures were grey-white, fuzzy and unimpressive. In contrast the colour transparency pictures taken by lads in the mess are brilliantly sharp. Tansy tells me about a NAAFI system called a Contract Sales Agreement to help those like me on relatively low pay to buy expensive items.

Fez suggests that I go to the shop that sells the model junks down by the laundry. The bloke who owns the place is a Chinese known to everybody as Clicka who has a supply of new and secondhand cameras in the back.

'Why do they call him Clicka?'

'Because he sells cameras.'

'Makes sense.'

'Beware his wife ... she doesn't like us.'

'Why?'

'I don't know.'

I'm impatient. That evening I'm in the mood to do some bartering, so I shuffle off down to the place that sells model junks. From the back a large round-faced Chinese with a long-stemmed pipe in his mouth appears. 'Yes, young sir, wha can I dew for yew?' He is wearing an embroidered skullcap with a bright red tassle and appears slightly unsteady on his feet.

'I'd like to buy a camera through NAAFI.'

He takes a lengthy lungful, taps the bowl of his pipe and blows his smoke over my head. He swerves and flicks the light switch. As though summoned, a small stooped, grey-haired woman wearing shiny black pyjamas appears at his elbow. A smoking brown cheroot is clamped in the corner of her mouth and she has a bowl of steaming noodles in her hand.

Clicka says something Chinese and she totally ignores him as she sits on a stool at the end of the counter, extracts a pair of chopsticks from somewhere inside her pyjamas and shovels a rope of noodles into her small mouth.

Clicka disappears into the back and reappears with a tray full of cameras.

'How much you wanna pay, young sir?' he inhales on his pipe.

'About a hundred dollars.'

'One huner dolla only?'

'About that, yes.'

'No much for one huner dolla.' He blows smoke over my shoulder.

He removes some of the cameras from the tray. 'Olympus, Pentax and Nikon much too expense.'

I have three to choose from. 'How much are these?'

'If yew buy threw NAAFI ... I not offa goo discoun.'

'How much then?'

Clicka says something to the small stooped woman who stuffs another wodge of steaming noodles into her mouth. The ash from the end of her cheroot drops into her bowl.

'Yew say your top price one huner dolla?' Clicka whispers.

'Yes.'

He removes two of the three cameras. 'This one exact pry one huner dolla.'

I pick it up. It's pleasantly heavy and has a load of dials and numbers on the top and around the lens.

'Samoca make. Goo Nippon company. Goo Ezumar lens. Goo value camma.'

'Can I have it for ninety dollars?' I mumble.

Clicka cups his ear. 'I not hear yew clear sir.'

The small, stooped woman does a drum roll on the counter-top with her chopsticks. She says something, belches and dribbles some noodles onto the counter.

A small sinewy dog rubs itself against my bare leg.

'Can I have it for ninety dollars?' I blurt.

Clicka holds his hand out and I pass him the camera.

'Sir. I make paper for sale price one huner dolla and I give you twenty-four exposure colour film total free.

'I don't know.'

'Bes deal in town.'

'Camera and twenty four films?'

'Naah ... you not listen correct sir. Camma and one free film with twenty-four exposure.'

'Oh.'

'This fine camma sir. Fast, fast syncro shutter. Extra goo focus system. Samoca M-35 ferkin good value.'

'Lang ... idj,' the small, stooped woman shouts, glaring and pointing chopsticks at Clicka.

I think I should conclude matters before violence erupts. 'OK I'll take it.'

'I fine box and book. Don move sir,' says Clicka.

I wait. Trying not to watch the small, stooped woman as she drains the ashed liquid from the bottom of her bowl.

Clicka and I fill in the paperwork and he promises to make sure the camera will be available at the *Terror* NAAFI shop tomorrow evening.

The small, stooped lady sticks one chopstick in her mouth, threads the other through her hair and shuffles away, leaving her empty bowl on the counter.

The following evening I present myself at *Terror*'s NAAFI shop where I sign the Credit Sales Agreement, pay a cash deposit and, as *Lincoln* will be at sea for the next three or four months, arrange to pay my monthly instalments to the Pay Office onboard.

I walk back to the mess the proud owner of a proper camera and my very first colour film. Instead of going down to the Armada Club with Lash, I lie on my bed and read my Samoca manual. Within an hour, I am totally confused. Shutter set signal, synchro select lever, aperture ring and distance scale have me partially confused. The Depth of Field table at the back is a complete mystery to me, particularly the bit about something ironically called the 'circle of confusion'.

After a week's difficult swotting I think I've mastered the 'depth of field' business. With the help of Gringo and Lash, I manage to get my free film loaded in the relative darkness of a wardrobe ... and I'm ready to take pictures. I take a series of pictures of *Terror* parade ground. Gringo takes some of me and Lash, I take some of Lash and Gringo, and Lash takes some of me and Gringo. We manage to squeeze 25 pictures from a 24 exposure film ... how brilliant is that – one extra picture?

I take the film down to Clicka who acts as a development agent for a downtown photographic shop. He tells me that I have to specify colour slides and that the developing process will take three days. Although I didn't pay for the film, I have to stump up four dollars and thirty five cents for it to be developed.

The small, stooped woman pokes her head around the door at the back, screws her nose up at me and disappears.

'I hope results goo,' says a smiling Clicka.

'Me too.'

'You will wan a projecta to see pictures, young sir.'

'Will I?'

'Fo sure, sir.'

'Do you have any?'

'Plenty, sir. Good, very good pry.'

I'm not in a projector-buying mood, so I make an excuse and leave.

We have a small Riot Control Party onboard. During our final week alongside it is exercised almost daily on a large open area adjacent to the dockyard gate. Every member of the Party is issued with a metal shield – a bit like a domestic dustbin lid – a tin hat and a metal-tipped wooden nightstick. Lots of dockyard workers volunteer to be rioters so that they can throw bricks and other missiles at us. The local police are in attendance and regularly call a halt to things when the rioters threaten to get out of hand. There is a rumour that the dockyard is planning a strike and that our Docking & Essential Maintenance period will not be completed on time. We know that when we leave Singapore we will be into our first period of serious Borneo Patrol. Nobody in the mess knows what that will involve.

In the evening I get my developed film back.

Clicka looks at me with apologetic eyes. 'No brilliant for fis try sir. Camma good ... but operator shit.'

'Oh.'

'Yew wanna other film?'

'Yes please.'

'Wanna projecta?'

'Not right now.'

Back in the mess, I secret myself and open my little box of slides. I have to hold each one up to the light to view them. Every slide is in a cardboard frame and they are terrible. Only one of the six parade ground pictures is in focus. All those taken by Lash, Gringo or me are either unfocused, badly framed or just rubbish. They all have lots of colour though, so at least the colour part worked.

I obviously have more work to do on this depth of field business. Maybe 'the circle of confusion' is important.

It is rumoured that we are leaving tomorrow. So Lash and I hot-foot it down to the Village to celebrate Suzie Right's birthday number 24. She is wearing a stunningly attractive white cheongsam: her soft-pack of Camel cigarettes is stuffed into her ample cleavage. I don't know where her matches or lighter are secreted. She gives me a brief hug before settling herself on Lash's lap where she wriggles and stays for a good half hour.

'I don't know who enjoyed that the most, Suzie or me,' says a flushed Lash.

Burma and I exchange lengthy, meaningful glances and as we leave I put my arm around her shoulders and give her a friendly goodbye squeeze. Burma manages a smile as Mama San, mouthing something unpleasant, ushers her into the back away from the main bar.

I enjoy my last Nasi Goreng for a while and Lash slurps his favourite Mami soup.

'I enjoyed Suzie on my lap,' says Lash. She hasn't done that before. I was getting quite excited.'

'You should have done a deal with Mama San.'

And with that, Lash skips back to the bar.

Next morning, he makes it back onboard with only minutes to spare. Because we both have hangovers, we are detailed off to help the unberthing party, as the dockyard workers responsible for un-berthing Frigates are on strike. The physical stuff helps in some small way to clear our heads.

Down the mess Lash explains where he thinks Suzie keeps her cigarette lighter. He confirms that for a 24-year-old Chinese bird, she's magic. She took him to a small shack just a ten-minute stagger from the village. He slept using her rolled-up cheongsam for a pillow.

'She looked OK in the morning as well ... and she made me tea,' states Lash.

'She made you morning tea?' asks Apple.

'Yeah ... and I'll tell you what ... she's got a couple of dragons, one tattooed on each of her bum cheeks, facing each other with claws up.'

'Claws up where?' asks Apple.

'At each other,' replies a suddenly embarrassed Lash. 'And she told me that I owe her four dollars fifty.'

'Fifty cents was probably for't tea then,' suggests Gringo.

By the time Lash finishes telling us how wonderful Suzie was, *Lincoln* is turning north up the west coast of Malaya.

We anchor briefly opposite Penang in the hope that there is mail for us. It turns out to be a hoax and we quickly continue our way north. The forecastle Petty Officer is beside himself as his immaculate starboard anchor has been soiled for no good reason. He has a couple of unfortunate blokes over the side scrubbing and painting it before the salt takes hold.

Having just got on top of Polly's out-of-control letter writing, Brick is thankful that we have no mail. He breathes a serious sigh of relief.

Off the Island of Lankawi, close to Malaya's northern border with Thailand, *Lincoln* once again drops her starboard anchor into the clear blue waters of the Malacca Straits. The forecastle

Petty Officer almost blows a fuse. Apparently the bridge has a good reason for not using the port anchor ... they know that the starboard one had been repainted only days previously.

The bridge orders an 'alcohol free' banyan for anyone who wants to spend a couple of hours on the beach of a deserted tropical island. Banyan is the name used by the Navy for a picnic held ashore. Our mess puts two fingers up at the Tannoy and decides to stay onboard. Personally I'd done Lankawi ... there are no girls there. However, somewhere in a hole close to the shore, are some bottles of Frazer & Neave orange juice.

The following day we trundle our way south. According to George's latest news-sheet we are on our way to relieve *HMS Cavendish* on Borneo Patrol.

We rendezvous with *HMS Cavendish* off the Island of Balambang near to the northern tip of Sabah. It's a while since our last jackstay transfer at sea and it takes a while for us to rig everything correctly. *Cavendish* approaches us from astern and throws a perfect heaving line onto our Quarterdeck. Nobody down aft is quick enough to catch it and it flops into the oggin. Someone catches the second one. The concrete test weight is transferred over to us and back again without any problems. Onboard *Cavendish* a bloke wearing a life-jacket and what looks like a flying helmet is strapped to the traveller. We have control of the main jackstay line and, at a signal from a bloke onboard *Cavendish*, we are told to 'Take the weight.' The jackstay line is hauled back until the bloke in the flying helmet is dangling high above *Cavendish's* deck. As we haul in the traveller *Cavendish* unexpectedly comes closer, the main jackstay line dips and the bottom half of the bloke in the flying helmet is well and truly submerged in the pounding waters. We quickly pull the main jackstay line taut and the bloke in the flying helmet springs up out of the waters, water cascading from his lower regions and his arms flailing.

The Captain, accompanied by a long line of officers in spanking white shirts and shorts, appears from the bridge area as the dripping wet bloke in the flying helmet is landed gently on our deck. The Captain salutes our new arrival who stands motionless, a large puddle forming at his feet. He is unshackled by a pair of Officers and politely escorted away.

'Who the ferk is he then?' asks someone.

'Dunno.'

'Aren't we expecting an Admiral or something today? It's on Daily Orders.'

'Is it?'

Petty Officer Oakley is quick to explain that it wasn't our fault that *Cavendish* suddenly altered course and dunked Vice Admiral Sir Desmond Dryer in the water.

'Flag ... flag. We've got to find a Vice Admiral's flag,' screams the Buffer.

Within the hour, a Vice Admiral's flag flutters from the yard of *Lincoln*'s mainmast.

Tomorrow's Daily Orders confirm that we are honoured to have a rather damp Vice Admiral Sir Desmond Dryer, the Commanding Officer of the Far East Fleet, onboard.

Popeye pokes a finger at Daily Orders. 'That's a fitting name, isn't it?'

'What is?' I ask.

'Dryer ... Vice Admiral Dryer. Just the right name for the bloke we dunked in the water ...'

'DO YOU HEAR THERE, THE CAPTAIN SPEAKING. YOU WILL BE PLEASED TO KNOW THAT VICE ADMIRAL SIR DESMOND DRYER IS NOW FULLY RECOVERED AFTER HIS BRUSH WITH THE ELEMENTS, AND HAS DECLARED AN INTEREST IN INSPECING THE SEAMEN'S MESS TOMORROW.'

'The bugger,' says Popeye.

It's blind, uncontrolled panic for a couple of hours after breakfast the following morning. Loose gear is crammed into large black plastic bags and spirited away somewhere. Everybody has something to do. My task is to clean the fronts of a bank of eight lockers with metal polish. I had honed my metal-polishing skills onboard *Bermuda* and I do a timely and efficient job.

At one point I stop to watch an Ordinary Seaman from the mess opposite do battle with a cockroach. He stomps around like an Irish dancer slapping his feet on the floor and shouting, 'You big ugly bastard.'

Every time he stamps on it, the cocky just shrugs itself and carries on walking. It's about 3" long, not including antennae, and built like a miniature tank.

'Pick the bastard up,' yells Tansy.

'Whah?'

'Pick the bugger up and give it a float test.'

'Have you seen the size of him?'

'It's a cocky.'

'But it's huge.' He stamps on it again as it trundles its way towards a gap in a bank of lockers.

Tansy picks it up and hands it over. 'Ditch it.'

The youngster climbs the mess ladder one-handed.

'That was a big one,' I say to Tansy.

'There are bigger ones. Singapore Dockyard is reputed to have the largest cockroach population in the world – a special monster breed.'

Vice Admiral Sir Desmond Dryer pops his head in the mess, makes a light-hearted comment about the Seamen being responsible for his dunking the other day, and leaves. So much for messdeck rounds.

After the morning watch on Monday, Lash and I are told to report to the Buffer. This is unusual – the Buffer normally has nothing to do with us watch-keepers.

'Your seamanship documents, young Broadbent, say that you're experienced at boats crew,' says Petty Officer Oakley.

'Do they, PO?'

'They do. While we are on Borneo Patrol you are no longer a watch-keeper – you are Kumpit Boarding Party crew in the motor-whaler along with Ordinary Seaman Trainer. Your Coxswain is Leading Seaman Chaplin. You will muster on the Quarterdeck at 13:30 when the Kumpit Boarding Party will be briefed by the Kumpit Boarding Party Officer. Understand?'

'Yes, PO.'

Down the mess I ask Tansy what a Kumpit is. He doesn't know, nor does anyone else. George Wild, in the next mess, says he thinks it's a boat.

After dinner Lash and I, along with Leading Seaman Chaplin and an unknown Stoker, muster on the Quarterdeck along with half-a-dozen other blokes dressed in No 8s, boots, gaiters and tin hats. Armed and dangerous, they are all equipped with the latest version of the MOD's metal-tipped wooden stick.

We wait.

Eventually a Petty Officer Gunner appears. 'Fall in. Those with tin hats muster in a reasonably tidy heap on the port side aft.' He watches for a moment. 'When I say a reasonably tidy heap I meant tallest on the right, smallest in the centre in a single straight rank ... no, make it two ranks.' He reorganises us. 'You're not as tall as you think you are, Stumpy – move over to your left. That night-stick is to be on your right hip, lad, not hanging between your legs like a bargirl's best friend. Leading Seaman Chaplin, you and your crew fall in on the other side.'

The Petty Officer stomps away forward.

'Who's he?' I ask Charlie.

'Petty Officer Cole. Smokey by name, Smokey by nature.'

The wind is getting up and we are rolling a bit more than normal. One of the lads in the tin-hat brigade loses his footing and nearly ends up over the side. His hat falls to the deck and nearly rolls under a guardrail.

'Chin stays down,' shouts Charlie.

Five minutes later a Lieutenant appears dressed in whites and carrying a clipboard. Smokey is two paces behind him. He stands in front of the tin hat brigade. 'Kumpit Boarding Party ... Kumpit Boarding Party SHUN!'

They didn't expect to be shouted at ... and react badly.

Smokey colours puce. 'Kumpit Boarding Party ... Kumpit Boarding Party ... that was an utter shambles!'

Charlie motions to me, Lash and the Stoker to stand up straight.

'Stand at Hease! Kumpit Boarding Party ... Kumpit Boarding Party SHUN!' It's a little better this time. The Lieutenant nods to Smokey who salutes smartly. 'Kumpit Boarding Party mustered and correct, sir!'

The Lieutenant strolls up and down in front of us. 'My name is Lieutenant Bell. I am the Kumpit Boarding Party Officer. You have been specially selected for the delicate and dangerous task of boarding Kumpits. Any questions so far?'

'What are Kumpits, sir?' someone asks ... thankfully.

'Kumpits are wooden craft used by the local Indonesians who mainly make their living from the sea. They can be fishing boats or cargo boats of any size. They are reportedly being used to smuggle arms throughout the region. Our job is to intercept, board and inspect any suspicious vessels. As Kumpit Boarding Party you will remain at a heightened state of readiness throughout our period of Borneo patrol and will respond immediately when required. Any questions?'

'Will we be armed, sir?' asks someone from the back rank whose voice sounds familiar.

'You ... no. I will be armed with a Naval issue side-arm. Any further questions?'

Silence.

'Carry on, Petty Officer Coke.'

'Cole, sir. Petty Officer Cole,' Smokey corrects him.

'Carry on, Petty Officer Cole,' says Lieutenant Bell as he struts away.

'Right then.' Smokey takes a deep breath and glares at the Kumpit Boarding Party each in turn. 'Muster in the Starboard waste at precisely 18:30 this evening to practise a boarding system. Clear?'

Silence.

'Dismiss.'

Down the mess, Lash is not his usual relaxed self. 'I'm not comfortable about this boat's crew thingy.'

'I'm not happy about having to remain at a heightened state of readiness,' I add. 'Glad we're not armed. The GI in charge of the shooting range at Ganges said I should never be given a shooting stick ... under any circumstances.'

'That bad eh?' asks Tommy.

'Yeah.'

At 18:25 the Kumpit Boarding Party is mustered on the Starboard waste and told to re-muster on the Quarterdeck. A motionless *Lincoln* wallows. Charlie and I start the motor-whaler's engine at the third attempt. Charlie and the Stoker have a tin of magic stuff they squirt somewhere.

We are lowered into the water, release ourselves from the boat's falls and drift aft to the Quarterdeck where a scrambling net has been rigged over the side. Both Lash and I have long boat-hooks and it's our job to keep the whaler alongside so that the Boarding Party can board us.

Lieutenant Bell, dressed in Officers No 8s, is the last to board and he instructs Charlie to take us some distance from *Lincoln*. The water is inky black and within minutes the mother ship is but a distant line of yellowed lights. We are surrounded by silent, dark water. There are a few nervous coughs.

'That's far enough, Coxswain,' says Lieutenant Bell, brandishing a large walkie-talkie. He clicks a few switches. 'Lincoln this is Motor-whaler over... Lincoln this is Motor-whaler over.' He clicks a switch and listens to static.

He tries again: 'Lincoln this is Motor-whaler over... Lincoln this is motor-whaler over.'

There is no response. The Kumpit Boarding Party sits in expectant silence, like coiled – or rather uncoiled – springs ready to pounce.

Lieutenant Bell tries one final time: 'Lincoln this is Motor-whaler over... Lincoln this is Motor-whaler OVER.'.

He tosses his walkie-talkie on the after thwart. 'Coxswain – take us in. Port side aft. Kumpit Boarding Party, remember the drill.'

'What ferkin drill?' someone whispers.

Charlie places us on the port side, the opposite side to where the scrambling net is. I grab *Lincoln*'s gunwale with my boat hook. Lash is unsteady on his feet and fails to grab anything at his first attempt. Eventually he manages to get his hook around a guardrail stanchion and Charlie flips the engine into neutral, bringing us to a halt.

'Kumpit Boarding Party ... BOARD,' yells Lieutenant Bell as he swings himself up and onboard. He stands on *Lincoln*'s Quarterdeck with his walkie-talkie in one hand and his other hand resting on his side-arm. He watches as the Boarding Party scrambles up and over *Lincoln*'s guardrails. One of the Party loses his tin hat and another gets his night-stick jammed in someone's gaiter.

We wait until Lieutenant Bell briefs his Boarding Party and then we make our way back to the starboard side where we are hoisted back onboard.

'You're not comfortable in a boat are you, Lash?' asks Charlie.

Lash shakes his head.

Next day, Lash is taken off boats' crew and replaced by Ordinary Seaman Sooty Stacks. He is the youngster who recently did battle with the cockroach.

Because the conflict between Malaya, Indonesia and Borneo is reportedly getting serious, the Kumpit Boarding Party is exercised daily. Charlie and the Stoker become experts at starting the Motor-whaler's engine and Sooty and I become pretty good at clagging the Motor-whaler alongside *Lincoln*'s Quarterdeck.

This evening I witness a bombardment of some kind. Sitting on the upper deck, having a quiet, relaxing smoke and an evening-dream, I can see the bursts of starshells and the rumbling sound of what I think is heavy artillery.

I decide to have some uniform shoes tailor made: my *Ganges*-issued shoes are almost three years old now and are beginning to show their age. Most of the lads in the mess have had a pair made to measure from our resident shoemaker. I make an appointment with Shoe-shoe, a crinkled old gentleman who occupies a small compartment on the upper deck. The compartment, that has a metal tally above the door identifying it as a 'Ready Use Store', is where he works, eats and sleeps – and it smells like it. He asks me to stand on a couple of sheets of paper, draws around my bare feet and takes some other measurements.

I watch his caged parrot as it adjusts itself against the roll of the ship: unnatural for a bird, I think.

'Six day OK?' says Shoe-shoe with a toothless smile, holding up two sets of three fingers.

'OK,' I reply. You don't disagree with someone who has a collection of very strange-looking knives dangling from his waist.

Sod's law. I'd had an extra couple of bottles of Tiger last night and am sleeping the sleep of the partially inebriated. Consequently I miss the 02:35 broadcast.

Charlie turns my hammock upsidedown and I land, face down, on the mess table.

'We've been called out ... night time Kumpits.'

Off our starboard beam is a wallowing, wooden vessel about a hundred feet long with a small wooden superstructure at the stern. A light on the end of a pole hangs over her stern. There are no people to be seen. We have lowered the Motor-whaler to deck level by the time the Kumpit Boarding Party is assembled.

Lieutenant Bell whispers last-minute instructions to those who will be boarding the Kumpit. 'You, lad ... you keep a close eye on the Kumpit in case anything is thrown over the side.'

'What do I do if I see anything being thrown over the side, sir?'

I recognise Asker's voice.

'Tell me lad, just tell me.'

Along with the riot-sticked Boarding Party is an interpreter, a small local man who I've not seen before, and a Radio Operator with a radio set strapped to his back.

There is a warm breeze blowing and the surface of the sea is slightly ruffled. The half moon is occasionally visible behind small areas of dense, grey cloud.

Once 'Dinger' is satisfied that everything is OK, the Boarding Party clambers onboard. The bloke with the radio sits in the stern next to Dinger. I'm isolated up forward.

The whaler is lowered to just above the water. Charlie and the Stoker start the engine on the first attempt and we slip ourselves. There is a swell running which I hadn't noticed.

There is a splash.

'Shit!'

'What has happened amidships?' asks Dinger.

'Lost my hat, sir. It just bounced over the side and into the oggin.'

'What is your name?'

'RO Atkins, sir.'

'You will board last ... understand?'

Dinger shouts his approach instructions to Charlie. 'Fast as you can, Coxswain, put us alongside ... midships on the lee side.'

'Aye aye, sir.'

Within minutes we approach the unpainted lee side of our first Kumpit. There is nothing on the hull I can easily hook onto, but the Kumpit's gunwale is just above head height and I'm able to lasso a line over a wooden bit.

Lieutenant Bell is the first up and over, followed by the rest of the Boarding Party. When everyone is on board, Lieutenant Bell hangs over the side and tells Charlie to lay off about ten yards or so. I can hear the crackle of radio static.

We lay off. Our tin-hatted colleagues mill about as Lieutenant Bell stands in the centre of the Kumpit's main deck with his hand on his side arm, talking to a small bearded man wearing a sarong and something red wrapped around his head.

Charlie and I take the opportunity to have a cigarette. Between the three of us we figure out that if anybody wants to throw stuff over the side they will do it over the side not seen by *Lincoln*. We can see a large hinged opening on the transom. 'We'll do a once-around,' says Charlie.

We circle the Kumpit twice, once clockwise and then, to confuse the Kumpit's crew, anti-clockwise.

Eventually Dinger calls us back. He leans over the gunwale waving his arms at us and flashing his torch. The guy in the sarong is by his side leaning on the gunwale smoking.

On the way back to *Lincoln* Dinger tells Charlie to organise some spare tin hats to keep in the boat and cross-examines the Communicator as to why the radio doesn't work efficiently. A couple of the lads sitting up forward tell me that the Kumpit stank of fish and that there were women, children, a couple of goats and some caged chickens onboard. The Captain had offered all the Boarding Party tea and a lungful of smoke from the end of a rubber hose that was connected to a complicated bubbling contraption. But Dinger flatly refused all offered hospitality.

Once safely back onboard, Dinger takes the Boarding Party to one side for a secretive de-brief. We secure the whaler and go back to bed. It's 03:55 and the morning watchmen are crawling out of their pits.

'Where you been, Charlie?'

'Kumpit boarding.'

'Find anything?'

'Piss off.'

Off the south-western tip of the Sulu Archipelago, close to the Sibatu Passage in the Sulawesi Sea, is a small deserted island which has been unofficially seconded as part of the Commonwealth and named Battleship Island on behalf of Her Majesty. This is because, in silhouette with the sun shining over your starboard shoulder, it looks like *HMS Vanguard* without the Forecastle gun turrets and her Quarterdeck awnings rigged. I have to admit it takes a bit of imagination to see the likeness.

We anchor off Battleship Island on our way to Jesselton. Once again our freshwater evaporators have packed in, so we have no fresh water and the Captain wants us to smell reasonably good before being allowed ashore. We anchor a short distance away from the Island.

'OUT BOOMS AND LADDERS. HANDS TO SWIM. THE SHIP'S BOATS WILL BE RUN A SHUTTLE SERVICE TO BATTLESHIP ISLAND FOR ANYBODY WISHING TO SWIM ...'

There is general excitement down the mess as people rummage in their lockers searching for their swimming costumes.

'THE SHIP'S COMPANY ARE ADVISED THAT IT'S NOT UNCOMMON FOR THERE TO BE SHARKS IN THE NORTH SULAWESI SEA ...'

The search for swimming costumes slows to a halt.

'BUT THERE WILL BE ARMED CREW MEMBERS ONBOARD THE ISLAND AND ONBOARD BOTH BOATS. ALL SWIMMERS ARE TO WEAR SWIMMING COSTUMES: NAKED SWIMMING AND DANGLY EQUIPMENT IS NOT ALLOWED. HANDS TO SWIM.'

'I won't be swimming naked. If a shark sees my dangly-bits waving around he won't be able to resist,' says Apple.

'Sharks don't wear glasses, do they?' jokes Tansy.

Charlie, Sooty and I are crewing the Motor-whaler. None of us are given a gun, so the bit about both boats having an armed crew member onboard is complete bollocks. The other whaler does, however, take a couple of gunners armed with rifles ashore. The lush green vegetation of Battleship Island comes down almost to sea level. I have never seen palm trees as tall. Even the slightest breeze makes the vegetation sway and rattle. It's a strange coconut-type rattle that welcomes us from an apparently deserted island.

I suppose there are about 30 or 40 people in the water by the time we land our final boat-full of swimmers.

Charlie takes us around a headland and strips down to his underpants.

'Take the helm, Pete,' he says before diving over the side.

He swims around for five minutes or so then climbs back onboard. 'Your turn, lads.'

So Sooty and I strip down to our bare essentials and have a swim. It's great. The water is warm and sparklingly clear. With my head underwater, I see large, brightly coloured fish. I suddenly remember the sharks and clamber back onboard.

'No sharks then?' asks Charlie.

'They wouldn't ferkin dare.'

The next day, while I'm doing some artistic painting at the base of the mast, I see an inverted island high in the sky. I can clearly make out the trees, the beaches and the rolling surf – all upsidedown. To make sure it isn't an illusion, I asks Gringo, who is round the other side of the mast, if he can see it.

'Ferkin 'ell. It's a ferkin island in the ferkin sky.' When he puts his mind to it, Gringo can swear for England after tot time.

'Can you see the waves breaking on the beach?'

'Yeah ... I ferkin can,' he replies.

I unexpectedly meet Petty Officer Rogers later in the day. I explain to him about the upsidedown island in the sky and he explains, in very simple terms, that it's probably caused by something called atmospheric refraction that can cause images to bounce large distances between the surface of the sea and a very dense layer of atmosphere experienced in the tropics.

I find Gringo and pass on as much of Roy's information as I can accurately remember.

'Well ferk me rigid,' he says. 'Could be a load of bollocks, of course.'

'Could be, yeah.'

6

JESSLETON, SANDAKAN, TAWAU AND BEYOND

Tommy and Apple are established as the official mess cribbage champions. Apple has a habit of mumbling his score and is too quick for any opponents to follow. Lash and I beat them once ... and they didn't speak to us for days.

The Uckers mess champions are not yet established. Lash and I have won nine games against Tommy and Popeye, who have also beaten us nine times. In the inter-mess competition, Lash and I beat the Stokers' champions, played on the neutral ground of the awning deck.

'DO YOU HEAR THERE. THE INFORMATION OFFICER SPEAKING. WE SHALL SHORTLY BE ENTERING JESSELTON, THE CAPITAL CITY OF SABAH.

JESSELTON WAS RAZED TO THE GROUND BY THE RETREATING BRITISH FORCES DURING WORLD WAR 2 TO PREVENT IT FALLING INTO THE HANDS OF THE INVADING JAPANESE,' (sniff) 'IN 1945 THE ALLIES BOMBED AN OCCUPIED JESSELTON FOR 6 MONTHS, LEAVING ONLY A SMALL NUMBER OF BUILDINGS STANDING. WE ARE ONE OF THE FIRST ROYAL NAVAL SHIPS TO VISIT JESSELTON AND WHAT TYPE OF RECEPTION WE WILL RECEIVE FROM THE LOCAL POPULATION IS NOT KNOWN. SHORE LEAVE WILL NOT BE GRANTED UNTIL THE LOCAL SITUATION IS ESTABLISHED.'

We berth alongside a rickety wooden jetty. The Captain, resplendent in his official 'going ashore' gear, paces up and down the deck waiting for something to happen. He is accompanied by a handful of silent, watchful Officers standing to one side. Eventually an elderly black Mercedes car draws up at the bottom of the gangway. The Captain steps ashore and is whisked away.

A couple of open-backed army trucks screech to a halt opposite the brow and disgorge about thirty dark-skinned soldiers each carrying a rifle and a large bag. They are marched over the brow and down to the Quarterdeck.

According to Tansy, they are Gurkhas.

'Gurkhas?'

'Yep.'

'Are they joining us and where are they going to sleep?'

'I don't ferkin know do I? In the passageway outside the galley or on the Quarterdeck maybe ... I don't know.'

A couple more open-backed trucks arrive containing six long narrow boats which are carried to the Quarterdeck.

Another truck arrives with bags of equipment and a number of outboard motors.

I'm not quick enough to avoid being detailed off as Outboard Motor humping party ... and they're ferkin heavy.

The Gurkhas busy themselves checking the equipment, and securing the boats. They appear to be very efficient.

A few hours later ...

'CLOSE UP SPECIAL SEA DUTYMEN, PREPARE FOR LEAVING HARBOUR. ASSUME DAMAGE CONTROL STATE ONE CONDITION ZULU ALPHA. CLOSE ALL UPPER DECK SCREEN DOORS. HANDS OUT OF THE RIG OF THE DAY CLEAR OFF THE UPPER DECK. THE QUARTERDECK AND ADJOINING PASSAGEWAYS ARE OUT OF BOUNDS UNTIL FURTHER NOTICE. THE MAIN GASH CHUTE IS NOW LOCATED IN THE PORT WASTE.'

Could I say, in future years, that I had been to Jesselton in Sabah? I don't think so. The distant outline of the double peaks of Mount Kinabalu is an impressive sight as we slowly edge our way away from the rickety wooden jetty with our metaphorical tail between our legs. We give the town a farewell blast on our horn.

'DO YOU HEAR THERE. WE ARE HONOURED TO HAVE ONBOARD A GROUP OF GURKHAS WHO WE ARE TRANSPORTING ALONG THE COAST WHERE THEY WILL BE USED TO PATROL INLAND RIVERS. THEY WILL BE ACCOMMODATED DOWN AFT. THE SHIP'S COMPANY ARE REMINDED TO TREAT OUR GUESTS WITH RESPECT PARTICULARLY WHEN USING THE GASH CHUTE. FRESH WATER IS AVAILABLE IN THE AFTER BATHROOM ONLY WHICH IS OUT OF BOUNDS TO THE SHIP'S COMPANY UNTIL FURTHER NOTICE.'

The following morning I wander down aft to ditch the breakfast gash and to watch the Gurkha's recover their long boats after a nighttime trip up one of the narrow rivers. They're a seriously busy and intent lot.

We launch and recover the long boats the next day. Instead of wallowing at the mouth of river, we head south east ...

'DO YOU HEAR THERE, THE INFORMATION OFFICER SPEAKING. WE SHALL SHORTLY BE ENTERING SANDAKAN. SANDAKAN IS THE SECOND LARGEST CITY IN SABAH AND WAS THE CAPITAL OF BRITISH NORTH BORNEO UNTIL 1946. IT HAS AN AIRPORT THAT WAS BUILT BY 6,000 JAVANESE CIVILIANS AND ALLIED PRISONERS OF WAR IN 1945 WHILE UNDER JAPANESE CONTROL. SANDAKAN IS PROMINENT IN THE TIMBER EXPORT INDUSTRY. THERE ARE FEW, IF ANY, PLACES THAT SERVE ALCOHOL IN SANDAKAN.'

There are snorts and mumbles from everybody in the mess except Brick, who is busy scribbling to Polly.

On the upper deck I watch as we leave a large island to starboard before entering a narrow gap between sloping land-masses covered in lush green vegetation. As we enter a long bay,

I see clumps of wooden houses built on stilts overhanging the shore to starboard. Amongst the steep green hills are red and yellow painted buildings. *Lincoln* comes to anchor about twenty yards from a deserted and dilapidated wooden jetty. Judging from the length of time the anchor chain rattles out, we are in deep water.

'Only a couple of places that sell booze then,' says a contemplative Lash.

'He did say ... if any.'

'Fancy going ashore then?'

'Can't come to a place like this and not give it a try can we?'

'Suppose not.'

Rumour has it that we are here for a couple of days. Leave is be granted from 14:00 till 18:30 each day for a part of the watch, so Lash and I have to wait until tomorrow to experience the delights that Sandakan has to offer.

The Captain is the first to go ashore, resplendent in his sparkly white official uniform and sword. We ferry officialdom back and forth and play host to a number of military bigwigs and Sandakan elders draped in colourful sarongs and strangely wound cloth headgear.

Reports from those who venture ashore confirm that the town is devoid of anything remotely alcoholic. There are no paved roads or pavements. The locals are friendly enough but the women are totally covered.

Our second Sandakan day dawns bright and early at a few minutes after 06:00. On the upper deck I can smell Sandakan: it's a mixture of pungent fish combined with overpowering jungle green vegetation and early morning bodily waste.

My morning is spent helping the Gurkhas launch their boats and making sure that all the outboard engines are in working order. After Stand-easy, I am given the job of filling the long boats' fuel tanks from a large fuel drum that has miraculously appeared from somewhere. I have to use a stiff hand pump contraption and by dinnertime my upper arms ache: at least I am doing my bit to help the War effort.

I don't take all my money ashore with me. According to those who have already explored Sandakan, there is nowhere to spend it. At about a quarter past two the whaler drops us midway down a small wooden jetty. There are about a dozen of us venturing ashore, dressed in white fronts, white shorts, white knee length stockings, black shoes and cap. At the bottom of the jetty we are faced with a terrace of elderly wooden shacks with red-painted tin roofs, built high on stilts. There is nobody around. We sniff the air: our inbuilt booze navigation system is not working.

Lash and I wander. Some men we pass greet us with raised eyebrows and a smile, but most don't acknowledge us. There is a distinct sense of haphazard lunacy about the place. Flat-topped mud and stone buildings, with small shuttered windows and staunchly studded doors, line narrow alleyways. The air is humid and still. Between quiet buildings is one open-fronted shop. A lounging owner is slumped partly out of sight fanning himself with a sheet of cardboard and smoking something brown and needle-thin. Behind him are shelves of dusty tins and bottles, their labels faded and peeling. I recognise a few familiar brands – Ideal milk, Oxo, Camp coffee, Bovril and a couple of packets of Lipton's tea.

Down a narrow street between walls of dirty, shuttered buildings. I stand in the centre and can almost touch both sides. Hundreds of years of compressed rubbish and filth have formed a solid, concave corridor. On either side the natural curve of the surface banks high against the flanking buildings. Wooden, grilled shutters stand firmly closed on rusting hinges. The air is super hot and smells as though it hasn't moved in years.

We disturb swarms of lethargic flies as we pass a pair of sleeping dogs huddled in a deep shaded corner.

It's ages before we see another human being. It's a middle-aged bloke in a ripped sarong, wearing a multicoloured scarf wrapped around his head. He avoids looking at us as he pushes his cart piled high with empty jars and bottles.

'Friendly lot,' remarks Lash.

'Watch that,' I point. Lash side-steps a fresh, steaming canine deposit.

Lash and I are alone where a narrow alley of shuttered, silent windows opens on to a square area. The high afternoon sun illuminates a narrow strip down one side. At the far end is an elderly saronged man, sporting a chin of long wispy strands of greying hair, slowly turning the handle of what looks like an ancient grinder. At his elbow is a pile of something vegetable and he is feeding pieces into his machine and collecting the juice in an elderly tin bowl. As we approach he makes the internationally accepted sign for 'Can I sell you something?'

Silently he offers a bowl of a urine-coloured liquid for our inspection.

I sniff it. It smells of sugar. 'Those sticks could be sugar cane,' I say to Lash.

'Don't give a shit what it is, I'm not having any.'

The old man disappears through a wood-slatted door behind him and returns almost immediately holding a couple of grimy glasses.

I hold my forefinger up to indicate only one and he fills one glass with the piss-coloured liquid.

As a West Yorkshire man, I'm not used to trying new things and it takes me a while to pluck up the courage to take my first tentative sip. When I do, I'm pleasantly surprised: it's exceptionally sweet but not that bad. It would be nicer refrigerated.

I empty my glass and smile at the old man. I offer him my Singapore coins as payment but he shakes his head. This is a problem – it's all the change I have. The old man points a gnarled finger at the outline of the cigarette packet in my shorts pocket. After a few misunderstandings we agree a payment of three export Woodbines for the glass of sweet stuff. Inhaling deeply on his Woodbine, the old man smiles broadly as we leave.

The following morning, after a few hurried visits by local Army Officers, we depart the well-concealed delights of Sandakan.

We retrace our way back to the river where our Gurkha contingent has been patrolling. As though by magic, or radio, we arrive at exactly the same time as the six longboats emerge from the mouth of the river. The Gurkhas look dishevelled. Onboard they throw Pusser's buckets over the side, haul them back in and shower each other down. We help hoist the boats onboard.

We remain close to the shoreline as we slip along the coast to our next destination, which lower deck rumour says is a place called Tawau.

'DO YOU HEAR THERE, THE INFORMATION OFFICER SPEAKING. WE SHALL SHORTLY BE ENTERING SEMPORNA. SEMPORNA WAS FOUNDED SOON AFTER THE BRITISH NORTH BORNEO COMPANY ESTABLISHED SANDAKAN. IT WAS INITIALLY SETTLED BY CHINESE TRADERS AND WAS CALLED TONG TALUN. SEMPORNA WAS THE HOME PORT OF A PIRATE ADMIRAL CALLED PANGLIMA BUM-BUM.'

'Did he say Bum Bum?'

'He did ... yeah.'

Lash, Tommy and I sample the delights of Semporna as soon as we berth, alongside a badly decaying concrete jetty. All the wooden, open-fronted shops are unlicensed and the dirt alleys and roads lead to yet more alleys. In Lash's considered opinion Semporna is as exciting as Jesselton on a blank week. It's another small, isolated village cut into the lush Sabah vegetation, teetering on the edge of civilization.

We're relieved to say farewell to Semporna and scuttle up the coast in search of badly behaving Kumpits.

'DO YOU HEAR THERE. THIS IS THE INFORMATION OFFICER. WE SHALL SHORTLY BE ENTERING TAWAU. TAWAU WAS FIRST OFFICIALLY SETTLED IN THE LAST CENTURY BY 25 PEOPLE OF THE BUGIS WAJO TRIBE WHO WERE COCONUT PLANTERS. THE FIRST BRITISH RESIDENT OF TAWAU WAS A MR ALEXANDER RANKIN DUNLOP WHO IS RECORDED AS LIVING HERE IN 1899. DURING THE SECOND WORLD WAR MANY OF THE TOWN'S INHABITANTS WERE MASSACRED BY

THE JAPANESE.' (cough) 'MAIN EXPORTS ARE RUBBER, HEMP AND COCONUTS. YOU WILL FIND TAWAU A REFRESHINGLY WELCOMING PLACE WHERE ALCOHOL CAN BE PURCHASED. LEAVE DETAILS WILL BE BROADCAST SHORTLY.'

We berth on a reasonably stable wooden jetty. There is a small crowd of impassive, saronged men standing watching as we rig our own berthing ropes and drag an elderly brow from the far end of the jetty to the Quarterdeck. No help is offered. Once again, the Captain waits at the top of the gangway for someone to collect him. Eventually, a stretched black Mercedes arrives and whisks him away.

The Gurkhas unship all their equipment and stack everything on the jetty. They all wave us goodbye when their transport arrives to take them away.

'DO YOU HEAR THERE. THIS IS THE INFORMATION OFFICER SPEAKING. WE SHALL BE STAYING IN TAWAU FOR FOUR DAYS. LEAVE WILL BE GRANTED FOR NONE DUTY PARTS OF THE WATCH FROM 14:00 UNTIL 22:00 ON EACH DAY. THE SHIP'S COMPANY ARE REMINDED THAT DRUNKEN BEHAVIOUR IS CONSIDERED OFFENSIVE IN SABAH.'

'Drunken behaviour. I'll have a little of that,' says Tommy.

Apple nods in agreement.

Brick nods agreement. He only has two of Polly's latest letters to answer.

'MAIL IS READY FOR COLLECTION.'

Brick holds his head in his hands.

Tansy distributes the mail. Brick has six and I have another disgustingly sexy letter from Wilco. She confirms her possible transfer to Singapore. Tansy has a letter that makes him slap his thigh with satisfaction. I notice that it has a Japanese stamp. He doesn't explain anything.

Lash and I go ashore the following afternoon. Yesterday's 'scouts' have found a bar on the eastern edge of town that has a generator and a large chest-freezer full of alcoholic stuff.

The town of Tawau is a melange of single-storey wooden huts, sheds and go-downs with tin or rattan roofs separated by dusty narrow alleys There is no paving anywhere and the surrounding lush green vegetation, overhanging the town on three sides, looks as though it is waiting to reclaim the place. It smells of rank fish and rubber. Rumour has it that Tawau is the centre of operations for Royal Naval and Royal Marine operations.

We find the bar with the generator easily enough. Those crew members with years more experience in tracking down licensed premises are already seated around tables full of beer bottles and full ashtrays. The bar is an open-fronted lean-to overlooking the Sulawesi Sea. The old man who owns the bar accepts all forms of payment including cigarettes. As we do naturally in most bars where English is not spoken, we establish a sign-language rapport with those who serve us. We quickly learn that the toilet facilities are the surrounding jungle. What is slightly annoying about this particular bar is the fact that the number one man continually tries to sell one of his staff to us. She is a young girl of about twelve with a deformed leg who limps around keeping the tables reasonably clean and well stocked. We ignore his offers of course. The number one man has a continual twitch that makes his right eye open and close: we have therefore Christened the bar 'Blinkers'.

By 21:45, we have all downed our final drink and slurring the Oggie song we make our way back to the jetty ... and home.

'And we'll all go back to Oggie land,
To Oggie Land, to Oggie Land,
And we'll all go back to Oggie land,
Where they can't tell sugar from tissue paper,
tissue paper ... marmalade and jam.

I am quietly settled in my hammock with loads of beer sloshing around my stomach when the Tannoy clicks into life: unusual for this time of night.

'DO YOU HEAR THERE. THERE WILL BE NO MOON TONIGHT. I SAY AGAIN, THERE WILL BE NO MOON TONIGHT.'

There is a theatrical thirty-second pause.

'BELAY MY LAST. THERE WILL BE A SMALL MOON TONIGHT ... FOR OFFICERS ONLY ... ON THE QUARTERDECK AT ZERO ONE THREE FIVE.'

*

The day we leave Tawau, a small group of smiling residents stand silently on the jetty to watch us leave. Some of them wave a gentle farewell. The old guy, who owns Blinkers, stands waving something that could be his bank statement.

It's 04:25 and I'm in the bow of the Motor-whaler bouncing through an invigorating swell beneath a bright full moon. *Lincoln* has her main armament pointing directly at a stationary Kumpit a couple of hundred yards distant. The Boarding Party are tin-hatted and ready. The Interpreter sits in contemplative silence. The radio operator twiddles with his knobs and Lieutenant Bell is adjusting the chinstrap of his helmet while chewing the inside of his cheek.

I hook a small stanchion on the Kumpit's bulwark. Sooty, down aft, does the same and Stokes flicks the engine into neutral.

Above us a female face appears, looking down at us. She has a grubby green bandana around her head and she is puffing vigorously on a long wooden pipe clamped firmly in the corner of her toothless mouth. She taps the top of her head with the wide blade of an enormous panga. She inhales deeply, removes her pipe and spits a line of amber-coloured phlegm at us.

Everybody instinctively ducks and swerves. Everybody that is, except Asker. A glistening amber line appears on his shoulder.

'Why me?' asks Asker.

Dinger unbuttons his holster and points his sidearm at the grinning pipe smoker. 'Back away, madam!'

The Interpreter says 'Eh?'

More female faces appear above us. All sporting a panga.

Dinger faces the Interpreter. 'Tell her ... tell them that we are going to board their vessel.'

The Interpreter shouts his version of Dinger's instruction. All the faces disappear and the Boarding Party follows a gun-toting Dinger over the gunwale.

From our position, we can clearly hear Dinger telling the Interpreter to muster the entire crew on the main deck. The sound of shuffling feet and the whimpering of disturbed babies eventually settles. One woman with a distinctively gravelly voice says something.

Dinger stutters. 'Tell those two ladies to put something over their – err – chests.'

The Interpreter tries to translate.

'And can they desist from ch ... chest feeding babies?'

Charlie, Sooty and I look at each other in silence. The Radio operator, with his huge earphones clamped to his head, listens to static. Sooty and I wrap our lines around a convenient stanchion. Stokes sits there glaring at his spluttering engine.

There is the sound of running feet above us. Still the babies grizzle.

Within half an hour the Boarding Party is back onboard the whaler.

One of them explains. 'The crew are all women, topless with babies hanging off their tits, some of 'em. They've got cages full of monkeys with ...' He places the heel of his flapping hand on the bridge of his nose. 'Those funny floppy noses.'

Once everyone is safely onboard, Dinger gives the necessary instructions and we arch away from the Kumpit. As we put distance between us and the Kumpit, we can see half a dozen or more women cradling babies in their arms.

'The monkeys were very quiet,' one of the Boarding Party says.

'Wonder why that was, then?' asks Asker.

'Maybe they were dead.'

'Dead monkeys?'

'Why not?'

By the time we have secured the whaler correctly and have a wash it's 05:55. The galley has been flashed up for some time and Charlie and I are hungry. 'Let's see if we can cadge a bacon butty from the galley before the rush starts.'

We don't get a butty but we manage to get some bacon bits and a couple of slices of deep fried white bread to make our own.

Eating an early morning, self-made warm bacon butty while sitting on a washdeck locker dripping grease over the deck ... is unbelievably brilliant: the perfect way to restart the day. I think I know how to take a photograph of myself, so I give it a try. I won't know if it has worked until I get the film developed back in Singers.

During breakfast a Communicator from the adjoining mess shouts: 'There's a ferkin animal in the mess.'

Tansy, who is head-down reading, looks up. 'I know ... I've got half a dozen in my mess.'

Asker comes bounding in, flailing an arm at the deckhead. 'It's up there ... up there. It's the size of a rat.'

'Rats don't climb up amongst the deckhead pipes and stuff,' explains Popeye.

'This one ferkin did,' someone says.

'Did anyone else see it?' asks Tansy.

Silence.

There is a scuffling noise above the inoperative main air inlet. We all look up.

'It's not a rat ... it's a ferkin monkey,' declares Tommy.

'It's an ugly ferkin monkey,' Popeye expands. 'And if it goes anywhere near that rum fanny it's dead meat.'

We are officially relieved by *HMS Brighton* at dinner time.

One of the Able Seamen in the mess opposite admits that he brought the monkey back onboard in a bag during our last day in Tawau. Apparently he paid someone a hundred fags for it and intends to sell it for a profit when we are next in Singapore or Hong Kong. Tommy puts the monkey in one of his net diving bags and hangs it from the edge of one of the bunks.

'You fed it?' Tansy asks the owner.

'Yeah, some mashed potato and baked beans last night.'

'I'll put a bucket underneath it then.'

The monkey sits motionless and wide-eyed, watching everybody. It doesn't appear worried or in any way distressed.

Tommy tries to tickle it and it snarls at him. 'Ferk you then.'

'You sure you want to keep this thing?' Tansy asks the bloke who brought it onboard.

'No ... not really.'

Before dinner, we do a jackstay transfer with *HMS Brighton*. We officially transfer concrete sinkers, some paperwork and a young Officer in exchange for some fresh milk. On the Quarterdeck, away from the prying eyes of those on the bridge, we rig a couple of heaving lines from our respective quarterdecks. Tansy places the monkey in a canvas bag and transfers it to *HMS Brighton*. Those onboard Brighton promise to look after it and to pass it over to whoever relieves them.

'What shall we call it? Does it have a name?' someone on *Brighton*'s Quarterdeck shouts.

'Call it what you like,' Fez replies.

'We'll call it Professor then ... as it will have been the most intelligent individual onboard Lincoln,' someone onboard *Brighton* shouts.

'Have a nice patrol. Jesselton is a fabulous run ashore,' shouts Tommy.

On the official jackstay, mail is transferred. Unbeknown to Brick, the blue nylon bag contains seven letters from Polly.

Down the mess, Brick counts and recounts his latest batch of letters. He extracts his writing pad from his locker and wanders off to find somewhere quiet.

'Poor sod,' says Popeye.'Doesn't do to have a UK girlfriend when you're doing trips like this.'

'Particularly when she looks like Polly,' splurts Lash.

We meet up with *HMS Hermes* off The Philippines in mid May and do Plane Guard duties for her. This involves us stationing ourselves some distance forward of her and plotting and reporting the surrounding air situation. It gives me the first real chance to do some long-range aircraft detection which I find surprisingly interesting. I'm no longer a basic Radar Plotter and can lord it a bit over the less experienced members of the Air Reporting team.

In the quiet of the Middle watch we have the opportunity to chat with the Ops Room team onboard *Hermes.* Tansy, who is in charge of our watch, learns that his opposite number was on the same course as him at *Dryad*, so we spend a lot of the time listening to boring banter about people that the rest of us don't know.

Our fresh-water situation has been serious for some days now, and as the Officers are beginning to 'hum' a bit, it's decided to try and do a fresh-water transfer with *Hermes*. Refuelling at sea is something that we have done before but the transfer of fresh water involves different pipes and valves.

When an Aircraft Carrier comes alongside a Frigate at sea, you realise just how small you are. Hundreds of people look down at us from *Hermes'* flight deck as they establish contact with us and we haul our fresh-water pipes across the turbulent waters. The wind increases and we have to abandon the first attempt. We both alter course in the hope that a change in the wind direction will help. We manage to establish a safe and stable transfer connection and water is transferred for half an hour or so before the wind gets up and almost blows little *Lincoln* onto *Hermes'* flight deck. There is panic and an emergency breakaway is ordered. Everything is slipped and we arch away with our fresh-water transfer hoses dangling over the side.

It's decided that the best method of transferring fresh water between us is alongside the jetty in Hong Kong, so we both make a course for the fragrant harbour. Cold San Miguel, the Old Toby Bar, Ruby and fresh clean water: I can't wait.

We berth on the outer mole near to *HMS Tamar*. It's unusual for an Aircraft Carrier to berth in the dockyard. An army of uniformed Chinese is on hand to ensure the whole operation goes without a hitch. There is enough room for us to squeeze in astern of *Hermes* who blocks out the evening sun. Surprisingly Hong Kong has a fresh water shortage and *Hermes* is asked to supply water to a shore-side tanker.

'Probably for one of the hotels,' someone says.

By the time *Hermes* has finished there is no fresh water left for us.

'DO YOU HEAR THERE, THE INFORMATION OFFICER SPEAKING. THIS IS OUR SECOND VISIT TO HONG KONG.'

'Yeah, we ferkin figured that out for ourselves,' someone shouts.

'THIS IS OUR SECOND VISIT TO HONG KONG. THE SHACKS ON THE SLOPES OF HONG KONG ISLAND ARE STRICTLY OUT OF BOUNDS. IN KOWLOON, THE WALLED CITY AND SURROUNDING AREAS ARE STRICTLY OUT OF BOUNDS.'

Lash and I are determined to explore more of Hong Kong. We spend our first free afternoon wandering around the Victoria area of town, window-shopping: it gives us both the added confidence to explore further than The Wanch. We visit a large Chinese Emporium that sells exotically carved Chinese furniture, ridiculously inexpensive full-length black leather coats, and translated copies of Chairman Mao's *Little Red Book*. It's the nearest I can get to Communist China and it's fascinating. The same evening, we catch the Star Ferry across the harbour to Kowloon but neither of us find it very appealing: somehow Kowloon doesn't have the atmosphere of Hong Kong Island.

On payday we visit the Peak and later enjoy a black pepper steak at the Hong Kong Hilton. I put my film in for developing. Inevitably, the call of Wan Chai interrupts our cultural pursuits and before we know what we are doing, we are back in the Old Toby Bar where, after a number of San Migs, I pluck up the courage to ask Ruby if she would like to go to the Floating Restaurant with me.

In a polite Chinese way she smiles sweetly and tells me 'No than yew.'

Lash has latched on to a new cheongsamed lady with exceptionally long legs called Pearl. During a visit to the heads I ask Lash to ask Pearl to take us to the Floating Restaurant.

Pearl asks Mama San and tells Lash how much it will cost.

Lash's response is typical. 'I'm an Able Seaman ... not Admiral of the ferkin fleet.'

That appears to draw a line under the Lash and Pearl relationship.

We learn that Brick has been saving his money ever since the last visit to Hong Kong and now has enough to buy Polly an engagement ring from one of the many Hong Kong jewellers.

'What do you want to buy an engagement ring for?' asks Tommy.

'To get engaged of course,' replies Brick.

'You'll need to know her finger size before you buy her a ring,' says Tansy.

Someone giggles and it starts the rest of us off.

'She's a size W,' says Brick. 'She told me. I asked her ages ago ... in one of my letters. Just in case I thought of buying her something like a ring.'

'Size W,' exclaims Gringo. 'That's the size of your average Cumberland sausage!'

Brick picks up his pile of letters, stuffs them in his writing case and scuttles away.

Nothing like a bacon sandwich to put a smile on your face

Lash, Tommy and I are granted a weekend off and we book a room each at the China Fleet Club. It's a great break from the ship's routine and the first time I have ever stayed overnight at something resembling a hotel.

I collect my developed slides. Surprisingly most of the photographs are OK, even those I took of myself using the delayed shutter on the morning of the upper deck bacon sarnies.

All three of us find it difficult to get out of our comfortable beds on Saturday morning. By eleven, we are showered, in what could be *Hermes* water, and are seated expectantly in the breakfast restaurant on the second floor. I'm a little unsettled as this is only the second time in my life that I have sat down for a meal that is to be served to me – forgetting the thousands of times that Mum has done exactly that, of course.

A little Chinese bloke appears unexpectedly at my shoulder. He looks from Lash, to me, to Tommy. 'Nee ha,' he places a thumb behind his name tag and waggles it. 'Mi name Tim. Yewwa wanna Chinee fewd … or yewwa wan Ingliss fewd?'

'English food please,' says Tommy instinctively.

I nod agreement: I'm not up for anything foreign at this time of the morning.

Tim extracts a pad and pencil from a rear pocket. 'We have speshew tew dayya … isa sossy ehh an cheep.'

'What?'

'Sossy ehh an cheep,' Tim smiles, his pencil poised to write.

I mimed the shape of a sausage. 'Sausage and chip?'

'Anna ehh?' asks Tim.

'What the ferk is an ehh?' Lash asks.

Tommy clicks his fingers. 'It must be a ferkin egg … isn't it? Sausage, egg and chips, that's it. Sausage egg and chips.'

I take charge of the ordering. 'We'll have three of those then Tim please. Three Sossy eh an Cheeep.'

'Yewgowin fo igliss… vely gew!' says a smiling Tim.

The 'sossy eh an cheeps' are great and put an effective lining on my stomach in preparation for an afternoon sesh' down the Wanch.

Part way through a Saturday night session, Tommy disappears with a resident lady from the Mermaid Bar.

It's mid-morning Sunday when Tim, who had served us 'sossy ehh an cheep', appears at my shoulder as Lash and I are enjoying our breakfast orange juice. 'Yew wanna go Floatin' Feesh Restran ah Aberdeen?'

'Yeah, how did you know?'

'Ching Lan from Old Toby Bar tol' me.'

'Ching Lan?' I asks.

'Rubee,' Tim explains.

'Ah ah.'

'Gentelemens ... I ave a too girl who will be appy to take you to Floatin' Feesh Restaurant ah Aberdeen for meal price.'

'Chinese girls? asks Lash.

'Ingliss. Beautiful girl both. Live in Happy Valley.'

'Beautiful girls?' I check.

Tim gives a double thumbs-up sign and smiles. 'Beautiful girl both.'

'When?' I ask.

'Tonigh goo?'

'Tonight yeah,' says Lash.

'Leh mee may telephone ca,' and he scuttles away.

I nudge Lash. He nudges me. 'Have we cracked it or what?'

'Have we ever?'

Within a quarter of an hour a smirking Tim slips me a note ...

Connie & Sandra
Lobbi 20:00

I nudge Lash and show him the note.

He nudges me back.

I shower under low water pressure, smother myself in something pleasantly aromatic and iron my shirt.

Tommy arrives, borrows ten dollars from Lash and I, and explains that he's going back to The Mermaid Bar. He's spent the morning at the wet fish market buying the makings of Sunday lunch for the girl's family. 'She's got extraordinarily long legs,' says Tommy. 'Not much in the tit department but brilliant pins.'

'Ah well – can't have everything Tom,' says Lash.

Lash and I arrive in the Lobby at exactly 19:55. It's empty.

'We're early.'

'Yeah.'

At exactly 20:00 a couple of unappealing females wearing matching quilted anoraks shoulder the main entrance door open.

The one with a round blotchy face, wearing a headscarf, asks, 'You our companions for the night then, boys?'

Her colleague, dark yellow skinned, sporting a noticeable moustache, silently examines each of us top to toe.

I cough into a clenched fist. 'Are you Connie and Sandra?'

'I'm Connie,' says the one wearing the headscarf. 'My mate here is Sandra, she's shy and doesn't speak much until she gets to know ya.'

Lash is silent and open mouthed.

Sandra thrusts a straight arm at Lash. She's wearing a fingerless woolly glove. 'Hello, I'm Sandra from 'appy Valley.'

'I've got to go to the heads,' says Lash, pulling a disturbed face.

'Do you both live in Hong Kong?' I ask. I can't think of anything else to say.

'Her dad is my dad's boss. Both at Tamar in the Pay Office,' explains Connie.

From behind the girls I spot Lash beckoning me from the partially opened heads door.

'Excuse me one moment ladies.'

Lash slams the door behind me. 'I'm no snob, Pete, you know me – but I'm not spending an entire evening with those two.'

I nod, torn between the delight of the Floating Restaurant and the frustration of an entire evening with Connie and Sandra.

'How do we get out of this then?' I ask.

'Dunno.'

We both take a seat in adjoining cubicles and I study my feet.

After ten minutes of silent contemplation I open the main door a little and scan the lobby. 'They've gone.'

'Are you sure?'

'I can't see 'em.'

'They could be hiding somewhere.'

'They could yeah.'

'Waiting for us. Take a better look, Pete, and if the coast to the main door is clear ... we'll leg it.'

'OK.' I take a deep breath and venture out. Neither Connie or her mate are to be seen. I wave an arm at the heads door and sprint across the lobby. Outside I take a series of deep breaths.

Lash sprints past me. 'That Sandra piece has spotted me ... quick, let's go.'

We jog the length of Lockhart Road and stumble breathlessly into the Old Toby Bar.

I put a Johnny And The Hurricanes record on the jukebox.

Ruby beckons me over. 'Yew luck fluster Peter Bee.'

'Ran all the way here.'

'Why run?'

'To see you.'

'Yew nice man Peter Bee.'

On Monday morning Brick tells us that he has ordered and paid a generous deposit for Polly's engagement ring.

'So you'll pick it up next time we're here then?' I ask.

'Yeah.'

'What if we don't come back?'

'It's on the programme that we're coming back later in the year.'

'But what if the programme is changed?'

'Shit. Never thought of that.'

Neither Apple's or Gringo's hammock was slung last night. Leave expired at 06:30 and neither of them have appeared. Everyone in the mess is 'gearing up' to give them both the standard breakfast grilling reserved for those who have spent all night ashore in Oriental arms.

Tansy sends me to the gangway to check: the Quartermaster confirms that neither of them have returned onboard.

I have the forenoon watch on the gangway when Apple and Gringo arrive back onboard escorted by a couple of Patrolmen from *HMS Tamar*. Gringo has a blood-stained bandage wrapped over one eye and around his head, his shirt is torn and he is carrying his shoes. Apple's left cheek is smeared with blood, his normally well-groomed hair is all over the place and his lips are swollen.

Fez hands one of the Patrolmen their station cards as Clink arrives.

'What have you two diplomats been up to?' Clink asks.

Both Apple and Gringo shake their heads.

'Let's take them down below,' says one of the Patrolmen.

I wave at Apple as he is led away: he doesn't respond. Gringo is trying to put his shoes on.

'Must have been some woman, eh?' says Fez, as all five of them disappear through the screen door.

'You are joking.'

'Nothing surprises me in this place.'

At dinnertime in the mess, Gringo refuses his tot. Everybody looks on, astonished.

Popeye pours Gringo's tot back into the rum fanny. 'Queen's then?'

Apple's mouth is sore. He takes a painful slurp of his tot and passes the rest of it round.

'So tell us then,' says Tansy.

Apple nods at Gringo. 'Motor mouth over there had a go at a departing group of Americans.'

'Not the Cinderella remark?' asks Tommy.

'We've done it before,' mumbles Gringo. 'The Cinderella thing.'

'Last night they didn't like it,' groans Apple.

'Complete sense of humour failure,' explains Gringo, stroking his bandage.

'They laid into us ... there were about six of 'em.'

'Big blokes.'

'We put up a good fight but in the end ...'

'We were outnumbered,' explains Gringo.

'Then the Naval patrol appeared and carted us away. The Yanks just walked off.'

'I think you're much better looking with your bandage on, Gringo,' says Popeye.

'Piss off,' replies Gringo.

The following day we take onboard a load of brightly painted playground equipment. There is a double swing frame, a couple of seesaws and a bag of dressing-up clothes courtesy of a well-known Portsmouth-based Naval tailor.

As far as I know, Apple is the only person in the Forward Seamen's Mess who has been to Japan before. He explains that, although he had never visited Osaka or Kobe, Japan is culturally very different from Singapore or Hong Kong. Very few Japanese speak English, so communication will be difficult. During his short visit to Tokyo some years ago he found that having American dollars in his pocket would buy you anything and suggests that we change some of our Hong Kong or Singapore dollars into American dollars before we leave.

Half a dozen of us queue inside the Victoria branch of the Hong Kong & Shanghai Bank the following day to change some of our local currency. It's the first time I've seen American money. Apple had advised us to ask for low-denomination one- or five-dollar bills. 'You don't want to be relying on the Japanese to give you change: they'll only give you local Yen that doesn't have the same purchasing power.'

Less than an hour before we leave Hong Kong we welcome onboard a man of the cloth. Typical of his calling, he flounces onboard smiling and with a word of greeting for the gangway staff. The Officer-of-the-Day orders a few young unfortunates, who are close to the brow, to carry his numerous cases and boxes down to the Officers' Cabin flat.

We leave Hong Kong on a sun-drenched morning. Those remembered, yet totally ignored, words of advice from the older hands ring in my ear. 'Don't spend all your money in Honkers, save some for Japan – it's a far better run.'

George publishes his **Malayan Crisis Report #2 ...**

The last elements of the TNKU, including its commander, have been captured in Kuching and Tawau. Several UK and Gurkha infantry battalions are deployed in mopping up operations.
Radio Operator George Wild.

We spend a week doing anti-submarine and helicopter direction exercises with *HMS Hermes*: the vivid lights and atmosphere of Hong Kong are a slowly fading memory. On the seventh day *Hermes* takes her leave and steams away south as we head north into a cooling northerly wind and straight into the tail end of a vicious typhoon named Olive.

7

'KONNICHI WA'

Typhoon Olive gives *Lincoln* a good battering for a few days. We turn tail and thankfully manage to find ourself a quiet place where we are able to do some upper-deck work in preparation for our formal arrival. Apparently we are one of the first Royal Naval ships to visit Osaka since the second World War.

There is an air of expectation down the mess, fuelled by Apple's enthusiasm.

'PREPARE FOR ENTERING HARBOUR PROCEDURE ALPHA. HANDS OUT OF THE RIG OF THE DAY CLEAR OFF THE UPPER DECK. CLOSE ALL SCUTTLES, UPPER DECK SCREEN DOORS AND HATCHES. SPECIAL SEA DUTYMEN CLOSE UP.'

At first glance, Osaka is a disappointment. Apple has described Japan as a picturesque place of oriental promise, but the skyline we encounter as we approach our allocated berth is of large spidery cranes, monumental gas storage tanks and square, uninspiring buildings.

To make a depressingly overcast, misty morning worse there is nobody to berth us, and definitely no welcoming party. We are all dressed in white fronts, matching shorts, caps with chin-stays down, blue stockings and shined shoes.

Her Majesty's Ship *Lincoln* wallows yards from the jetty in the hope that a team to help with our berthing ropes will materialise ... but it doesn't.

'KUMPIT BOARDING PARTY WHALER'S CREW MUSTER BY THE STARBOARD WHALER.'

That's a strange and unexpected broadcast. There is a hint of panic in the voice of whoever makes it. I look at Charlie who shrugs his shoulders and slopes off in the direction of the starboard whaler. Sooty and I follow.

Lieutenant Bell, the Stoker and the Radio Operator arrive as the whaler is lowered to deck level.

We wait.

Annie Oakley arrives with half a dozen Seamen. 'Leading Seaman Chaplin, you are now the nominated Berthing Officer. Take these six strong and willing young men, clamber onto the jetty and berth us. Understand?'

'Yes, PO,' says a rather perplexed-looking Charlie. Lieutenant Bell, the Stoker and the Radio Operator slope off as we are lowered to the placid, grey Osaka water. I see something that looks like an inflated condom float past.

Charlie takes the whaler around *Lincoln*'s bows in search of a ladder on the jetty wall. There is nothing so we place the boat under a stout-looking piece of timber. One of the lads grabs hold of something metallic and someone scrambles over his back and onto the jetty. Within minutes, the nominated berthing party is ashore.

Charlie turns to me. 'Wait right here. Keep the boat here while I'm on the jetty.'

I wrap a bow rope around a rusted piece of Japanese iron and relax. Sooty manages to grapple a piece of the jetty with his boat hook and pulls the stern in. We are secure and partially protected from the drifting rain that blows over our heads.

'Not much of a place is it?' says Sooty.

I pull a face. 'And Apple told us to change our Hong Kong dollars into Yankee money because Japan is a better run ashore.'

'Has he ever been to Osaka before?'

'He only went to Tokyo apparently.'

'It's probably different there.'

'Probably.'

I watch another fleet of inflated condoms bobble past.

Lincoln's head rope is secured to a less than adequate jetty bollard and slowly the bow is pulled in towards the jetty. *Lincoln* has put a line of rattan fenders over the side, not only to protect our ship's side but to prevent damaging Osaka's jetty, which look as though it doesn't have much purposeful life left in it.

Charlie appears above us, his shoes and the bottom part of his trousers covered in a wet brown mud. 'Stand back, I'm coming down. Someone has just arrived with a gangway, so the lads can organise that while we get the whaler back onboard.'

By the time the whaler is stowed and we are back onboard, *Lincoln* is securely berthed and there is a small queue of Burberry-clad non-combatants hanging around the gangway waiting to hand in their station cards and go ashore.

We are cold and wet.

Down the mess, Apple is having a hard time.

'So this is exotically wonderful Japan is it?'

'Don't ferkin blame me.'

'We do.'

'Why?'

'Because you told us that Japan would be brilliant,' says a tired looking Tommy who had been part of the berthing party.

'It looks crap,' says Lash.

'It's the weather,' explains Apple.

'It's a miserable looking place out there, I can tell you,' says Tommy. 'Mud everywhere.'

I'm duty so I have to wait until tomorrow before I can sample the delights of Osaka.

At 13:00 the Duty Part of the watch are mustered and we are told that a children's party has been arranged. Some are given the simple task of rigging a screen and reorganising the furniture in the Wardroom so that we can show some cartoons and feed our visitors if the weather doesn't improve. Gringo and I have to figure out how to rig a high-wire and traveller from 01 deck to the jetty just in case the weather improves.

Gringo manages to secure one end of the wire to a shackle that he finds buried in the jetty mud, when an elderly yellow bus slurps and slides its way down the jetty and skids to a halt opposite the brow.

An elderly gentleman with a wispy beard ushers a gang of children off the bus. They are all wearing coats with hoods and stand in wide-eyed silence staring at *Lincoln*. Fez, who is the stand-in Quartermaster, telephones the Officer-of-the-Day.

It starts to rain. The Officer-of-the-Day skips over the brow, protected by his Wan Chai Burbs, and ushers the gentleman with the wispy beard, five other adults and the children onboard. They gather on the back end of the awning deck while the Officer-of-the-Day tries manfully to communicate to the elderly gentleman in a slow, high-pitched English. All our Japanese guests shake their heads.

'Pipe for the Padre to come to the gangway immediately. Apparently he can speak some Japanese,' says a rather flustered Officer-of-the-Day.

Gringo and I get on with the business of installing the traveller and securing the inboard end of our wire to something substantial.

The Padre arrives, protecting his hair from the rain with a purple clipboard. All six adults bow as though choreographed. The Padre coughs into his fist, 'Konnichi wa.'

The six adults bow again. 'Doozo yoroshiku,' says the tallest.

The Padre hands the old gentleman his clipboard and points to the top of the exposed page. The old gentleman clasps his hands together as though in prayer, smiles and shakes his head. He says something to the other adults who scurry off to where the children are becoming bored and beginning to disperse.

'Can you actually speak any Japanese, Padre?' asks the Officer-of-the-Day.

'Only a polite, formal greeting I'm afraid.'

'That's no blasted good, is it? How in heaven's name are we supposed to communicate with these people?'

The Padre shrugs his shoulders. 'I have a sermon to put together.'

The Officer-of-the-Day turns on the Bosun's Mate, 'Take this lot down to the Wardroom and tell the Petty Officer Steward to show them some cartoons.'

'English language cartoons, sir?'

'Don't you get smart with me, young man. Just do as I say.'

The Padre and the Bosun's Mate usher everybody down below as the rain turns serious.

Gringo and I are soaking wet as we finish rigging our wire. I connect a Bosun's Chair to the traveller, hoist myself into it and Gringo gives me a shove. I slide over the ship's side and onto the jetty. The wire is a bit slack but that doesn't matter, I'm much heavier than any of the Osaka children.

Another elderly yellow bus skids to a halt at the bottom of the brow. A small dumpy lady, protected from the rain by a transparent raincoat, clomps her way over the brow. The rain stops. She looks up at the Officer-of-the-Day who towers a good foot and a half above her. She bows and clasped her hands together. 'Who do I have the pleasure of addressing?'

'The Officer-of-the-Day onboard Her Majesty's Ship Lincoln madam. And who, may I ask, are you?'

'The headmistress of the school you invited onboard for a party.'

The Officer-of-the-Day blinks and whirls to face the Quartermaster. 'Get the Padre up here.'

The little lady flicks the hood of her flimsy, plastic raincoat back to reveal a little round face with a tiny nose and bright red mouth. Her straight hair is short and ink black.

The smiling Padre arrives. He clasps his hands together and bows at the lady in the transparent raincoat. 'Konnichi wa.'

'Good afternoon Padre. As arranged I have brought a bus full of schoolchildren who are really excited about visiting your ship this afternoon.'

The Padre gulps and look wide-eyed at the Officer-of-the-Day. He shows the clipboard to the headmistress who, after a bit of a search, finds her spectacles. She reads the paper. 'Yes … that's us.'

'Then who the heck are …?' the Padre asks a sullen looking Officer-of-the-Day.

'Pipe for the Petty Officer Steward to come to the gangway.'

Gringo and I have sorted the wire out as the first load of children and five adults are politely ushered off the ship and back onto their bus.

The old gentleman with a wispy beard and the headmistress are having a few words some distance away.

The headmistress explains to The Officer-of-the-Day. 'They only came down here to look at the British ship. They come from an orphanage fifty kilometres away and forewent their breakfast to get here in time to see you arrive.'

The Petty Officer Steward confirms to the Officer-of-the-Day that all the food that had been laid out in the Wardroom has been consumed.

'We can organise some more food though, can't we Petty Officer ... can't we, for these children?'

'I suppose so sir, yes.'

'Pipe for the Petty Officer Chef to report to the Wardroom ... immediately.'

The headmistress waves welcoming arms to the children looking out of the bus windows. They exploded out of the bus doors and up the brow, screaming and shouting.

It's time for a cup of tea, so Gringo and I tell the Duty Petty Officer that the high-wire is rigged. Then we slope off below to change into something dry and presentable. The sun is making an occasional appearance, although Osaka still remains wreathed in a low-lying blanket of pale grey mist. The town is unusually quiet: there is little activity or the expected traffic noise.

I tell the lads down the mess that we have fed the wrong children and there is a panic to dredge up some more food. A group of lads are sitting in the back section of the opposite mess dressed as pirates and strumming guitars. Tansy says they are 'Black Jake and his Pirates' who have been cobbled together to entertain our guests this afternoon.

Despite a confusing start, the party proves to be a great success. The sun makes a reluctant appearance, and a local TV crew arrives to record everything. We lower the whaler and give some of the children boat rides up and down the river. Gunga organises a limbo-dancing competition. The cartoons are popular, as is the food. Our high-wire works well and we don't damage anyone. All the children scream as they skim over the ship's side onto the jetty. They scramble back up the brow caked in mud, chattering and smiling, wanting to do it again and again. An enjoyable scream doesn't need translating.

Eventually, as daylight disappears behind the largest of the gas storage tanks, the children carrying balloons, sweets and wearing paper hats make their way back to the bus. Before they board, the headmistress lines them all up and they sing us a farewell song and dance in the jetty mud for us. It's brilliant and in the gloom they board the bus full of smiles. Osaka is a much nicer place all of a sudden.

'DO YOU HEAR THERE, THE RECREATION OFFICER SPEAKING. A NUMBER OF ADMIRALTY APPROVED CONTRACEPTIVE ITEMS ARE AVAILABLE AT THE GANGWAY. IT'S RECOMMENDED THAT CREW MEMBERS AVAIL THEMSELVES OF THESE ITEMS ... AND RETURN ANY UNUSED ITEMS TO THE QUARTERMASTER WHEN RETURNING ONBOARD. THAT IS ALL.'

'Admiralty-approved Johnnies!' exclaims Tommy.

'Got a Pusser's arrow on them,' explains Brick, without looking up from the letter he is writing.

'To show you virgins the way to insert it,' adds Tansy.

I'm not a virgin, so it doesn't apply to me.

In the morning the mess is full of hung-over individuals who had gone ashore the previous night.

Apple in particular looks awful. He had gone ashore with Tommy, who refuses his breakfast bacon.

'The local fire-water is evil stuff,' declares Tommy. 'Suntory whisky and Asahi beer ... be aware.'

'And very cheap,' says Apple, holding his head in his hands.

Fez appears in our mess at dinner time: he has earned 'gulpers' of Tansy's tot.

'How did the Johnnie situation work out then, Fez?' asks Tommy.

'Waste of time as usual. They only gave us nine. The Wardroom took one, Stokers' Mess and the Senior Rates' mess had one each and the Forward Seamen's mess had the rest ... six.'

'That's good then,' says Tommy.

'The Wardroom returned theirs this morning – they couldn't work out what to do with it.'

'DO YOU HEAR THERE, THE RECREATIONAL OFFICER SPEAKING. THE SHIP WILL BE MOVING TO THE PORT OF KOBE TOMORROW. YOU ARE REMINDED THAT LOCALLY DISTILLED WHISKY AND BEER CAN BE DANGEROUS. CREW MEMBERS ARE ADVISED TO DRINK MODERATELY. KOBE HAS AN ACTIVE RED LIGHT DISTRICT ADJACENT TO WHERE WE WILL BERTH AND CREW MEMBERS ARE ADVISED TO AVOID THIS AREA. KOBE HAS MANY INTERESTING ARCHITECTURAL AND GEOGRAPHICAL ...'

Tommy throws a steaming boot at the Tannoy and it sparks out.

'An active red light district, eh ... must write and tell mummy about that,' says Popeye.

'Did you hear that, Brick,' asks Tommy. 'A red light district adjacent to where we will berth in Kobe.'

Brick, who is scribbling frantically, looks up briefly and pulls a face.

'MAIL IS NOW READY FOR COLLECTION.'

Brick's shoulders droop and his head slumps onto his chest, eyes hard shut.

'Another sack full from Polly,' exclaims Apple.

'That's not ferkin funny.' Brick opens one eye slightly.

George collects the mess mail and is almost apologetic as he hands Brick a wodge of letters.

'How many, Brick?' asks Apple.

Brick flicks through his pile. 'Seven ... ferkin seven.'

I have one from Wilco which I decide to open later. Wilco has an uncanny knack of unsettling me.

A couple of blokes dressed in blue shirts and trousers arrive on the jetty the following morning and without any communication remove our main berthing ropes from the jetty bollards and toss them into the water. I suppose that is Japanese for 'Sayonara' then. The two blokes slope away to Osaka having done their bit for Anglo-Japanese relations.

A team of hung-over Seamen is quickly scrambled onto the upper deck and the jetty to reinstall the ropes in a way that we can remove them ourself when we are good and ready.

The upper deck Tannoy is working.

'PREPARE FOR LEAVING HARBOUR PROCEDURE ALPHA. ASSUME DAMAGE CONTROL STATE ONE CONDITION ZULU. SPECIAL SEA DUTY MEN TO YOUR STATIONS. CLOSE ALL UPPER DECK SCREEN DOORS. HANDS OUT OF THE RIG OF THE DAY CLEAR OFF THE UPPER DECK.'

We unberth and dump the borrowed gangway in the mud. It rains as we muster in Procedure Alpha to say a disciplined farewell to Osaka.

'What a dump,' says the bloke standing to attention next to me.

'Did you go ashore then?'

'Naah ... didn't ferkin bother.'

Kobe isn't far away. It's so close it could be a suburb of Osaka. Within a couple of hours, the Japanese sun once again makes an appearance and a team of uniformed men and women welcome us alongside the Kobe spit. They take our berthing ropes and provide us with an attractive gangway that they install for us. As soon as we are secure, the Captain welcomes a group of local dignitaries onboard.

The sun shines brightly over the skyline of Kobe that is devoid of anything tall or industrial. Kobe looks to be one storey high and attractively colourful. Crisp, curled Japanese roofs of varying colours flow away into the sunlit distance.

A uniformed brass band appears from nowhere and plays a rather strange version of 'Hearts of Oak'. I tap my feet to the rhythm: it's great.

Osaka is yesterday's memory, and down the mess there is an atmosphere of expectation.

'Red light district eh?' Apple reminds us.

'DO YOU HEAR THERE, THE RECREATION OFFICER SPEA ...'

Tommy throws his other steaming boot at the Tannoy and misses.

'MISSED. DO YOU HEAR THERE, THE RECREATION OFFICER SPEAKING. LEAVE WILL BE GRANTED FROM 13:30. A NUMBER OF ADMIRALTY APPROVED CONTRACEPTIVES WILL BE AVAILABLE ON THE GANGWAY. IT IS S T R O N G LY RECOMMENDED THAT ...'

Tommy's second attempt hits the Tannoy fair and square and it sparks out.

Tansy packs a small bag and leaves the mess without any explanation. Fez takes over as Killick of the mess.

Lash and I decide that it's about time that Japan had the benefit of our presence. Resplendent in white trousers, white front, cap and with American dollars stuffed in our pockets we skip expectantly over the brow after dinner.

No sooner have our feet hit the jetty than a smiling young man approaches us and offers to take us to 'Bes bar in Kobe with beautiful womens.'

We don't want to waste time and money negotiating with taxi drivers so we accept his offer and squeeze ourselves into the back seat of a small Japanese car.

The 'Bes bar in Kobe with beautiful womens' is brilliant.

We are each given a complimentary bottle of Asahi beer accompanied by lots of smiles and head bowing.

A small group of women sit demurely in the corner looking at us.

A group of four other '*Lincolns*' arrive. Lash and I raise our glasses in a welcoming salute. 'The Asahi beer is good,' I explain.

'Try the Suntory Whisky, that'll knock your head off,' says a bloke who I know to be an Electrician.

A couple of the women appear at our table, smile and bow. 'Konnichi wa.'

Both Lash and I repeat 'Konnichi wa' as two other ladies skirt around behind us, lean over our shoulders and place a bottle of chilled Japanese beer in front of each of us.

They ask to sit down and we agree.

There is a jeer from the Electricians' table.

It takes a while to come to terms with the language barrier: we don't have a common language between us. We exchange names, which is a well practised process. The one who pours my beer calls herself Harumi and is attractive in a Japanese way. She has shoulder-length straight black hair, good shoulders and great hips. The woman sat next to Lash introduces herself as Katsumi.

I don't know what it is, but Harumi's eyes and mine meet and something lustful and titillating immediately passes between us.

'Lash is similarly taken with Katsumi. 'I think I've a yen for a Kat ... get it?'

I smile, then I get it. 'I've only got American dollars.'

We both laugh. The ladies look at us and smile politely. They understand not a word.

Harumi extracts the silver foil from the inside of my empty cigarette packet and within minutes produces a long-beaked bird with folded wings. Harumi offers the bird to me in her upturned hands. She looks me straight in the eyes and says something to me in Japanese that makes Katsumi smile. I gently take the foil bird, examine it, extend each wing and stand it on the table.

Harumi mimes for me to put it safely in my pocket, which I do.

'Maybe it's a love token of some kind,' says Lash.

Katsumi is busy folding a paper napkin. Lash looks on in anticipation, wondering what will emerge.

Harumi goes to the bar and returns with fresh bottles of Asahi beer and glasses of what looks like pale orange juice for herself and Katsumi.

Katsumi places her folded napkin on the table; it looks like a giraffe.

Harumi waves an arm and giggles. Katsumi offers the paper giraffe to Lash who accepts it with uncharacteristic politeness. Harumi nudges me in the ribs and smiles at Lash and Katsumi in turn.

To celebrate, I order a round of drinks. Surprisingly both the girls ask for a Suntory, so Lash and I order the same.

Suntory whisky takes my breath away but isn't that bad. We all clink glasses and repeat a Japanese version of cheers that sounds like 'Kan-pie'.

'Kan-pie.'

'Kan-pie.'

'Kan-pie.'

Both Harumi and Katsumi signal that we have had enough to drink and we settle the bill with a mixture of Yen and American dollars. It isn't as expensive as I expected.

Outside the bar, Lash and Katsumi go one way; Harumi and I go the other.

We zigzag through Kobe's narrow streets for ten minutes or so before climbing a short series of steps into a suite of pure white rooms. She opens the curtains to show me *Lincoln* in the distance.

She invites me to take my clothes off and ushers me towards the bathroom. The last time someone bathed me was when I was too young to wash myself. In a two-tiered pale blue bath full of warm sudsy water, a naked Harumi sits above and behind me. She bathes me, feeds and waters me and indoctrinates me into a series of complicated water-borne activities.

Cleansed, we spend a long time in a variety of enjoyable, adult performances. I'm glad that the messdeck rumour about Japanese women being physically different is complete rubbish.

At the end of the bed is a colour television showing American programmes dubbed into Japanese. It's the first colour television I've ever seen. We cuddle up and watch it; Harumi giggles occasionally.

The last thing I remember is watching a late evening black and white, dubbed episode of The Beverly Hillbillies whilst Harumi ...

There is a slightly salacious expression on my face as I collect my station card from the Quartermaster at 06:55 the following morning. I'm sparkly clean and absolutely knackered. My American dollars and Identity card are still in my back pocket. 'Has Lash come back yet?' I ask.

'Ten minutes ago with a similar expression on his face,' says the Quartermaster.

Down the mess, Apple is dishing out breakfast. Lash is changing into his number 8s.

Fez is sitting at the end of the mess table eating a sausage sarnie. 'Oh oh, here's the other one of the gruesome twosome. Where've you been then?'

'Don't know exactly ... but I could see Lincoln from the window.'

'Good night was it?'

'Great. I spent more time in the bath ...'

'You had a ferkin bath?' interrupts Lash.

'Can I do mess cleaner this morning Fez?' I ask.

'No chance. You get your leg-over all night and then expect special treatment. No chance.'

'I don't suppose either of you took advantage of the Admiralty approved articles available from the gangway then?' asks Apple.

We both shake our heads.

'I think both of you should have a word with the Padre,' says Tommy.

I find myself some simple brass tallies to polish. After dinner I have a couple of bottles of Tiger and both Lash and I are almost ready to hit Kobe again. We both agree to have a quick nap and sling our hammocks in a quiet corner of the mess.

It's 21:00 when our young, recovered bodies awake. The mess is empty apart from those who are duty. We move our hammocks to our normal slinging points and go back to sleep. So much for another run ashore.

We are duty the following day and the ship is open to visitors. I bring up the subject of removing the backs of ladders, saying that it was a habit onboard *HMS Bermuda* whenever we were open to visitors. Female visitors always have trouble with our relatively steep ladders and if they are wearing skirts it always give us something to approve of. Apple, Tommy and Tansy confirm that it's normal practice throughout the Navy. However, nobody volunteers to remove the backs of any of our ladders.

The queue of visitors stretches a long distance down the jetty. Dressed in our second-best suits, we wait for the word to remove the rope barrier at the bottom of the brow and let them onboard. I decide to position myself at the top of the gangway where I can help those who need a guiding hand to negotiate the small wooden steps. I wonder if Harumi or Kat will visit us and a few times during the course of the afternoon I think I see them: most of the Japanese females look much the same to me. By far the largest contingent of our visitors are schoolgirls. They skip up the gangway in large giggling groups and noisily make their way around the visitors' route. We have clearly restricted access to our accommodation, but the young girls ignore the barriers and are soon swarming around the forward Seamen's mess and the Stokers' mess down aft. The Officer-of-the-Day gets wind of this infiltration of boisterous young girls to the messdecks and panics.

'DO YOU HEAR THERE, THE OFFICER-OF-THE-DAY SPEAKING. WE ARE CUTTING SHORT OUR OPEN TO VISITOR HOURS. ALL CREW MEMBERS ARE TO ESCORT VISITORS TO THE MAIN GANGWAY. CREW MEMBERS ARE REMINDED THAT VISITORS ARE NOT ALLOWED INTO MESSDECK AREAS.'

Fez and the other Killicks have cleared our mess area of schoolgirls by the time I go down to help. Our bathroom, however, is overflowing with chattering young ladies and it takes a while for us to clear everybody out.

'DO YOU HEAR THERE, THE OFFICER-OF-THE-DAY SPEAKING. WILL ALL CREW MEMBERS SEARCH ALL THE SHIP'S COMPARTMENTS FOR LOST VISITORS. ALL VISITORS ARE TO BE TAKEN TO THE GANGWAY WHERE RELATIVES AND FRIENDS OF SOME MISSING INDIVIDUALS ARE WAITING.'

'Don't say that we have stowaways,' says a smiling Apple. 'I'll go and check the heads.'

It's 19:00 before all our visitors are accounted for and *Lincoln* is officially declared a schoolgirl-free zone.

Everybody, apart from those of us on duty, goes ashore. Most stagger back onboard between midnight and 02:00, all declaring that Suntory whisky, Asahi beer, Sake and Kobe are ferkin brilliant.

I find Wilco's unopened letter under my pillow and decide to read it once we are at sea.

Lash and I are the only two in the mess without a hangover the following morning. Exaggerated stories of last night's run ashore abound.

'This is a cracking place.'

'Everybody is so ferkin friendly.'

'Apparently we're the first British ship to visit Kobe since the Second World War.'

After dinner, only Lash and I are in any fit state to go ashore. While we get dressed in our whites, everybody else slings their hammock and 'crashes'.

Once over the brow we have to decide what to do.

'Let's go to the same bar?' I suggest.

'Let's try somewhere different. Let's try this way,' Lash points towards the less picturesque part of town.

For about an hour we stroll up and down narrow streets and alleyways until we find a reasonably comfortable-looking bar with Asahi beer and Suntory whisky signage outside. Inside it's dimly lit. The only female in the place is a wizened, toothless lady dressed in black sitting on a tall stool behind the bar. There is a jukebox in the corner that has the names of the records in both Japanese and English. We decide to enjoy the music and some cold beer.

We don't hear them enter. I realise that we have been tracked down when Harumi gently squeezes my ear lobe. She smiles, says something to the old lady behind the bar, and sits herself down. Kat follows suit.

Large glasses of Suntory are placed in front of us. Lash slips away, changes a Japanese note for some coins and selects more music on the jukebox. To the strains of a new Elvis Presley song, we empty our glasses. Katsumi and Lash leave first. Harumi and I have another round of drinks and listen to a couple more records before leaving.

On the way back to our 'lust nest' we spend some time in a small bar listening to a group of four young Japanese boys with long hair playing what they called Beatle music. It sounds OK, but nothing spectacular.

'Inglis?' asks Harumi.

'Dunno.' I shrug my shoulders.

The Beverly Hillbillies is once again on the TV. The bath is full and Harumi and I spend the next thirteen and a half hours utterly naked.

I fully intend to meet up with Harumi the following afternoon. The mind is willing, but the body has other ideas. Lash makes it ashore to see Katsumi for the last time before we sail, but I don't manage it. I stay onboard with Apple and play a civilised game of Uckers. It's later on in the evening that my body has recovered enough to say farewell to Harumi in the prescribed Naval fashion, but the Officer-of-the-Day doesn't let me to go ashore at midnight.

Next morning I regret not having made more of an effort.

'PREPARE FOR LEAVING HARBOUR. SPECIAL DUTYMEN WILL CLOSE UP AT 09:00. WE SHALL LEAVE HARBOUR IN PROCEDURE ALPHA. WE MAY ENCOUNTER SOME BAD WEATHER DURING THE FORTHCOMING TWENTY FOUR HOURS SO ENSURE THAT ALL LOOSE EQUIPMENT IS CORRECTLY STOWED.'

Lash and I stand shoulder to shoulder as *Lincoln* slowly drifts away from the jetty. A small group of dignitaries are lined up to see us off.

Lash nudges me in the ribs and nods towards two ladies who are enthusiastically waving small Union flags. 'She said she would come,' he says out of the corner of his mouth. 'Harumi has given me her address in English and a photograph for you.'

It's forbidden to wave, so we don't. I feel rather pleased with myself. In some small way, I have done my bit for Anglo-Japanese relations. I have most of my American dollars in my locker, I have learned a good deal about the Oriental female anatomy and I have been bathed and massaged in the most exquisite fashion. I feel good with myself. I could do with another week in Kobe.

George Wild comes down the mess waving a copy of the following day's Daily Orders. 'Read that,' he says, pointing to a small article at the top of the page.

CONGRATULATIONS TO LEADING SEAMAN LEE WHO HAS BEEN EXAMINED BY THE JAPANESE NATIONAL JUDO ORGANISATION AND BEEN AWARDED HIS BLACK BELT 5TH DAN (GO-DAN).

Shit! Tansy is a Judo black-belt. And it's only a few days ago that I'd arm-wrestled him. He could have killed me ... or severely damaged me.

'So you're a black belt in Judo then, Tansy?' Popeye asks.

'Yep.'

'A ferkin black belt?'

'Yep.'

'Shit.'

We all adopt a new, respectful attitude towards Tansy. Personally I don't fancy being on the receiving end of a Judo black belt.

Wilco's letter is disgusting ... full of Anglo-Saxon spelling mistakes: the underlying message is crystal clear though.

The typhoon that hits us a few days out of Kobe is Rose. We head south and Rose follows us.

'ASSUME DAMAGE CONTROL STATE ONE CONDITION ZULU ALPHA. CLOSE ALL DOORS AND HATCHES. WE SHALL SOON BE ALTERING COURSE TO PUT SOME DISTANCE BETWEEN OURSELVES AND THIS SPIRITED FEMALE CALLED ROSE.'

Lincoln was designed to withstand the worst that the North Sea could throw at her. She isn't prepared, or capable, of doing battle with a typhoon no matter what her name is.

I had experienced bad weather onboard *HMS Bermuda* whose Second World War armour-plating had groaned under the strain when battered. In contrast, *Lincoln* is constructed of corned beef tins, and she snorts and squeals when put under pressure. Deckhead pipework bounces and flanged joints spring leaks. Rose certainly has the edge over us.

In the wheelhouse, trying to steer a direct course is impossible. Eventually, it's officially sanctioned that *Lincoln* and Rose should immediately part company. Repair teams are working throughout the ship fixing leaks, buckled structure and wrecked equipment. We head through the Korean Strait aiming for the relatively tranquility of the west coast of Kyushu Island.

The Sea of Japan is initially calm and serene until, just off the small island of Oki-Shoto, we get wind of a lady called Shirley who is all set to swirl her underskirts at us.

'ASSUME DAMAGE CONTROL STATE ONE CONDITION ZULU ALPHA. CLOSE ALL DOORS AND HATCHES. WE SHALL SOON BE ALTERING COURSE TO PUT SOME DISTANCE BETWEEN OURSELVES AND YET ANOTHER SPIRITED FEMALE.'

The upper deck is strictly out of bounds to all but Seamen who rig safety lines. All hatches and doors are clipped closed. The main forecastle hatch has developed a twist, consequently it can't be closed completely.

We hit a particularly solid 'milestone' ...

'DO YOU HEAR THERE. WE NOW HAVE A REASONABLY GOOD IDEA OF SHIRLEY'S COURSE AND SPEED AND WE WILL BE ALTERING COURSE SHORTLY TO PUT SOME DISTANCE BETWEEN US. FRESH WATER RESTRICTIONS WILL BE BROADCAST SHORTLY.'

We head south-west to the relatively protected waters west of Kyushu. It's a while before *Lincoln* settles herself into a more manageable roll. Down the mess, we have lost some plates and a substantial amount of water has found its way into the ventilation trunking, onto the deck and under lockers.

The plan is for us to join the United States seventh fleet off Okinawa, to demonstrate our aircraft direction skills. Unfortunately a typhoon called Tallulah is in our way and we have to turn tail and run for it. We have a few clear days and then, as we pass the Batan Islands, we are caught and battered by super-typhoon Ursula. She's a real bitch who forces us to run for the safety of the Bohol Sea between the Philippine Islands of Samar and Mindanao.

We then head south-east for Singapore. Unfortunately, we are spotted by other warships and get ourselves involved in some pointless exercises. We are used to our independence ... and enjoy doing our own thing.

We change our American money back into Singapore dollars only hours before ...

'DO YOU HEAR THERE: WE HAVE RECEIVED A SIGNAL FROM THE COMMANDER-IN-CHIEF FAR EAST. INSTEAD OF A PERIOD OF SELF-MAINTENANCE IN SINGAPORE WE HAVE BEEN DIVERTED TO TAWAU TO RELIEVE *HMS LOCH FADA* ON BORNEO PATROL. FRESH WATER WILL BE RATIONED AS FOLLOWS: THERE WILL BE NO FRESH WATER IN THE JUNIOR RATES BATHROOMS UNTIL FURTHER NOTICE.'

I'm taken off watch-keeping and transferred to the Top part of ship. Petty Officer 'Smokey' Cole, tells me to tie a Turk's Head around one of the handrails that runs around the screen bulkhead. It's a strange and unexpected order and I fumble a little as I start. However, I like ropework and within minutes I'd tied a tight three-stranded Turks Head using Coston gun-line as instructed.

'What are you like at sewing canvas?' asks Smokey.

'Never done any, PO.'

'That's a pity. If you can sew canvas as well as you can tie Turk's Heads I could use you to canvas all these handrails. There are forty two of them which could keep someone gainfully occupied for a couple of months.'

It sounds like a brilliant way to pass a couple of months. 'I can learn to sew canvas,' I declare.

After dinner, Smokey shows me how – and when to soak canvas so that it shrinks to fit and where to tie the Turk's Heads to cover the ragged canvas ends. The first section of handrail takes me ages to complete but it's a learning length. It's a nice relaxing way to earn a living.

'ABLE SEAMAN BROADBENT REPORT TO SUB LIEUTENANT PINKERTON IN THE WARDROOM.'

I'm in the middle of tying a particularly tight Turk's Head.

Someone says. 'Did you hear that, Pete?'

I knock on the main Wardroom door and a smartly dressed Chinese Steward opens the door.

'Able Seaman Broadbent. I've been piped to report to Sub Lieutenant Pinkerton.'

'Wait there, I fin' him for yew.'

A young Officer, smartly dressed in a crackling starched white shirt and shorts, knee length stockings and white shoes, appears. 'Able Seaman Broadbent?'

'Yes, sir.'

'You knew Sir Len Hutton, I believe.'

'Yes sir.' It's a lie: as a schoolboy I shared a wooden bench with Len at Pudsey St Lawrence's cricket ground on a couple of occasions.

'You come from Pudsey?'

'Yes, sir.'

'Not only home to Sir Len but also the Bedser twins?'

'Yes, sir.'

'The heart of Yorkshire and England cricket?'

'Yes, sir.'

'I've organised a game against the Tawau first eleven tomorrow. Will you play?'

'Yes, sir.'

I follow him to his cabin where he rummages in a cardboard box full of white trousers and shirts. 'Try these on – if they are too small I'll change them. If they are too big, take them up to Sew-sew and get them altered. Tell him it's for the cricket team.'

'Thank you, sir.'

'Bat at number six. Is that OK?'

'Yes, sir.'

'Can you bowl?'

'A little. Fast, not much spin.'

'I'll keep that in mind. Might give you a crack once I've established what the opposition is capable of. 11:00 sharp at the gangway tomorrow.'

'Aye aye, sir.'

We berth alongside Tawau's wooden jetty at sunrise the following day.

By exactly 11:00, I've finished loading – with the help of a Junior Seaman – all the cricket equipment into the back of a tin-roofed truck. The driver keeps the spluttering engine running and stands watching us while we wait for our transport to arrive.

A tall Officer resplendent in well-ironed whites paces up and down. He stops, towering above the small saronged driver.

'Where is our transport, my good man?' He waves a hand that encompassed all of us dressed in white.

The driver smiles and points to the truck. 'Tranpo Padang.'

'Yes, my good man,' says the Officer.' We are waiting for our transport to the cricket pitch.'

The driver, whose smile doesn't fade, points at the truck. 'Tranpo Padang.'

'Yes I understand perfectly, my man. But how long will it be before our transport arrives?'

Sub Lieutenant Pinkerton intervenes and speaks slowly and directly to the driver. 'We ... require ... transport ... to ... the ... Padang.'

'Tranpo Padang.'

'Lieutenant Pinkerton turns to the tall Officer. 'I think that the truck could be our transport sir.'

'The truck?'

'Yes, sir.'

Sub Lieutenant Pinkerton points at his chest then at the truck. 'Is this the transport to take us to the Padang?' he asks the driver.

The driver smiles and nods. He waves a welcoming arm.

'Well, I'll be blowed,' says the tall Officer.

There are no seats in the back of the tin-roofed truck. As instructed by the tall Officer, we all stand as close together as possible for safety.

The truck growls and splutters over tracks full of holes and ruts. We bounce and sway around as one homogenous white group.

'This is a bugger isn't it, Pete?' asks Asker, standing behind me.

'Yeah, certainly is. You batting?'

'I think so. Are you?'

'Number 6, I think.'

'This is not a good start, is it?'

'Not really, no.'

'Wonder what the Tawau team is like?'

'Dunno.'

We come to a halt on the edge of a dark brown clearing double the size of your average football pitch.

The truck engine continues to run and belch thick grey smoke over us as we scramble over the tailgate. The tall Officer spends some time removing a dark grey stain from the knee of his trousers.

The still smiling driver waves an arm towards a small isolated hut to our right where a small group of saronged individuals sit on rattan chairs smoking.

As we approach, the saronged individuals stand as one to welcome us with wide grins. Not a word is spoken. Sub Lieutenant Pinkerton raises a friendly hand in salute. One of the saronged crowd does exactly the same and Sub Lieutenant Pinkerton extended a friendly hand.

'Welcome, welcome,' booms a cultured voice from the veranda of an adjacent hut. 'A most hearty welcome to our guests from HMS Lincoln. Here to do friendly battle on the not-so-green sward of Tawau's Padang.'

The tall Officer immediately takes charge and marches over to where our host stands resplendent in perfect whites and pads with a cricket bat resting nonchalantly on his shoulder. The tall Officer holds out a hand. 'Lieutenant Jeremy Lancing-Browne, Royal Navy.'

They briefly shake hands. 'Very good,' says our host, casting a friendly eye over us. He does a quick head count. 'There are only ten of you.'

'It's the best we could do at such short notice ... sir. My apologies.'

'Bad show. Bad show.' Our host expands his chest and waves his bat in the air. 'The Tawau first eleven are thirteen in total. Eleven to play and two to assist.' He waves a hand at the hut. 'Come inside out of the sun where we have laid out some refreshments and nibbles for ... for all ten of you.'

Inside are tables laden with cakes and jugs full of liquid fruit.

'Before you eat, let me introduce myself.'

I stop, a succulent donut midway between table-top and my mouth.

Our host leans nonchalantly on his bat. 'My name is Prince Jabar, Ex Wellington College and London School of Economics.' During the game I will appreciate it if you can address me as Your Highness ... for propriety's sake, you understand.'

Lieutenant Jeremy Lancing-Browne Royal Navy and Sub Lieutenant Pinkerton clip their heels together in acknowledgement.

Lieutenant Lancing-Browne replies. 'Thank you, Your Highness, and may we, on behalf of Her Majesty's Royal Navy, extend our heartiest appreciation for this opportunity to ... err ... play cricket with ... against you.'

'My team outside,' the Prince waves an arm at the door, 'are fully briefed on the rules of the beautiful game.' He points to a small table at the back of the room on which is a thick yellow book. 'We have this year's copy of Wisden to ensure that we correctly apply any recent rule changes.'

Lieutenant Lancing-Browne loses the toss because he doesn't understand which side of the used coin is heads and which is tails. Prince Jabar chooses to bat first. I field at silly mid on for the first half-dozen overs then Sub Lieutenant Pinkerton, our designated fielding strategist, moves me to square leg as one of the opening pair for Tawau favours that area. Later I despatch Tawau's number four and five during a three-over bowling spell. Number 5 is particularly gratifying as he is a large bloke who, if he had connected with any of my balls, would have scored well. 'Pinkers' catches Prince Jabar, who is the last man, and we have Tawau all out for a creditable 56.

Lieutenant Lancing-Browne makes a few tactical changes while we enjoy some Kuih Pandan rice cakes and orange juice. He confirms what we already know: that the wicket is terrible and there is a distinct hump on the leg side of the crease at the south end. We will have to bat cleverly, keep an eye on the field positions, exploit any gaps they may provide – and punish sloppy bowling. 'Remember, team, it's getting hot out there so we don't want to be out there any longer than necessary.'

We aren't out there long. Tawau have a bowler with magic fingers. He takes a deceptively short run up and makes the ball swerve, skid and bounce in the strangest of ways. He is also uncannily accurate. Sub Lieutenant Pinkerton and Lieutenant Lancing-Browne Royal Navy, who open for us, are both despatched in the first over without scoring.

We are nine for the loss of five wickets by the time I stroll out to the wicket, convinced that I will go the way of my predecessors. I'm not wrong: the lad who alternates with the demon bowler is getting his length and with his second ball has my leg stump laid flat. It takes a couple of lads some minutes to find both bails. The only member of the team not to be clean bowled is Asker. He is run out when his opposite number shouts to him to 'take a quick one,' and Asker cups his ear. 'What?'

In the end we score sixteen. Prince Jabar thanks us for playing and then organises team photographs. He ushers us back onboard the tin-roofed truck and that's it. We are a morose and well-beaten team who stand and sway in embarrassed silence as we are transported all the way back to the jetty.

We take some stores onboard along with a couple of local gentlemen the following afternoon before unberthing.

Down the mess we are all a little disappointed, as we expected at least a weekend in Tawau and the opportunity to get 'legless' at Blinkers at least once.

Two days later, I return my whites to Sub Lieutenant Pinkerton's cabin. He tells me that he has been sacked as cricket strategist and that I should contact Lieutenant Lancing-Browne for any future cricket fixtures.

For the first time in my life, I consider giving up the game. Our recent defeat was a humiliation at the hands of a mainly saronged team. The 'stick' I get down the mess is embarrassing.

'Thought you people from Pudsey West Yorkshire have this game of cricket all sussed?' asks a sarcastic Fez.

'We have.'

'But you are thrashed by a group of natives wearing sarongs and flip-flops.'

'Thrashed is an unnecessarily strong word ...'

'What would you say then?'

'Well beaten.'

'Like a Pusser's omelette,' says Apple.

'DO YOU HEAR THERE, THE INFORMATION OFFICER SPEAKING. WE SHALL SHORTLY BE ENTERING LAHAD DATU. A SETTLEMENT IS BELIEVED TO HAVE EXISTED HERE AS LONG AGO AS THE 15TH CENTURY, AS RECENT EXCAVATIONS HAVE UNEARTHED MING DYNASTY CHINESE CERAMICS. JUST EAST OF LAHAD DATU, IS THE VILLAGE OF TUNKU, A NOTORIOUS BASE FOR PIRATES AND SLAVE TRADERS IN THE 19TH CENTURY. LAHAD DATU IS HOME TO SABAH'S POPULATION OF ORANG BAJAU AND OTHER ETHNIC MALAYS, WHO SETTLED IN THIS AREA IN THE 1950'S WHEN THE COCOS ISLANDS BECAME PART OF AUSTRALIA.'

Today is to be unforgettable: etched in my memory forever. Nobody in our mess complex has been to Lahad Datu before.

Even the grey-haired bloke in the mess opposite, who has been everywhere, says it's new to him.

I enjoy my breakfast and am washing my plate when ...

'PETTY OFFICER COLE, LEADING SEAMAN CHAPLIN, ABLE SEAMAN BROADBENT, ORDINARY SEAMAN STACKS AND M.E. LAMB REPORT TO THE BRIDGE IMMEDIATELY.'

'That's the Kumpit Boarding Party,' says Popeye, who is as sharp as a tack this morning.

I follow Charlie up to the bridge where Lieutenant Bell is in discussion with the Captain on the port bridge wing. He spots us and with a wave of his hand instructs us to stay where we are – at a distance.

Dinger grabs the main Tannoy microphone ...

'DO YOU HEAR THERE. A RAF HELICOPTER HAS REPORTED AN INCIDENT ON A SMALL UNINHABITED ISLAND AHEAD OF US. LINCOLN HAS VOLUNTEERED TO INVESTIGATE. THE MOTOR-WHALER'S CREW WILL BE DESPATCHED AS WE GET CLOSER. BOTH WATCHES OF SEAMEN TO MUSTER.'

In the whaler we have Smokey Cole, Sick Berth Attendant 'Dagga' Dawes and a large pile of brand new sheets. Charlie, Sooty, 'Larry' Lamb and I are somewhat confused. We ask Smokey what's going on, but he says that he doesn't know.

Lieutenant Bell is talking to the Captain as the whaler is lowered to deck level. We wait until the Captain and Dinger have finished. Dinger jumps onboard wearing his sidearm and a strapped walkie-talkie slung over his shoulder. He signals to the Buffer: 'Lower away, Chief.'

Larry has the engine ticking over nicely as we are slipped. Dinger instructs Charlie to take us towards a smudge of an island about quarter of a mile away. Midway there, he tells Charlie to put the boat into neutral. We bob uncomfortably in a deep blue sea with a bit of a roll on.

Dinger braces himself against the engine casing and the after thwart. 'Right then gentlemen. An RAF surveillance helicopter has spotted what they think are a number of dead bodies on this island along with a pair of abandoned local craft. Apparently, there are no other occupants on the island. We shall do a slow circuit to see if there is anybody around and to find the best place to beach ourselves. Any questions?'

'Did you say dead bodies, sir?' Larry asks.

'Yes.'

'How do we know they are dead, sir?'

'The RAF said so.'

'Must be ferkin right then, sir,' mumbles Larry.

Dinger continues. 'If the bodies are dead we shall collect them and take them back to Lincoln who will take them to a medical centre in Lahad Datu. If there is any sign of life we shall act on the advice of Sick Berth Attendant Dawes before taking them back to Lincoln and then to Lahad Datu.'

The island is more or less elliptical in shape and a little larger than *Lincoln*. Along the central spine is a line of palm trees and some low-lying shrubbery. The entire water's edge on both sides is a narrow rising strip of sand. On the southern point are two small wooden canoes and Dinger decides that this is the place to beach ourselves.

Dinger adjusts his holster. 'Petty Officer Cole, the SBA and I will wade ashore and assess the situation.'

Dagga glares at Dinger. He doesn't look too happy. Neither does Smokey.

Charlie beaches us nicely alongside a wooden canoe.

The chosen three shuffle and splash ashore.

I secure our small anchor to the bow rope and paddle ashore to dig it into the sand. The sand is warm; there are loads of footprints around both the wooden canoes.

Charlie tells me to look in the two boats for anything. Thankfully they are both completely empty apart from a small number of empty tins and a bucket containing some dry, long-dead fish. I'm about to rejoin the whaler when Dinger shouts from the edge of the shrubbery. 'Able Seaman Broadbent – grab the pile of sheets that are in the whaler and bring them over here along with Ordinary Seaman ... whatever his name is ... quick as you can.'

Oh shit.

Dagga meets us halfway to the peak of the island and takes the sheets from me. 'Four bodies. We'll need eight sheets.'

There are butterflies in my stomach.

'Hurry up with those sheets,' shouts Smokey from somewhere in the shrubbery.

We follow Dagga. By the time I crest the island's highest point, two of the four bodies have been covered. The uncovered pair are teenage boys wearing shorts and nothing else and covered in what I assumed is dried blood. Before Dagga covers them with a sheet, Smokey tries to waft the flies away using a spare sheet. Lieutenant Bell has a camera and is taking photographs. As I stand there, not knowing what to do, a smell hits me.

'You will each carry one of the bodies back to the boat,' says Dinger. 'Petty Officer Cole and I will lift each body and place it in your outstretched arms. SBA Dawes will be first. Lay them out gently in the bottom of the whaler, side by side. Treat them with respect ... it's the very least we can do.'

Dagga carries his body towards the whaler. I hold out my arms as a white sheeted body is given to me. It's surprisingly light and warm. I settle myself, take a deep breath and carefully make my way to the whaler. Dagga waits for me and between us we gently lay our bodies alongside each other.

'I suppose it's OK to place them head to toe?' Dagga says.

'Suppose so.'

Lieutenant Bell accompanies Petty Officer Cole and Dagga carrying the last two bodies. They are gently placed on top of the first two.

'Not a perfect arrangement,' says Dinger. 'But we haven't the room to do much else.' He fiddles with his walkie-talkie as I collect the anchor line and Charlie slowly backs us away from the island.

I perch myself as far forward as I can in order to avoid the nearest body. I can make out the head and shoulders of the two uppermost bodies. I gently remove a curl of dried palm from one of the sheeted bodies. Through the sheet I can clearly see his blood-splattered blue shorts.

'*Lincoln* this is motor-whaler over,' shouts Lieutenant Bell into his walkie-talkie.

Static.

Dinger places the microphone closer to his mouth '*Lincoln* this is motor-whaler over.'

Static.

'Blast,' says Dinger. He tosses his walkie-talkie to Larry. Larry catches it, looks at it, switches the transmit switch to on and offers it to Dinger.

Dinger waves a dismissive hand.

Lieutenant Lamin, RPO Warden and a bunch of Wardroom stewards are waiting on *Lincoln*'s Quarterdeck. We secure ourselves alongside where the guardrails are dropped. Dagga and I lift each body and hand it inboard where it's put onto an unrolled hammock, strapped in and carefully carried through a screen door and away.

There is a puddle of blood in our bilge water.

We are hoisted and secured in silence. Lieutenant Bell thanks each of us as we secure the whaler's gripes. 'Well done lads: that wasn't a nice job. Well done.'

Back down the mess there is a degree of sympathy for the boat's crew. Personally I feel strange. I smoke a series of cigarettes one after the other and have a couple of bottles of Tiger. Then I go and have a long, cleansing shower before the water is switched off.

'DO YOU HEAR THERE, THE INFORMATION OFFICER SPEAKING. WE SHALL SHORTLY BE ENTERING LAHAD DATU. A SETTLEMENT IS BELIEVED TO HAVE EXISTED HERE AS LONG AGO AS THE ...'

Lahad Datu is a slightly larger version of Sandakan ... or was it Semporna?

Two jungle-green trucks are waiting for us as we berth alongside a partially constructed concrete jetty. A small group of what probably pass for policeman in this part of the world waits patiently as a bunch of local stevedores organise a number of wooden planks to act as a temporary brow.

The Buffer is beside himself and is discussing with some of his working party how he can rig some safety lines. The four hammocks containing the dead bodies are laid out underneath the port lifeboat. Dagga stands guard. Some paperwork is given to the Officer-of-the-Day, who disappears for a few minutes before returning with the Captain. There is an un-ceremonial handshake between the Captain and a policeman: the papers are handed over and the four bodies are carried over our planked brow, placed unceremoniously in the back of the trucks and driven away.

'Are they rats?' asks Asker pointing to a pair of squatting animals beside an overflowing dustbin.

'Yeah, look like rats to me,' I reply.

'What was it like bringing those bodies back then? I bet you feel a bit strange don't you?'

I walk away. There are times when Asker is impossible to talk to.

The Buffer also notices the rats and makes sure that the largest of our rat-guards are installed on all our berthing ropes and wires.

Instead of going ashore to partake of the few strip-lights of Lahad Datu, I stay onboard. I spend a couple of hours sitting on an upper deck wash-deck locker watching three rats trying to negotiate the rat guard on our forward spring. They scamper along the wire and back to the jetty a number of times. Eventually two of the rats form a platform on the outboard face of the rat-guard while the third clambers over. I tell the Quartermaster what I have just seen.

I don't sleep too well tonight. If it isn't the bodies on that deserted island, it's rats as big as dogs climbing onboard my ship.

Late in the morning we unhitch ourself from Lahad Datu and scuttle off east towards Battleship Island.

It's a beautifully calm afternoon and *Lincoln* has stopped a larger-than-average Kumpit to the east of Lahad Datu. It does as we ask and cuts its spluttering engine and sits wallowing in a gentle swell.

Without much urgency, we board the whaler and make our way across to the Kumpit only 50 yards distant. A single face gazes at us over the gunwale as Lieutenant Bell explains the well-rehearsed boarding procedure. The Boarding Party boards. The Communicator onboard the whaler does a successful radio check with *Lincoln*. Sooty and I secure ourselves and sit down aft with Charlie. We keep an ear cocked for any unusual sounds from onboard the Kumpit, but everything appears normal. The Interpreter explains what is happening. Lieutenant Bell bellows his orders to the Boarding Party who busy themselves searching everywhere. There is an occasional shouted exchange of words but nothing unusual.

Half an hour later the Boarding Party climbs over the side of the Kumpit and back into the whaler. As I let go of my bow rope and Charlie lets the bow drift away from the Kumpit, that has started its engines, the contents of a number of buckets are emptied over us. The smell of human excrement and fishy urine is overpowering. The solids hit everybody apart from Sooty and myself who are standing at the extreme ends of the boat. Everybody else is caught and they are jumping around in an effort to rid themselves of the stuff.

Faces appear over the Kumpit's gunwales above us: they are all smiling and waving empty buckets as the Kumpit slews her back end and splutters away.

'Shit.'

'I think so yes.'

'Bastards.'

The Buffer organises the rigging of hoses at the davit. As *Lincoln* hoists us out of the water we remove the whaler's drain plug and sit in hunched silence while we are hosed down. The smell is stomach-churning.

'Mi ferkin fags are soaking wet.'

'And mine.'

Ten minutes under the hoses is considered long enough. We are hoisted to deck level and we disembark. It looks as though most of the solids have been dispersed as Sooty and I ensure that the boat is secured correctly before disembarking ourselves.

Those operating the davit winch are still complaining about the smell as we explain what happened.

Thankfully, we have water in the main forward bathroom so I'm able to immerse myself, and everything I'm wearing, in a tepid shower. Lash has lent me a tin of scented foo-foo that I use liberally and give the rest to Sooty.

I'm part-way explaining the latest Kumpit boarding story to those in the mess when Charlie arrives with his arm crooked round Sooty's neck. 'Did you replace the main drain plug, young Peter?'

'Err ... no. I thought Sooty was doing it.'

'And Sooty here,' he tightens his grip on Sooty, 'Sooty here says he thought that you were doing it.'

'Shit.'

'Indeed,' says Charlie. 'If that boat is to be used in an emergency right now ... we'd be in deep shit. Get up top both of you, find the plug and make sure it's installed correctly.'

We can't find the ferkin plug. It's obviously been hosed overboard during our cleaning procedure. Thankfully, Charlie manages to find a replacement in the Sailmaker's store. Both Sooty and I give it a ceremonial 'stamp' to make sure that it's tightly installed.

'DO YOU HEAR THERE. THE KUMPIT CO-ORDINATION OFFICER SPEAKING. WE HAVE RECEIVED A REPORT OF A SUSPICIOUS KUMPIT IN THE AREA. WE ARE DIVERTING TO TAWAU TO PICK UP SOME SPECIALIST PERSONNEL AND EQUIPMENT. DARKEN SHIP. NO SMOKING OR NAKED LIGHTS ON THE UPPER DECK.'

We nudge a couple of wooden craft out of the way so that we can berth on Tawau's pitch-black wooden jetty. The moment we have the gangway rigged, four armed Gurkhas scramble onboard and report to The Officer of the Watch. The Quarterdeck lads are busy hoisting a large inflatable boat onboard.

'SPECIAL SEA DUTYMEN REMAIN CLOSED UP. WE SHALL BE SAILING IN THE NEXT TEN MINUTES.'

We don't unship the brow: we are obviously waiting for somebody or something.

It's fresh milk. A crate of fresh milk cartons is dumped at the bottom of the gangway and the Duty Wardroom Steward is called to bring it all onboard. The gangway is slipped and we drift away from Tawau.

Annie Oakley and a small group of Quarterdeck seamen are working on the Rigid Inflatable, installing a large black outboard engine.

After sunset, we darken ship and the inflatable, with four armed Gurkhas onboard, is launched and streamed aft on a short tow-rope. Tansy is Coxswain.

'KUMPIT BOARDING PARTY TO MUSTER.'

We wait to be launched. Dinger is on the bridge receiving his instructions, so we sneak a quick cigarette despite the fact that the ship is officially darkened.

Dinger appears and we quickly flick our cigarette ends over the side. 'There is a report of a suspicious Kumpit in the area. Apparently it's currently two miles due east of us and is been tracked in the Ops Room as Bogey Oscar. We will intercept it along with the Gurkhas in the inflatable. The Gurkhas, who are fully armed, will board the Kumpit – we will act as support if required.'

We are launched and as we round *Lincoln*'s stern the Inflatable takes station on our starboard beam. Arm signals are exchanged. The outboard engine of the Inflatable is strangely silent; maybe it's a special type for this kind of work. Our tin-hatted Boarding Party sits silently on the thwarts anxious about what lies ahead onboard Bogey Oscar.

A Communicator, wearing headphones, is in contact with the someone on *Lincoln*'s bridge. 'Bogey Oscar is less than five cables dead ahead sir. Speed four point five knots.'

Dinger nods. 'Complete silence from now on.' He scans ahead with his special type of binoculars. 'Tell the bridge I have Bogey Oscar visible.'

By the time those of us without special binoculars can focus on the stern of Bogey Oscar, the Inflatable is alongside and the Gurkhas are onboard.

There is a large splash and Dinger directs Charlie to slew round to the opposite side from the Inflatable. By the time we pull alongside the port side, the splash has disappeared.

A Gurkha leans over the port quarter and gives a silent thumbs-up. We secure ourself alongside. There is no noise from the main deck above us.

Dinger makes sure that his hat chinstrap is secured correctly. 'Kumpit Boarding Party prepare to board.'

The last person to clamber over the gunwale is the Communicator with the radio slung over his shoulder.

'Can I have a smoke, Hooky?' I ask.

'If you must. Make it quick,' replies Charlie.

So that's what I do.

Above us and on the other side of the wooden hull is the noise of things being moved around.

A series of shouted orders in a foreign tongue line up a pair of saronged individuals against the wooden rails above us. Something is happening. I toss my part-smoked cigarette over the side. A Gurkha, followed by two of the Kumpit crew, clambers over the side into the whaler. I inadvertently see much more than I want to under the flapping sarong of the second crew member. The second Gurkha follows.

'Leading Seaman Chaplin,' shouts Dinger leaning over the Kumpit's gunwale.

'Yes, sir.'

'Return to Lincoln. The inflatable will take the two remaining crew members and the other two Gurkhas. I am in radio contact with Lincoln and the Boarding Party will remain onboard.'

'Have you found anything, sir?' asks Charlie.

'Back to Lincoln, Coxswain,' says Dinger.

'Ignorant pig,' whispers Charlie. He glares at the two saronged individuals who are sitting, heads down and shivering, between the two Gurkhas.

The trip back to *Lincoln*, who is now partially undarkened, is silent. At the top of the Accommodation ladder stands a gaggle of Officers and RPO Warden with his cap on. We unload our two prisoners and the two Gurkhas.

'Stand off, Coxswain,' orders someone.

We take the whaler to a point just off *Lincoln*'s stern while the Inflatable unloads her two prisoners.

Annie leans over the stern and waves us in. He explains that *Lincoln* is to take the Kumpit in tow. We are to take one end of a heaving line to the Kumpit so that a tow-rope can be rigged.

Once the distance between Lincoln and the Kumpit is the same as the length of a standard Admiralty heaving line, we do as instructed. Dinger, Captain of his very own Kumpit, stands in the bows while a couple of Seamen from the Boarding Party secure the tow-rope.

'Can we return to Lincoln now, sir?' Charlie asks Lieutenant Bell.

'Yes, Coxswain, you are no longer required.'

'Aye aye sir,' says Charlie. 'Pompous git,' he whispers to the rest of us.

Onboard *Lincoln* the four saronged crewmembers are handcuffed to the Quarterdeck guardrails, watched over by an armed Gurkha seated on an adjacent bollard. They look scared, cold and as though they desperately needed the heads.

Annie stands looking at them.

'What would you do if they wanted to go to the heads, PO?' I ask.

'Don't you start, young Broadbent.'

'I'm not, PO ... I'm just int ...'

'Just ... JUST?'

I amble away, wondering if Annie had ever been a class Instructor at *HMS Ganges*.

In the early hours of the morning we enter Tawau. Charlie, Sooty and I are in the whaler transferring the tow-rope from the Kumpit to a group of local scallywags on the jetty. As the bows of the Kumpit are pulled towards the jetty, Dinger leans over the bows and shouts for fenders. There aren't any and the Kumpit scrapes noisily along the wooden piling.

A truck screams to a halt and a platoon of Gurkhas leap out. They muster in three straight ranks as *Lincoln* secures her brow. The whaler is hoisted and secured.

Our saronged prisoners are escorted over the brow and into the Gurkha truck: they look terrified. A good number of Gurkhas scramble onboard the Kumpit and begin to remove its cargo.

As Dinger walks up the brow, the gangway staff give him the special greeting reserved for visiting Captains. He salutes smartly at the top of the gangway, not realising that they are taking the piss.

We leave Tawau. Personally, I'm satisfied that I've done something significant for Queen and Country.

The starboard bridge lookout reports, 'HMS Vanguard bearing green 027 sir.' He is an Ordinary Seaman with a surprisingly mature sense of humour.

We anchor off Battleship Island for the second time.

'HANDS TO SWIM. THE SHIP'S BOATS WILL BE RUN A SHUTTLE SERVICE FOR ANYBODY WISHING TO SWIM.'

Down the mess people rummage in their lockers for their swimming costumes.

'THE SHIP'S COMPANY ARE ADVISED THAT SHARKS ARE NOT UNCOMMON IN THE NORTH SULAWESI SEA ...'

'Does that mean there are sharks or not?' someone asks.

A few swimming costumes are flung back into lockers.

'BUT THERE WILL BE ARMED CREW MEMBERS ONBOARD THE ISLAND AND ONBOARD BOTH BOATS. HANDS TO SWIM.'

As during our previous visit, Charlie, Sooty, Larry the Stoker and I are crewing the whaler. I make sure that I have my swimming costume on under my shorts just in case I get the chance for a dip.

We wallow off the designated swimming area until Charlie gives us permission to take our shirts off. Larry has an Engine Room tan that ends at his elbows, so he doesn't remove his shirt. The rest of us, who already have a deep upper deck tan, toss our shirts onto the engine casing. Charlie takes us around a headland, gives the tiller to me and dives over the side.

He swims around for five minutes or so then climbs back onboard. He tosses a sodden packet of cigarettes on the after thwart. 'Forgot to take mi fags out of mi pocket.'

I hand the tiller back and offer him one of my cigarettes.

Sooty and I remove our shorts and have a swim. Larry spots a large Wrasse in the water and doesn't join us.

Lincoln blows her horn three times and hoists the international recall flag that is our signal to round-up all the swimmers.

After all the station cards have been returned to their owners, we are missing a couple of the Chinese Cooks.

We take the whaler back and do one circuit of the island before beaching it. Charlie blows his whistle continually. Eventually a couple of pink-chested young Chinese stroll demurely out of the Island's vegetation, each carrying a couple of sheets bulging with something.

'What have you two been doing?' asks Charlie.

'Gatha nut,' says the shorter of the two.

'Get in the ferkin boat.'

One of the Cooks holds a coconut aloft. He smiles a satisfied smile.

Clink taps the Station cards of the two Cooks on his arm as we secure ourself to the bottom of the Accommodation ladder. 'It had to be you two ladies, didn't it?'

They don't understand a word and collect their Station cards with a smile before disappearing through a screen door with their crop of Battleship Island coconuts.

We stop and board at least one Kumpit a day until *HMS Loch Lomond* chugs over the horizon one fine morning to relieve us. We do a jackstay transfer and I exchange a friendly wave with 'Sugar' who is sitting having a fag on one of *Lo-Lo's* Quarterdeck bollards.

Instead of a farewell visit to Tawau, we skirt around the northern corner of Sabah and anchor off unfriendly Jesselton.

Nothing happens for a couple of days. None of our boats are lowered into the water and no vessels come to visit us. The Engine Room branch are kept busy working on the ship's fresh water evaporators, which is probably the reason we have anchored in a relatively calm stretch of water.

'HANDS TO SWIM AT 14:30. THOSE WHO ARE ABLE TO JUMP INTO THE WATER FROM THE FORECASTLE ONLY WILL BE ALLOWED TO SWIM. IT'S NOT UNCOMMON FOR SHARKS TO BE SEEN IN THE BALABAC STRAIT. ALL SHALLOW WATER DIVERS AND ANY CREW MEMBERS WHO HAVE ROYAL LIFESAVING ACCREDITATION ARE TO REPORT TO THE OFFICER-OF-THE-DAY ON THE BRIDGE.'

I have a Bronze Medallion from the Royal Lifesaving Society, but I also want to swim, so I don't report to the bridge.

Some lads who want a swim don't have the balls to jump, or dive, from the forecastle and access to the Quarterdeck is denied. I dive into the clear blue waters along with Tommy – who jumps. Lash has promised to station himself behind the after funnel with a pair of bridge binoculars to scan the surrounding waters for anything shark-like and dangerous.

I help a young Stoker, who has a touch of cramp, around to the Accommodation ladder. I see a huge red spotted Ray that flaps only a few feet below my dangling feet.

Down the mess I ask Lash if he had seen the spotted Ray.

He says that the bridge binoculars are rubbish.

8

WITH THE GURKHAS AT KOTA TINGGI

The familiar sights and smells of Singapore greet us as we berth alongside the corner of the Dockyard that is the furthest away from the gates. Messdeck rumour has it that we occupy the punishment berth again. It's going to be a lengthy trudge to Sembawang. Apparently we are here for a six-week Docking and Essential Maintenance Period. Unfortunately this means we will miss Exercise FOTEX and will have to rough it in *HMS Terror* while *Lincoln* is in dry dock and the rest of the Far East Fleet are out there playing war games.

George Wild tosses a two-week-old copy of the *Daily Mirror* onto the mess table. There is a picture on the front page of an attractive woman called Christine Keeler, so I whip it away to have a read. Apparently the Secretary of State for War, a bloke called John Profumo, has been giving Christine 'one' ... the lucky sod.

I scan the sports pages but there is no mention of Leeds United anywhere. That's typical.

In today's mail Brick only receives one letter from Polly. He panics and says that there must be more mail yet to be sorted: but there isn't.

Lash and I visit Lakki's on our way into downtown Singapore. Burma is glad to see me: I can tell by the way she keeps that part of the floor around my feet clean.

Popeye joins us.

I politely ask Mama San if I can take Burma down Bugis Street for the evening. She slaps me round the head with a wet cloth. 'Yew jokin' man. You no tek my cleanah woman into place like tha. It place for stupid mens.'

My second visit to Bugis Street is more focused. I'm with Lash and Popeye and we are early: there are empty stools and chairs at the stalls. The windows on both sides of the street are shuttered against the heat of the day. Today's washing is hanging from cantilevered bamboo poles, or draped bone-dry over windowsills in the airless atmosphere. The sun sets quickly. I pay a quick visit to the toilet block at the crossroads. It's relatively quiet. The Kai-ties won't make an appearance for hours yet; nevertheless, I empty my bladder as quickly as I can.

The evening's beer, the food and the music are excellent. The Kai-ties began to arrive as we are wrapping ourselves around our seventh or eighth bottle of Tiger. We are in the mood to offer encouragement to any of them who approach our table.

I have to keep reminding myself that the best-looking ones are blokes. For an 18-year-old Pudsey boy, it's a difficult concept to get my head around. With each Tiger they look increasingly attractive. A trio of particularly attractive Eurasian Kai-ties home in on us. They order extra chairs, that are immediately supplied by the stall owner, and sit down with us.

On an adjoining table are a couple of RAF families. The wives are looking on, open-mouthed. In comparison to our guests, their wives look distinctly dowdy. Like the bar girls, our guests flutter their long eyelashes and perfectly manicured hands and in their oddly pitched voices chat and joke with us. We buy them Tigers to keep them at our table. When the subject becomes overtly sexual, I realise how much out of my depth I am. Lash, in particular, is sweating uncharacteristically. The RAF family are nudging each other and looking on expectantly. Lash says he is hungry. Our guests take that as a signal, finish their Tigers in typical bloke's fashion and blow us kisses as they depart to tables new. I look over at our neighbours, exhale visibly and shrug my shoulders. One of the wives smiled uncertainly at me.

Hunger is seriously setting in.

We order food and immerse ourselves in large platefuls of steaming fried rice and mysterious bits of meat.

'You seen any cats?' asks Lash.

'Loads ... they farm them in this part of town,' says Popeye.

'Farm them?'

'Breed them for the Makan stalls.'

Notice anything strange?

'Naah.'

'This,' he holds a stringy length of rice-encrusted meat up to the light, 'could be a cat's penis ...'

'Oh for ferk's sake, Pops.'

Lash farts and a lady on the next table holds her nose.

'Sorry,' says Lash.

We stay until well after midnight when some of the Kai-ties start to leave. What they actually get up to, and with whom, after they disappear I can't imagine. I doubt if my friends in Pudsey would understand any of this.

Popeye, Lash and I make a pact that we will make a special effort to see the sun come up over Bugis Street before we leave Singapore.

We pack all our kit into our kit bags and take everything, including our hammock, into *HMS Terror*. Apparently *Lincoln* is to be fumigated while she is in dry-dock.

We are accommodated in a second-floor mess in *Terror*. Once again I am transferred to watch-keeping duties working with Fez.

I expect *Lincoln's* dry-docking to be similar to the one I had experienced onboard *HMS Bermuda*, but it isn't. We are manoeuvred into the jaws of a ballasted floating dock alongside the jetty. Once *Lincoln* is positioned correctly, the water ballast from the floating dock is pumped out and slowly raised. I'm off watch and observe the operation from the safety of a jetty bollard. Within a couple of hours *Lincoln* is high and dry.

'DO YOU HEAR THERE: ALL ONBOARD HEADS AND BATHROOMS ARE OUT OF BOUNDS. FACILITIES ARE AVAILABLE ON THE FLOATING DOCK. WILL THE PADRE MAKE HIS WHEREABOUTS KNOWN TO THE OFFICER-OF-THE-DAY ON THE GANGWAY.'

In addition to our standard pay, we are paid a Local Overseas Allowance. Singapore and Hong Kong don't attract a high level of LOA but Borneo and the surrounding areas do. Our first payday back from patrol is therefore a pleasant surprise and four of us plan to sample some of Singapore's less grotty Makan stalls.

'There's only one place,' says Tommy, 'and that's under the Flyer.'

'Rubbish,' replies Popeye. 'Newton Circus if you want authentic Singapore food.'

'What's authentic mean?' asks Tommy.

'Food you can write home about,' explains Popeye.

I'm confused.

'There's a brilliant place off Thomson Road by the flyover that does brilliant vegetable fry-ups,' says an animated Tommy.

'Not for me, mate,' says Popeye. 'I want a plate full of tiger prawns followed by stingray flaps from my favourite stall down Newton Circus.'

Tommy screws up his face.

I don't think I fancy stingray flaps. I'd seen pictures of stingrays and I remember the red spotted monster I saw off unfriendly Jesselton. That didn't look at all palatable.

After some heated negotiations between Popeye and Tommy, the four of us bundle ourselves into a fast-black and head for Boon Tat Street and Newton Circus. I envisage elephants, tigers and long-limbed girls in fishnet tights swinging from trapezes.

Unfortunately, Newton Circus has nothing to do with swinging girls in fishnet tights. It's a compact collection of rusted tin-roofed food stalls. The smell of fish is overpowering. Popeye knows exactly where to sit. We grab ourselves one of a bank of folding tin tables and unfold it on a small section of levelish ground where we hope it won't wobble. We each collect a small stool; Tommy finds himself a rusted tin folding chair and we order Tigers, plus a gin-and-orange for Tommy, and watch as a caravan of elderly wooden push-carts laden with a variety of sea creatures, smothered in chunks of milky ice, are trundled past. As the sun sets, the surrounding dark and dingy stalls burst into life. The lights from kerosene pressure lamps and the flashed-up woks cast eerie, flickering yellow lights. The tables surrounding us begin to fill with civilian families.

'It's a good sign when you see the locals eating here,' says Popeye. 'The Newton routine is that you select food from the stall that specialises in what you want and then hope that they can find your table.'

'Just the same as under the Flyer,' says Tommy. He spots an elderly Chinese lady on an adjacent table eating a bowl full of noodles and scampers over to ask her where she got them from.

Although she speaks good English it takes her a while to understand Tommy. Eventually she understands and points him in the direction of a fish-free noodle stall.

We order more drinks. The yellow, blue-tipped flames that flare up and around the sides of the blackened woks begin to roar as tossed seafood crackles and the spatulas of artistic fryers scratch and scrape.

Popeye scuttles away. Lash and I watch Tommy as he zigzags back through a maze of tables carrying a bowl full of steaming yellow stuff with a couple of chopsticks clamped in his mouth.

Popeye returns to tell us that he has ordered three plates of deep-fried tiger prawns.

I'd had a Yorkshire prawn cocktail once, so I'm relaxed and prepared for prawns.

Around us, people try to attract the serving boys carrying trays of steaming food.

I spot a group of about a dozen cats sitting patiently under a sloping, empty push-cart on the corner of the prawn stall. At least there are cats here.

An old man wearing a grease-stained apron over his sarong and carrying a tray, tries to interest us in something called Kacang Putih and a Bird's Nest drink. Even Popeye refuses.

A young boy appears with his pad and pencil and challenges Lash to a game of noughts and crosses. He ignores me: obviously my Bugis Street reputation has preceded me.

The prawns are monstrous. They are striped, steaming and the size of a baby's arm.

Lash is staring at his three monster prawns, speechless. He pays another dollar to his young opponent for losing his last game of noughts and crosses.

'How do I eat those?' I ask.

'Depends how adventurous you are,' says Popeye. He grabs a prawn and bites its head off.

Lash and I watch as he eats it.

'Oh no!' says a wide-eyed Lash. 'Never.'

'Tear the head and legs off ... if you don't fancy them,' says Popeye.

Lash pushes his plate towards Popeye. 'You take 'em off for me, Pops ... please.'

I watch as Popeye expertly removes all the strange dangly bits and the head with its pair of morose ink-black eyes. I clean up one of mine, everything coming away surprisingly easily.

Lash takes a nibble of one of his headless prawns. He closes his eyes as he chews. Slowly his eyes open and he smiles. 'They taste better than they look,' he proclaims.

That gives me the nerve to tackle mine.

It takes two further bottles of Tiger before I manage to finish all three of my prawns. My plate is overflowing with inedible prawn fragments. Popeye's plate is empty. Lash's plate is the same as mine. Tommy finished his noodles ages ago.

'Anybody for stingray flaps?' asks Popeye.

Lash and I shake our heads and massage our stomachs.

'Four ice balls to finish then?' suggests Popeye.

Ice balls are cold, circular and very, very nice indeed. They effectively mask the lingering after-taste of the prawns.

A large ginger cat nibbles my ankle and claws my knee.

'It wants your prawn bits,' says Popeye.

I put my plate on the floor. The large ginger cat runs off with a prawn head clamped firmly in its mouth. Other cats approach our table, form a semi-orderly queue and efficiently clear my dish of inedible prawn debris. A single head is left, and a couple of white cats stand guard until Ginger returns and collects the head, unmolested. Rank obviously has its privileges amongst the Newton Circus felines.

On the way back to the Dockyard we call at Lakki's Bar for a John Collins.

Burma spots me and comes over, her purple sweeping brush tucked under her arm. 'Pita hello.'

'Hello, beautiful.'

She doesn't understand the word beautiful. She smiles and sweeps the floor around my feet. I blow her a kiss as we leave. Mama San glares at me and threatens me with a wet bar towel.

I can still taste prawns the following morning.

Photographic slides are brilliant, but viewing them while holding them up to a poor light source is becoming a nuisance. So I stroll nonchalantly down to Clicka's, confident that I have been in the Far East long enough to know how to negotiate a good price for a slide projector.

Clicka's place is open but empty. I cough loudly and wait patiently until Clicka appears, inhaling deeply on a long, wood-stemmed pipe. 'Yes sir, welcome. How are yew today?'

'Fine thank you.' I reply.

'An how is your Samoca M-35 camma ... goo I hope.'

'Yes, fine thank you.'

He blows a thin sheet of grey pipe smoke over my head. 'Goo. Wha can I dew for yew today?'

'I want to buy a projector ... for slides.'

'A projecta. I knew you would ... at some time.'

'What do you have then?'

'I have bes range of slide projecta in Singapore.'

'How much?'

Clicka smiles and takes a long, slow lungful of whatever he is smoking. 'Pry depen on type of projecta required, young sir. How much do yew have to spen?'

It's time to play it cool. 'That depends on your prices.'

'I undersan sir,' says Clicka as he taps the bowl of his pipe on the counter-top.

As though summoned, his wife – dressed in her black silk pyjamas – appears from behind the back curtains. She has a small brown cheroot dangling from the corner of her mouth. In one hand she has a bowl full of steaming something. She settles herself at the end of the counter and deftly takes a pair of chopsticks from her tightly folded grey hair.

Clicka says something and she totally ignores him as she pokes food into her small mouth.

'How much did yew say that yew have to spen, young sir?'

'Depends on your prices.' I'm running out of answers.

'I have large projecta wi' cassette load system ... expensive top of range. At bottom of range I have small single load. All electric.'

'Can I have a look, please?'

'Sure, sir,' he disappears through the back curtain.

I turn to watch his wife poke the last of her food into her mouth. She wipes her mouth with a piece of white cloth and smiles at me. 'That was goo.'

I nod.

'Parrot goo when cook slow.'

I think I misheard.' Pardon?'

'Parrot goo when cook slow.'

'Parrot?'

'Brother who sell watch in Sembawang village,' she turns and points in the general direction of *Terror*'s main gate, 'his parrot die. We divide it down middle. Goo when cook slow ... particular brain and eye. Beak no good for eat but perfec' for clean finger.' She waves her stubby hands at me.

Thankfully Clicka re-appears. I can't believe that they can eat parrot. He is carrying two boxes. He places them on the counter-top and taps the largest box. 'This one go special pry today only.'

'How much?' I ask.

'Fifty nine dollar. Special pry.'

I blow a puff of exasperated air.

'That not goo pry for yew, young sir?'

'No ... far too expensive.'

'This one,' he taps the small box. 'Was on offa las wee ... but not this wee unfortunate.'

'That's a pity.'

'Sure, young sir. But that is retail business ... sorry.'

'How much?'

'Twenny two dollar,' he blinks and quickly moves to one side. His wife gives him a dirty look as she passes him. She mutters something as the curtain closes behind her.

'Tell yew, young sir. As you are return customa ... I can offa yew ten percen discoun.'

'Ten percent?'

'Two dollar and twenty cent reduct, sir.'

'Can I have a look at it?' I ask. I have thirty five dollars in my pocket to spend.

'New pry is twenny dollar ... ignore cent. Twenny dollar goo pry for yew, sir.'

I unwrap the projector from its layers of plastic and Clicka shows me how to install the simple slide mechanism. It looks good for twenty bucks. 'OK. I'll have that then.'

'I can do special pry on big one sir and sell threw NAAFI. I can offa ten percen reduct ... ignore cents.'

'No thanks, the small one is OK.'

'Yew undersan sir that guarantee is no' valid because sold for reduce pry.'

'OK then,' I nonchalantly place two ten dollar notes on the counter top.

Clicka holds each note up the light. He repacks my projector. 'Than you, young sir.'

The following day I see the exact same projector on display in one of the Sembawang village stalls.

I think I know the answer before I ask, 'How much is that projector?'

The smiling gentleman on the other side of the counter shakes his head. 'Cash pry this afternoon is fifteen dollar. Tomorrow full pry eighteen dollar.'

'Thanks.' I feel really seen-off. It's the last time I buy anything from Clicka.

There is nowhere in the mess where I can plug my projector in and view my slides privately, so I stow it away in the back of my locker.

On the mess noticeboard, George has posted his latest report ...

Malaysian Crisis Report #3

President Sukarno has declared to crush Malaysia. He says that Malaysia is a British puppet state, and that any expansion of Malaysia will increase British control over the region, with implications for Indonesia's national security. Similarly, the Philippines have made a claim for

Sabah, arguing that it has historic links with the Philippines through the Sulu archipelago.
Leading Radio Operator
George Wild

In Lakki's Bar this evening I put aside all thoughts of President Sukarno and his threat to crush Malaysia. I have a sudden overwhelming desire to get close to Burma. Despite Mama San keeping a close eye on both of us, I make sure that my toilet visits coincide with Burma's disappearance from the main bar. I manoeuvre her into a darkened corner and take both her hands in mine. She panics and looks towards the opening to the main bar where Mama San sits. I kiss her on her cheek. She whimpers, not knowing what to do. I tap one of her hands and stroll nonchalantly away, satisfied for the moment.

There is an uncharacteristic twinkle in Burma's eye as she emerges into the main bar some minutes later. She picks her moment to clear our table and sweep under our table. She smells of freshly applied perfume.

The following day, the entire ship's company is assembled on the jetty a quarter of an hour before dinner, wearing our caps. It's scorchingly hot and uncomfortable as we wait for something to happen. Those of us from the forward Seamen's mess don't have a clue what is going on.

The Captain and a bloke with over-starched shirt and shorts eventually appears and we are called to attention. The Captain has something to say. Apparently, despite *HMS Lincoln* being an Aircraft Direction Frigate, we have won the Fleet Anti Aircraft gunnery trophy. The bloke in starched whites is Admiral Scatchard, Flag Officer Second-in Command Far East Fleet, and he presents the Captain with a trophy of a swept-wing aircraft on a circular base.

Back down the mess, those in the gunnery branch explain that we have distinguished ourselves in tracking and shooting attacking aircraft under exercise conditions. Those of us not in the Gunnery branch don't have a clue what they mean. Daily orders for the following day tells us, in Wardroom speak, that we are a brilliant ship's company.

George Wild spends some time in the mess this evening telling Tansy all about something called The Great Train Robbery that has taken place in Buckinghamshire. The rest of us pay little notice.

I have finished *The Shadow of Tyburn Tree*. I return it to Tansy and exchange it for the next in the series, *The Rising Storm*.

Brick hasn't received a letter from Polly for the past ten days: he's a worried and confused man. Today he receives a letter that he opens slowly.

It's only a single sheet and he reads it and re-reads it. 'Thank goodness for that,' he says, as he taps his head on the mess table.

'For what?' I ask.

'Her mum has written to tell me that Polly is poorly.'

'You're relieved that she's ill?'

'Thought she'd dumped me.'

'How ill is she, mate?'

He scans the letter again. 'She doesn't say.'

'Hope she's not seriously ill, Brick mate.'

'At least she hasn't dumped me.'

'She must be really ill if she can't write to you herself,' says Popeye.

Brick stops in his tracks. 'You've got a point there, Pops.'

'Sorry, mate.'

'You'll have to write her a long letter of condolence,' suggests a grinning Tommy.

The Entertainments Officer posts a notice asking for volunteers to spend a week with the Ghurkhas in their jungle training camp in Malaya. Lash convinces me that it will be a laugh. After a bottle of Tiger at dinner time I put my name down.

A few days later Lash and I are summoned to Lieutenant Conway's cabin.

'I didn't have you pair down as the adventurous types,' says a rather bored-looking Lieutenant Conway. 'Radio Operator Atkins has also volunteered. To keep you pair in check, I have also volunteered Leading Seaman Parker to go with you. A happy band of four.'

'Thank you, sir.'

'Thank you, sir.'

'This is a wonderful opportunity for you to represent Her Majesty's Royal Navy in a unique way. The Jungle Warfare Training Facility at Kota Tinggi was recently established not only for jungle training but also to train the recently formed Gurkha Parachute Regiment ...'

Wha! ... Parachute? Nobody said anything about ferkin parachutes.

'I have arranged for you to draw jungle greens from stores in HMS Terror tomorrow. Transport for Kota Tinggi is arranged for 13:00 the following day, giving Leading Seaman Parker a chance to have his last tot for a week or so.'

We nod.

'You will need your passports. I've arranged for those to be given to you tomorrow from the Ship's Office.'

Down the mess I break the news about parachuting to Fez. 'Conway says this Kota Tinggi place is for training the Gurkha Parachute Regiment.'

'He's having you on,' says Fez.

'That's what he said,' confirms Lash. 'I was there when he said it.'

'Nobody's mentioned that to me,' says Fez who continues to stir his coffee.

The following day, I'm sitting with Fez, Asker and Lash in the Armada Club, having a Stand-easy Tiger. The place still has the smell of last night's beer and cigarettes, despite the best efforts of the cleaners. The deckhead fans rotate lethargically. A number of young, playful chit-chats scuttle across the deckhead. There is no wind and it's stiflingly hot.

Inwardly refreshed, we set out to find the Stores building. It's a single-storey white building with small windows and surrounded by masses of bright red flowers that Fez says are orchids. Behind the counter, an elderly Malayan gentleman with a wispy beard scrutinises the chit offered by Fez.

'Yew go jungle?'

'Yes,' replies Fez.

'Wi Gurkha at Kota Tinggi?'

'Yes.'

'Morrow?'

'Yes.'

He shakes his head and smiles. He scuttles away and returns ten minutes later carrying a pile of green clothing. We are each given a jacket, a pair of trousers, a khaki T-shirt, a pair of calf-length jungle boots and a green floppy hat. He waits patiently while we try them on. Surprisingly we are all happy with the cut and hang of our new equipment.

'These are good, aren't they?' asks Asker.

Back in the mess we are subject to some jungle observations from those who have never been there.

'You know there are tigers in the Malayan jungle?' says Tommy.

'That's not true – don't believe him lads,' says Fez.

'Haven't you heard the story of the tiger who walked into the snooker room at Raffles Hotel and spread himself out on the snooker table then?' asks Tommy.

'That's bollocks,' says Lash

'It's true,' confirms Tommy. 'Ask anybody.'

My stomach wobbles. Tigers!

'And on top of that. On top of that are all the poisonous snakes and things,' adds Apple.

Next day, at exactly 13:00, I muster on the gangway with my co-adventurers, decked out in my jungle greens. I have a plastic carrier bag containing all my washing gear, four pairs of clean underpants, a hundred duty-free cigarettes and my camera. I feel a bit special; I have my passport in my pocket and I'm on my way to Kota Tinggi ... in the Malayan jungle.

We have a forty-seater dockyard bus all to ourselves. Lieutenant Conway appears and gives the driver his instructions on a small piece of paper.

'Best of luck, gentlemen.'

Gentlemen?

'Remember that you are representing Her Majesty's Senior Service. Make sure that you listen to all the advice given to you by the experts. Enjoy yourselves and I'll see you back here in a week. Your point of contact upon arrival at Kota Tinggi is a Major Kyte.' He turns and waves an arm at the driver. 'Carry on, driver.'

'Do you know how long the journey will be to Kota whatsit?' asks Asker.

'No idea,' says Fez.

The bus takes us over the causeway to Johore Bahru where the driver unexpectedly tells us to disembark as we pull up alongside the main immigration building. He tells us to take our bags with us for inspection.

Inside the badly lit building, we join the back of a snaking queue of saronged individuals wanting to visit Malaya.

'It's a ferkin long queue, isn't it?' asks Asker.

Nobody replies. There is no air conditioning or deckhead fans and my jungle greens are beginning to stick to me. By the time we make it to the front, I've smoked three cigarettes. Fez offers the small, unsmiling Malayan gentleman behind a glass screen our 'Movement' chit. He reads it, mumbles something, stamps each of our passports and waves us through.

I'm in Malaya: another country to add to my list.

Outside we look around for the dockyard bus but it's gone -we're stranded.

'What are we going to do now?' I ask. I don't expect an answer.

Fez scratches his head underneath his floppy hat. 'Give it ten minutes, then we'll find somewhere we can get a drink.'

Within the allocated ten minutes, just as we are getting thirsty, a Land Rover, with a Gurkha logo of crossed knives on the door, screams to a halt alongside us. The driver, a small round-faced man wearing a green pillbox hat, leans out of his window. 'Are yew for waiting Kota Tinggi transpor?'

Fez waves a welcoming hand.

'I was looking forward to a Tiger,' says a disappointed Lash.

We jam ourselves into the Land Rover. Fez sits in the front seat and exchanges pleasantries with the driver who is dressed in a perfectly ironed dark green uniform. He has a short row of medal ribbons above his left shirt pocket.

We encounter little traffic on our two hour journey north on a partially tarmaced, two-way road. The jungle stands dense and green on both sides, patiently waiting its chance to regain its lost strip.

'That jungle looks serious, doesn't it?' asks Asker.

Nobody replies.

We all sit silently. Personally, I'm out of my environment and I'm feeling a little nervous.

More than once our driver has to swerve to avoid a large reptile or a snake of some kind on the road. Surely the Royal Navy wouldn't send me anywhere where there are wild creatures roaming free, would they?

'Did you see that?' asks Asker.

'What?'

'That ferkin great lizard thing. It's gone now. It was looking at us from the jungle. Didn't you see it? It was as big as a ... a ... ferkin Land Rover.'

'Never,' says Lash who is gazing wide-eyed at the jungle fringe.

'Didn't look too happy to see us,' says Asker.

We all sit in silence. My bowels begin to move when our driver casually mentions 'I see tiger two day ago. Beautiful.'

Fez looks at him with open mouth.

Lash farts.

'Did he say tiger?' asks Asker.

'He did yeah,' I reply.

We swerve off the main road and head upwards on a red dirt road.

'Win window up please,' says the driver. Within minutes the track narrows and the jungle fronds and branches abrade the side and roof of the Land Rover. There is an overwhelming unnatural smell to the place; a seriously intimidating smell – a jungle smell.

We emerge into a cleared area. A line of green camouflage tents stands erect against the jungle fringes. A fire burns smokeless under a wood-framed canopy topped with palm leaves.

A tall gentleman in camouflage uniform stands erect in the centre of the clearing. The driver screeches to a halt. 'Arry Kota Tinggi gentelmeh. Thank yew for journey.'

We all say 'Thank you,' in our own way as we disembark. The tall gentleman waits. 'Welcome to Kota Tinggi gentlemen,' he says. He has unusually long blond hair that escapes from under the rim of his dark green beret and drapes over the tops of his ears. He has penetrating pale blue eyes and an extraordinarily long pointed nose. 'My name is Major Kyte the Commanding Officer of the Gurkha Parachute Regiment currently undergoing training at Kota Tinggi. Let me tell you something about the place.'

A group of three Gurkhas appear and take position alongside Major Kyte.

'Kota Tinggi is the primary jungle warfare training facility in Malaya. Ideally situated in an area of the densest jungle on the Malay peninsula.'

I'm finding it difficult to maintain my level of concentration: I'm flagging. I notice behind Major Kyte a cascading river of red water tumbling down a bare rock face into a large pool of red-green water bordered on three sides by particularly well-watered jungle.

'The three people I would like to introduce to you are Sergeant Warrior Limbu,' he waves a hand towards the nearest gentleman who smiles briefly, 'Corporal Bibek Kandel and Cook

Asim Waggle. While you are our guests at Kota Tinggi you will refer to them as Sergeant, Corporal and Chef respectively.'

We all mumble something that is accepted as an agreement.

'Any questions?'

We expect Asker to have at least one, and he does.

'Are there tigers in the jungle, sir?'

'Yes. Any further questions?'

'Are these tigers anywhere near here … sir?' blurts Asker.

'We did see one a couple of days ago. We don't know exactly where it is now. It drank from the pond.'

'It could still be around here then, sir?'

'Possibly … but we are not here to track wildlife.'

'Shit,' whispers Fez.

'I wanna go home,' says Lash.

Major Kyte looks at his wristwatch. 'There will be food available within the hour. I trust that you will approve of our Nepalese cuisine. Corporal Kandel will show you to your tent. I hope that you enjoy your short stay with us. Tomorrow we will be doing a jungle trek.'

We all look at each other. We don't have to say anything: a ferkin trek … a ferkin jungle trek. I didn't expect to be ferkin trekking.

Major Kyte, the Sergeant and the Chef leave us in the company of a smiling Corporal Kandel who waves us towards the tent at the end of the row, its two sides hard up against the encroaching jungle.

Inside our tent are four camp beds, on top of which are a couple of blankets and a folded white fine meshed net. I toss my bag onto the bed furthest from to the door.

'Foo at seventee thirty exact,' says Corporal Kandel. 'Make you home.' And he leaves us.

'Didn't expect it to be like this, did you?' asks Asker.

'My grandfather told me when I joined up never to volunteer for anything. He fought in the First World War.' I say.

'Good advice,' says Fez.

'You should know better, Hooky,' says Lash.

'I didn't volunteer for this, I was detailed off,' says Fez. 'To look after you lot.'

I notice a family group of bright green chit-chats looking at us from a corner of the tent roof. They are directly above Asker's bed so I don't concern myself.

I decide that my belongings are safest left in my bag.

At 17:30 precisely we wander outside. The sun is below the jungle line and the mosquitoes are out. Corporal Kandel waves us towards a large tent. Inside are bench seats set alongside bare wooden tables. At one end the Chef who had been introduced to us earlier stands stirring a large bowl of something aromatic.

'Dal-bhat-tarkari ... jungle style,' explains Corporal Kandel.

There are no plates and we have nothing to put the Dal-bhat-tarkari in, so there is a panic until the chef finds four badly bashed bowls. We take our bowl full of the lumpy grey concoction and sit as far away from the chef as possible. Corporal Kandel tosses four spoons on the table.

'What is in this?' asks Asker, pointing his spoon at his bowl.

Corporal Kandel sits down opposite us. 'Dal-bhat-tarkari, traditional Nepalese dish. We eat every day.'

'But what's in it?' asks Asker, sniffing his bowl.

'Lentils, achaar, fermented pickle and animal.'

'What ferkin animal?' asks Asker.

'I don know how to say in English,' replies Corporal Kandel.

'Try ... please.'

Fez takes a mouthful. He wipes his mouth on his sleeve. 'It's not bad, lads.'

Outside, we wander over to the bank of the pool. The very dark jungle looks menacing

'Fancy a swim?' I ask.

'You won't get me in there,' replies Lash.

'Wonder what's in there?' asks Asker.

'Wonder where everybody else is. He did say that there are more Gurkhas here, didn't he?'

I spot a movement in the black jungle line to the right of our tent. 'Wha?'

We all turn as an old man, pushing a large wheeled pram, passes us without a sideways glance. He stops outside the large tent.

Major Kyte appears and strides purposefully towards us. 'Would you like a beer?'

It's a stupid question and has us perplexed for a moment. We stand in silence.

'Our daily supply of beer has arrived. The rest of the troop won't be back until the early hours so you may as well grab a couple of bottles each while they are still cold. We'll be doing a jungle trek tomorrow so you should get yourselves a good night's sleep.'

In the pram, amidst a covering of crushed ice, are a number of crates of Tiger beer. We each grab a couple of bottles and retire to our tent.

'Did you hear what he said about a trek?' asks Asker.

'I didn't come here for a trek,' says Lash.

'Particularly in this ferkin jungle stuff,' I say.

Fez, forever the optimist, says it will be an experience.

To say that Lash breaks wind would be an understatement. He explodes and almost raises himself off his camp bed. 'Must be something in the food.'

'Maybe the animal,' says Fez.

'Anything and everything makes him fart,' I explain. 'The medical staff onboard Bermuda were completely baffled.'

'You can sleep with your arse facing outboard,' instructs Fez.

'Wonder what the animal was?' asks Asker.

'Finish your beer and go to sleep.'

'Wonder where the heads are?' says Lash.

'That's a good point,' I say.

All four of us spend an uncomfortable night. We hear the Gurkha troop return in the early hours. Instead of going to bed they spend a noisy hour opening bottles of Tiger before retiring.

Maybe I managed a couple of hours' sleep.

Someone smacks the side of our tent. 'Brekfar' ready now.'

We roll out of our respective bunks.

'Shit,' says Lash. 'Look at these.' He points to two lines of large, black and red ants. Each line is tramping in the opposite direction. The two-way line runs from one corner of the tent to the other. They climb the bottom corner of Lash's bed and over our pile of bags.

'Look at the size of the bastards.'

'Are they ants?' asks Asker.

'No, they're ferkin elephants.'

'Brekfar ready NOW.' The side of the tent is slapped again.

Breakfast is a warm banana omelette that is surprisingly nice. There is no coffee, only an urn of milky sweet tea. The four of us sit at a short trestle table in the corner and watch in silence as the Gurkhas breakfast. They do most things in a dignified silence; there is little banter between individuals. They are a friendly lot, most of them acknowledging us with a wide toothed smile.

I never have sugar in my tea and I'm struggling with my first and only glassful when Corporal Kandel appears. 'We leave at 06:30.'

I look at my watch. It isn't the best timekeeper but accurate enough to show that we have about ten minutes. Fez takes a picture of me by the waterfall. I take a picture of Fez, just in case either of us don't survive the trek.

By the waterfall

The sun is behind the jungle canopy but rising like a rocket. Already it's sticky as we form an untidy group of four at a respectful distance from the perfectly straight lines of Gurkhas assembled by the side of the pool.

Major Kyte arrives and hands us each a green net scarf. 'You'll need these. Today we are doing a trek through the thickest part of the surrounding jungle. I strongly advise you all to ensure that all your buttons and flaps are firmly fastened. Particularly important is that your boots are correctly laced. Tuck the scarf tight around your neck to cover the gap below your chin and roll your sleeves all the way down. We will be out for approximately four hours. There will be an optional period of rest after two hours. You should find it easy to follow the man in front of you but as a safety measure we have a man who will always be behind you.'

The jungle envelopes us. The brightness of the sun is barely evident as we trek in single file through a variety of tough and sometimes dangerous-looking vegetation. The Gurkhas silently brush the jungle aside without much effort. The Royal Naval contingent, on the other hand, ploughs its way through the barely discernible jungle path, coughing, spluttering, and in Lash's case, breaking wind continually. Asker has taken up position downwind of Lash. My sweat glands suddenly explode. I'm continually wiping my face with my net scarf that has no absorbent properties whatsoever. The chatter and screech of the jungle's inhabitants surround us. Occasionally, there is an unnatural period of silence with only the crunching of dead vegetation beneath our boots. It's as though those that live here are listening to us. I blank my mind and try to ignore what kinds of animals are surrounding us, watching and following us.

It's a long two and a half hours before we stop in a small clearing. I'm wringing wet from head to toe. My jungle greens are like rags. In contrast the Gurkhas are smiling and looking every bit as fresh as they did at breakfast.

'That was a long two and a half hours, wasn't it?' asks Asker.

Major Kyte appears, wringing his hands. 'How do we feel, lads?' He doesn't expect an answer. 'That was a relaxing two-hour slog to get the blood circulating. You did very well to keep up.

Cook Waggle has some tea on the boil. You've brought a drinking vessel with you, I suppose?'

We haven't and we all shake our heads.

'No matter, I'll get someone to make some for you.'

We all look at each other, pull a face and do nothing. Lash spots a bright green and purple lizard scuttling around his feet, picking up fallen leaves, crunching them and spitting them out.

Five minutes later Chef Waggle appears carrying four leaves folded in the form of shallow cups. 'Chi now.'

We scoop the milky brown liquid from a steaming pan. Surprisingly our leaves don't leak.

I push my folded leaf into the breast pocket of my jacket as we prepare to set off on what I hope is the return journey.

Within minutes of our departure, a piece of the jungle with razor-sharp leaves strikes the side of my face. The whole of one side of my face begins to throb and itch. There is blood on my hand as I wipe the sweat away.

By the time we arrive back at Kota Tinggi my right eye has almost closed and my net scarf is covered in blood.

Sergeant Warrior Limbu examines me and slaps me on the shoulder. 'In water,' he says pointing at the pool.

I place my cigarettes, lighter and Naval Identity card in my bag and immerse myself in the pool along with Fez.

'Is it deep?' asks Asker who is standing on the bank with Lash.

I'm treading water. 'Yeah, but it's cool.'

'Any other things in there?' asks a concerned-looking Lash.

'Dunno.' I rub my face with my soaked net scarf. I'm already feeling better and I can see more.

Asker takes his boots off and dangles his feet in the water.

Lash walks away.

The old bloke with the pram appears and our eyes follow the crates of iced Tigers.

Sergeant Limbu joins us at our table. He is a few inches taller than your average Gurkha and has unnaturally wide, square shoulders. 'Tomorrow is Friday. We have special evening this evening. You welcome to join us after mealtime for drinking. Yew did good today. No more trekking for two day now.'

The evening meal is a variation on Dal-bhat-tarkari. It's a little thicker than yesterdays and has chunks of an unknown purplish vegetable floating in it.

All the beer is equally dished out followed by something milky and warm that they called Aela. 'Rice beer,' explains Corporal Kandel. He smiles when I take my leaf cup from my pocket.

The ants are still crawling through our tent, but after three cups of Aela none of us cares very much.

'What was that milky stuff called?' asks Asker the following morning.

None of us can remember.

'Must have been good though … I've got a stinking hangover,' I say.

'Navy logic,' explains Fez.

The side of the tent is slapped. 'Break-fa' ready NOW.'

Thankfully, today is the designated day off. We spend the day lounging around, topping up our tan and complaining about life in the jungle. Chef Waggle examines the cut on my face, gives me something to wipe it with and says something reassuring in Nepalese.

A Gurkha private called Gagan spends some time with us showing us how to make eating and drinking vessels from large leaves. In exchange we teach him some English swear words.

Fez and I swim in the pool.

Sergeant Limbu tells us not to venture into the jungle. In the afternoon the Royal Naval contingent sleep.

I awake as the old bloke with the pram appears with Friday evening's liquid refreshment: there are more crates than usual. The old man huffs and puffs his way up the short incline. I wonder how far he's pushed his pram.

I ask Gagan if there is a way of getting rid of the ants in our tent.

'Yew goh ferkin ants?' he says, practising one of his newly learned words.

'Yes.'

In the tent he looks and shakes his head. 'Ant going place ... import place ... no stop them. Ferkin ant eh?'

'Yeah.'

He picks an ant up and examines it. 'If bite yew, this one make you piss green.' He gently places the ant back in the line.

I sleep well and don't wake until I hear the side of the tent being slapped. 'Breakfa ready saylah.'

After breakfast, the Gurkhas are mustered with full packs and marched into the jungle.

Major Kyte addresses us. 'Got a little job for you lads this lunch time. I want you to dress as for a trek. I'll issue you each with a whistle and a compass and I want you to go into the jungle ... not too far ... and find yourselves a spot where you can observe any of the troop returning from today's trek. Make a mental note of how many you spot. Clear?'

Fez mumbles. 'Yes, sir.'

After a dinner of Dal-bhat-tarkari with Gundruk and something the chef says is Golbeda, Major Kyte gives us our approximate positions. 'If you feel as though you are lost, blow on your whistle and I'll send someone out to rescue you. Clear?'

'Yes, sir,' says Fez.

'Test your whistles.'

We all take a deep breath and blow our whistles. They all work. Chef comes running out of his tent, realises that it's only a test and strolls back, flicking his dish cloth on his thigh.

'No smoking outside of the camp area by the way,' says Major Kyte.

I'm detailed to protect the section of Malayan jungle on the opposite side of the pool.

'Walk in to the jungle until you can no longer hear the waterfall,' says a smiling Major Kyte.

I nod.

'All of you, keep your eyes and ears open. Filter out the noises of the jungle if you can. Don't smoke. When you hear chef banging on a pot you can come back. It won't be more than a couple of hours.'

We disperse. I climb over the large wet rocks at the foot of the waterfall and thread my way into the jungle. I feel a little vulnerable all by myself and have already decided that I'm not going to go too far. I brush aside the vegetation as I look for a distinguishing feature that will help me navigate my way back, but everything is the same. The sun has gone and I can hear yelps and growls around me. I stop. I can't hear the waterfall so I decide to squat down exactly where I am. There is nothing to squat on so I tear down a large elliptical leaf and sit on that with my feet facing the waterfall ... I think. The Malayan jungle encircles me, so close that whenever I move, so does the jungle: it rustles and vibrates angrily as though disturbed. There are animal noises everywhere. I suppose the chances of the Malayan tiger finding me here are slim. I decide not to think about that.

Despite what Major Kyte said, I have a cigarette. The jungle is damp and I'm very careful where I flick my ash and how I put it out.

My ears begin to filter out the noises of the jungle and the humidity quickly makes me drowsy. I watch white ants scurrying in and out of a hole not far from my left foot. They are each carrying something dead.

I must have dozed off briefly, because the next thing I hear is the distant clatter of someone banging on a pot.

Walking back is more difficult for some unknown reason. As I hop from one rock to another at the base of the waterfall, I realise that my bootlaces are undone.

Fez is the first one of us back. He is sitting enjoying a beer with Chef and Corporal Kandel.

Corporal Kandel looks at my boots and smiles. 'Goh yew eh?'

I look down and realise that the laces of both boots have been cut. 'Wha ...?'

'It's their exercise apparently,' says Fez. 'To see if they can find us. Cutting our bootlaces is an indication that they found us.'

'But I never ...'

'That's the exercise.'

'Ferkin Nora.'

'More or less what I said,' says Fez.

Lash and Asker hobble back into camp both with cut bootlaces.

Chef smiles as Major Kyte appears and hands us each a brand new set of laces.

'How did they manage that, sir?' asks Asker.

'If I tell you that, young man, I would have to kill you,' says a smiling Major.

'Really?' asks a wide-eyed Asker.

As we are re-lacing our boots, Gagan comes over and whispers in my ear, 'Smell your cigarette half an hour away.'

'How did you know it was mine?'

'Yew only one smoke Lucky 7 shit.'

Asker and I go for a refreshing splash and float in the pond. Asker screams as he stumbles out of the water holding one of his feet. 'I've been ferkin bitten, haven't I?'

The Chef, carrying a First Aid box, is on the scene immediately. Asker's lower calf muscle is already inflamed and swelling. We lay him on the ground outside the tent. 'What is it?' asks Fez.

'Dunno. Had ferkin sharp teeth whatever it was.'

'What's in the pond, sir?' asks Fez as Major Kyte arrives.

'Don't know, to be honest. The Gurkhas aren't great ones for swimming. Did you see what attacked you?'

'Didn't see it ... just felt it, sir,' replies Asker.

'Let Chef do his bit and we'll see how it goes in the next half hour or so. Does it hurt?'

'Yes, sir.'

Major Kyte claps his hands. 'Half an hour then, lads. We'll see what it's like then. In the meantime just keep him quiet and relaxed if you can.'

Chef rubs some jelly stuff onto Askers lower leg and wraps a tight bandage around his knee.

Major Kyte arrives after half an hour or so carrying two bottles of Tiger. He hands one to Asker. 'Any better, Chef?'

'No sir. Worse a little.'

'Pack your kit then, lads. I'll arrange transport back to Singapore. I think that this needs to be looked at in your Sick Bay.'

We pack our kit and wait in silence for our transport. We say goodbyes and shake hands with most of the Troop. Gagan gives me a special cup made from a dark green leaf – much better made than mine.

A blue Land Rover screams to a halt by the pond. We jump in and that is it: our Kota Tinggi adventure is over.

Fez, Lash and I are proud that we have spent almost a week in the Malayan jungle with the Gurkhas and have returned relatively unscathed. We try to explain to those in the mess about Dal-bhat-tarkari and Gundruk, but it's impossible. We explain the bootlace exercise, but everybody thinks we're bullshitting.

'You mean that while you were sitting in the jungle a bloke was actually able to sneak up on you unnoticed and cut your boot laces?'

'Yep.'

'Impossible.'

'Not to the Gurkhas it isn't,' I reply.

'You didn't hear them?'

'I did drop off once for a few minutes I think.'

'Lazy sod.'

'They've said yes. Albion have said ferkin yes,' PTI Dyne screams as he dances around the mess in his tight white singlet and not much else.

For its size, *Lincoln* has a great football team. It has won most of its matches and is the current holder of the Far Eastern Small Ships Trophy. Gunga is confident that our team can beat anybody and had issued a number of official challenges to *HMS Albion* over the last months. *HMS Albion* is an Aircraft Carrier, with a crew ten times larger than *Lincoln* and the current holder of the prestigious Far East Fleet Soccer Cup. If the game's a draw, they retain the cup: if we beat them, we take the trophy.

'Calm down Gunga,' says Tansy.

Tansy and I look at each other, not fully understanding Gunga's enthusiastic outburst.

'Next Saturday,' Gunga screams. He jumps in the air, almost bangs his head on an un-lagged pipe and claps his hands on his thighs. 'Next Saturday on Terror's number one pitch 19:30 under floodlights. Lincoln versus Albion.'

'Put some nicks on Gunga,' says Tansy.

Gunga skips over into the next mess, gives an unsuspecting Ordinary Seaman a kiss and goes through everything again. 'When we win ... when we ferkin win we will be the holders of the Far East Fleet Soccer Cup.'

'Strange people these PTIs,' says Popeye.

Gunga organises the banners. From somewhere he provides canvas strips and cajoles people to design their own individual placards. Apple is a bit of an artist and on our mess canvas he draws a colourful ship's crest and underneath scrawls 'Drinkin' Lincoln'. He is commissioned by other messes to draw a ship's crest for them in exchange for rum.

It's rumoured that our football team plus substitutes are given meat priority at meal times ... and are given the largest portion of 'duff'. In the adjacent mess Gunga is becoming a footballing nuisance.

9

HMS LINCOLN V HMS ALBION

Daily orders for Saturday encourages everybody to muster at *HMS Terror*'s main football pitch for a 19:30 kick-off. We are all issued with a chit entitling us all to a free pint of Armada Club Tiger courtesy of the ship's Tombola fund. Tommy exchanges his chit for 'sippers' at tot time.

Brick, who is duty and has a fresh pile of Polly's letters to answer, stays in the mess. We muster in the Armada Club well before the prescribed time. By the time the others begin to arrive we have spent our chits and are already well into our third round. Tommy is on to his second gin and orange. Senior Rates, who have their own watering hole in *Terror*, begin to congregate at our Club. We smirk as a few Officers appear, clearly out of their comfort zone.

'Women,' says Lash, pointing. A Midshipman, who has recently joined *Lincoln*, is standing outside talking to Lieutenant Conway. Standing alongside with their hands self-consciously clasped behind their backs, are two strikingly attractive ladies. One is wearing a patterned flowing dress; she has high piled fair hair and is old enough to be the Midshipman's mother. The younger one, wearing pink Bermuda shorts and a white singlet, is obviously related as she also has blonde hair and long, shapely legs. The Midshipman looks around and decides against entering the Club proper. He ushers his ladies away over the road towards the pitch that is already bathed in floodlights.

'Not bad eh ... the one in shorts?' says Lash.

'Legs up to her armpits,' explains Tommy.

We all nod. There is nothing the rest of us can add to that.

Tansy explains that some Officers and Senior Rates have paid to bring their wives and girlfriends out to Singapore for a short holiday while *Lincoln* is in refit.

Apple spots something worth mentioning. 'There's another woman ... just behind that column,' he points. 'There she is – look.'

Apple is absolutely right: it's a woman. Very much a woman with loads of bulging bodily bits. Definitely not the type of woman who should be allowed out wearing revealingly thin tropical clothing. Her enormous breasts look as though they are resting on her swollen stomach. Her backside is monstrous. There is a sweat line running down the back of her pale blue smock.

'I wonder who she belongs to?' asks Asker.

An unknown Petty Officer ushers her away towards the pitch.

'Poor sod,' someone says.

'Yeah, poor old bugger.'

'Who'd pay good money to bring that all the way to Singapore?'

'Who's round is it?' asks Tansy. 'About time we were making our way over the road to get seats.'

Over the road, the Officers and guests have naturally taken that section of the east stand that has the thicker seat cushions. The Senior Rates are occupying a section alongside that also has cushions, but slightly less plump ones.

A relatively small group of silent *HMS Albion* crewmembers sit on the un-cushioned end of our west stand.

We unfurl our banners. The Stokers' mess arrive and add significantly to the number of *Lincoln* supporters. On the opposite stand more people, including some women, take their seats. There are no banners in evidence on that side of the pitch. I spot the woman in the pink shorts sitting on the front row directly opposite our chosen positions.

We have each brought a couple of pints with us and we settle ourselves having erected our mess banner to the back and above us.

Someone decides that we should parade around the pitch, so we do. Carrying our banners and flying our flags, about fifty of us parade around the edge of the pitch chanting whatever we fancy as long as it contains the words *Lincoln* and Drinkin'. Those seated on the plump cushions politely applaud us. The woman in the pink shorts is visibly excited by our performance.

At 19:20 the team from *HMS Albion* take to the pitch resplendent in a strip of blue shirts and white shorts that sparkle under the floodlights. The goalkeeper is wearing a standard green jersey. The referee and linesmen take up position in the centre circle as the team from *Lincoln* stroll casually onto the pitch to a cacophony of support from the west stand and polite applause from those opposite. *Lincoln*'s first eleven are resplendent in Lincoln green shirts, shorts and socks. Our goalkeeper is wearing a jumper of bright yellow.

I drain my glass. We begin chanting as the referee brings the two captains to the centre for the ceremonial handshake, exchange of ships' crests and the tossing of a coin. Gunga is bouncing up and down as though he is on springs. In contrast, the captain of *HMS Albion* appears calm and confident.

Apple appears carrying a couple of empty galvanised buckets. 'For the next round,' he explains.

Lincoln kick off and are attacking the *Albion* goal immediately. The over-confident *Albion* are taken by surprise and are still organising themselves while the *Lincolns* scurry around, determined to score early. Our early burst of energy prove too much for our opponents and ten minutes into the game we score a much deserved opening goal. Five minutes later we score a second. We are 2-0 up and the *Albion* supporters have lost their voice. Our brave lads manage to withstand an *Albion* onslaught in the latter minutes of the first half.

The stand seats are filling up as the whole of *HMS Terror* has heard that little *Lincoln* are giving big *Albion* a footballing lesson.

Lash and I are collecting glasses to take back to the Armada Club when we are stopped by Apple. 'Leave the glasses, just fill the buckets.'

We check the insides of the buckets that look reasonably clean.

'Will they fill them for us?' I ask.

'Sure they will.'

'How many pints do you reckon they hold?'

'I don't know, do I?' says Apple. 'I'll come with you. I'm sure I can convince Nigel to give us a couple of buckets-full on tick.'

I feel a little self-conscious plonking a pair of galvanised buckets on the bar. Apple collars Nigel Lee, the Eurasian who manages the bar, and he agrees to fill the buckets for us. He uses his gun to squirt Tiger into the buckets as though this is normal procedure.

'Twenty-two pints in each, Apple,' says a pouting Nigel. 'Nineteen dollar in total. Pay me when game is finish. Who playing anyway?'

'Lincoln are playing Albion for The Fleet Soccer Cup,' I say.

'Fancy,' says Nigel. He's a touch on the effeminate side, is Nigel.

Apple takes one of the buckets. 'We'll sell the contents for sixty cents a pint.'

In the stand, there are plenty of lazy drinkers who prefer to buy our Tiger than walk to the Club bar.

Albion start the second half round of shoulder and heavy-legged. *Lincoln* are over-confident: our passing is going astray and we are not concentrating on the game in hand. Thanks to our goalkeeper we prevent Albion from scoring as they pepper our goal.

Halfway through the second half, we have emptied both buckets of Tiger and Apple and I have pockets full of money.

Albion eventually score and I notice the lady in the pink shorts jumping up and down.

Apple and I refill the buckets. We have timed it perfectly and are pouring out the dregs just as Lash, the unofficial timekeeper, is telling us that the ninety minutes are up. We are unfurling our banners and flags in preparation for a victory lap of the pitch. Someone has placed what we assume is The Far East Fleet Soccer Cup on a chair in front of the east stand. To me it looks like a silver finger bowl on a black plinth.

Then, horrors of horrors, *Albion* score a fluky equaliser. Before we can kick off again the referee blows his whistle and brings the game to an end.

The lady in the pink Bermuda shorts hugs the lucky bastard sitting next to her.

I, along with most of the west stand, look on in stunned silence as our team stroll off the pitch utterly dejected.

The lady in the pink shorts is being shown the Fleet Soccer Cup.

'Let's count our money,' says Apple.

'After the presentation.'

'Why?'

'I think that the girl in the pink shorts is going to do something with the cup.'

'Right then.'

We watch as the beauty in the pink shorts officially presents the captain of the *Albion* team with the Far East Fleet Soccer Cup to the polite applause of the east stand.

Apple and I have made a good profit each. We also have ourselves a couple of new buckets for the mess.

'That woman in the pink shorts is nice, isn't she?' I ask Tommy.

'Daughter of Loch Lomond's Engineering Officer apparently. And granddaughter of someone really high up in the Admiralty.'

'Naah.'

'So I'm told.'

'I wonder if she's bumped into Sugar yet.'

Tommy is determined to take me and Lash to the place under the Flyover. We pretend to be interested in a veggie evening. Popeye refuses to come with us.

We called in at Lakki's on the way to town. Tommy spends some time in a dark corner with Lilly while Lash and I down a couple of ice-cold Tigers.

'You're not going to have a veggie with Tommy, are ya?' asks Lash.

'Nope. I'm in experimental mode and I fancy Stingray flaps,' I say.

'You don't.' Lash pulls the face that normally accompanies any mention of seafood.

Burma smiles at me. 'Pita Hello.'

'Hello gorgeous,' I reply with a smile. She flicks a cloth over the tabletop and places a bowl full of shelled peanuts in the centre. She smells wonderful.

I blow Burma a kiss as we leave. She smiles nervously.

The place under the Flyover is a line of rusty, tin-roofed eating stalls under the concrete of the partially constructed flyover.

'I like this place,' says Tommy as he unfolds a tin table. A young boy wrapped in a bright yellow apron organises three plastic chairs and suggests that we move away from the monsoon drain that runs parallel to the flyover.

Tommy rattles off his order.

'Where is the Stingray flap stall?' I ask.

Tommy points to a stall that has a sign running along the top depicting flat winged fish of various kinds.

'It will take some explaining,' says Tommy.

But it doesn't. The bloke running the stall has a better command of the English language than some of my shipmates. He offers to organise noodles for Lash and suggests what flaps I should have for my first try.

You won't understand what an unbelievable experience eating perfectly fried hot Stingray flaps is, if you've never done it.

'What were you talking to Lilly about at Lakki's?' I ask Tommy.

'Trying to do a deal.'

'A deal?'

'Yeah, for Saturday.'

'And did you do one?'

'Don't think so.'

'Shame. What was her price today?'

'Eleven bucks with a discount of two bucks next time.'

'She offered Popeye a special eight-buck deal yesterday.'

'She didn't.'

'Did.'

'I'll talk to Popeye. How are the noodles, Lash?' Tommy asks as he wipes his bowl with his forefinger.

'OK. But not as good as those at Newton Circus.'

'See that building over there?'

'Where?' asks Lash.

Tommy waves a finger in the direction of pale blue three-storey building with brown louvered shutters over all the windows. 'That building over there, the blue one, is full of British airline stewardesses. They sometimes come over here for something to eat.'

Lash looks around. 'But not tonight eh?'

'Doesn't look like it,' says Tommy.

'Maybe they're flying somewhere,' I say.

'Let's have another round.' Tommy raises his arm and our young waiter in the bright yellow apron comes bounding over. 'You wanna girl or boy? I can arrange for yew not many dollar today. Yew wanna ...'

'On ya bike,' says Tommy.

'Yew sure?' asks the boy, suddenly downcast.

'Sure,' replies Lash.

'Ditto,' I say.

'What is ditto?' asks the boy, suddenly interested.

'On ya bike,' says Tommy. 'Just bring us two Tigers and a John Collins.'

We see a couple of lights go on and off in the light blue building, but no stewardesses appear.

Back in Sembawang, Lakki's Bar is full to overflowing with noisy Australians so we decide to call it a night and stroll back onboard.

Malaysian Crisis Report #4
The proposed member states of Malaysia met representatives of Indonesia and the Philippines in Manila in July. At the meeting, the Philippines and Indonesia

formally agreed to accept the formation of Malaysia if a
majority in the disputed region votes for it in a referendum
organized by the United Nations. The UN expects the
referendum result to be published by mid September.
Courtesy of Radio operator George Wild.

Early in September the Floating Dock is lowered and *Lincoln* is once again waterborne. All the deck protection sheets and the majority of the snaking pneumatic hoses and electric cables are removed. The repaired machinery disappears down below.

Once we are alongside and on Dockyard supply for electricity and water, the forward part of *Lincoln* is battened down in preparation for decontamination. At the last minute Fez and I remove our bedding from our mess and dump it on the deck in the after cabin flat.

'Where are we going to sleep tonight then?' I ask.

'We'll figure something out later.'

It's Sadiq that suggests we use a couple of the Officers' cabins.

I'm shaken at 03:30 for the Morning Watch. I'd had a blissful three-and-a-quarter hours sleep, luxuriating on a lump-free Officer's mattress. I don't want to get out of my bed.

'I'll have two heaped sugars in my tea please Steward,' Fez shouts from the adjacent cabin.

Fez and I catch the 08:30 bus back to *Terror* as the decontamination team arrive onboard carrying a variety of hoses, fan blowers and large yellow tins full of chemicals.

Twenty four hours later, Fez and I can smell decontaminated *Lincoln* before the bus turns the corner of a dockyard workshop.

After establishing how far the decontamination process has progressed, we decide to sleep on the upper deck as the Officers' cabin flat is the next on the decontamination schedule. While the after part of the ship is being battened down a continual stream of dockyard workers, each carrying a couple of buckets of dead cockroaches over the gangway, dump the contents into a special dead cockroach bin some distance away. I stop counting after thirty-two buckets full.

I sneak a quick look down my mess but it's still being vacuumed and the smell of whatever decontamination chemical has been used is still overpowering.

Fez and I grab a couple of Officers' mattresses before the cabin flat is sealed off.

Sleeping under the Singapore stars on a comfortable mattress is brilliant.

Some days later the crew moves back onboard. There is still a strong smell of decontaminant, but we quickly disperse it. Lash does his utmost.

Lash and I spend a quiet evening in Lakki's saying our farewells and promising that we will be back. The bar is full of Australians who are making themselves at home. One red-bearded Australian Stoker wishes us a 'Bonza trip' as we leave. Lash gives our Australian cousins a two-finger salute as soon as the main door closes behind us.

We join *HMS Loch Alvie* for a week's post-docking shakedown off the east coast of Malaya opposite a place called Kuantan.

Malaysian Crisis report #5

Malaysia was formally established on 16 September.
Brunei decided against joining. Indonesia reacted furiously,
tensions rose on both sides and the Malayan Ambassador
was expelled from Jakarta. Rioters have burned the
British Embassy in Jakarta and the homes of Singaporean
diplomats have been burnt. Crowds attacked the Indonesian
embassy in Kuala Lumpur.
George Wild

A leak has been reported in the bridge deckhead and I'm given the job, along with Popeye and Apple, of repainting the top of the bridge. Jenny's paint job is already cracking.

It's a brilliant day, hot and clear with a nice cooling breeze. *Lincoln* is at anchor and it's rumoured that we will be doing a

'Hands to Swim' later in the afternoon. The South China Sea is a deep turquoise and glass flat.

'Those waters look brilliant, don't they?' I say as I'm refilling my paint pot.

'You're into diving aren't ya, Pete?'

'Yeah.'

'Could you dive into the oggin from here?'

'Easy.' I shrug my shoulders.

'Go on then,' says Apple.

'Go on what?'

'Dive from here. We'll cover for you – say that you slipped or something.'

'Yeah go on,' says Popeye. 'A day's tot from each of us.'

'From here?' I ask.

'Not as high as the top platform at the swimming pool, is it?' asks Apple.

'I'll do it from the next deck down – it's too far inboard for me to clear the ship's side from here.'

'Go on then, Pete. Two days' tot if you do it.'

I descend to the next deck down, place my fags and lighter on the top of a wash deck locker near the base of the main mast, look around me, see nobody and perform a reasonably good, straight-legged dive in to the undisturbed waters of the South China Sea. I surface and swim down aft towards the Quarterdeck. Popeye scuttles aft and throws a heaving line over the side for me.

By the time I scramble over the Quarterdeck guardrail Regulating Petty Officer Warden is standing waiting for me.

'I slipped, PO,' I say.

'Bollocks,' replies Regulating Petty Officer 'Clink' Warden.

I look down at the puddle of seawater I'm standing in.

'You were observed by the Officer of the watch from the bridge wing ... putting your fags on a locker before executing a deliberate dive.'

'It's a natural reaction to finding myself falling over the side into the oggin,' I explain. It's a terrible excuse but all I can think of.

'Bollocks,' repeats Clink. 'Get dried off and report to the Regulating Office in ten minutes.' He turns to Popeye. 'You as well. With your caps.'

Down the mess Apple confirms that I've earned myself a couple of days' tot.

In the Regulating Office, Clink is busy scribbling on a pad as Popeye and I stand silently waiting for him to finish.

'DO YOU HEAR THERE. HANDS TO SWIM. AWAY SEA BOATS CREW. ANYBODY WISHING TO SWIM WILL BE REQUIRED TO ENTER THE WATER FROM THE QUARTERDECK ONLY. THE WATER TEMPERATURE IS ESTIMATED AT EIGHTY TWO DEGREES FAHRENHEIT. WE ARE NOT IN A KNOWN SHARK AREA. I REPEAT WE ARE NOT IN A KNOWN SHARK AREA. THE DEPTH OF WATER IS CHARTED AT ONE HUNDRED AND EIGHTY FATHOMS.'

Clink looks up and stares directly at me and grimaces. 'I hope that you have thanked Able Seaman Barrat for throwing you a life line over the side as quickly as he did?'

Popeye looks at me and back to Clink. 'Able Seaman Broadbent has already thanked me, PO.'

'That's good.' Clink taps his pad with the end of his pencil. 'I've been putting your charge sheet together, Broadbent. Incomplete as yet, but so far you will be charged with leaving the ship without permission, leaving the ship improperly dressed, leaving Her Majesty's Ship Lincoln without handing your Station card in, leaving the ship while the ship is under sailing orders.' He smiles, obviously enjoying himself. 'I like this one: returning onboard improperly dressed and endangering your own life. Within the next hour I will be able to add plenty of others.'

Popeye coughs.

'Thank you, PO,' I say.

'You, Able Seaman Broadbent,' he points a menacing pencil directly at me, 'will be seeing the Officer-of-the-Day within the next half hour. After some deliberation I should be able to put together the longest, most comprehensive charge list of my career. Go back down your mess, get yourself cleaned up and report back here in ten minutes with your cap ... a clean, presentable cap.'

I nod.

'You, Able Seaman Barrat – consider yourself severely reprimanded. I know you were involved in this ... escapade. Off you go.'

The Officer-of-the-Day is quite obviously annoyed that he isn't able to join the rest of the crew who are enjoying a swim.

Clink reads out all my charges. It takes almost two minutes. The Officer-of-the-Day blinks. 'I will have to refer these charges to higher authority, Able Seaman Broadbent. First Lieutenant's report.'

Back down the mess both Lash and Brick are busy writing letters. Tommy is wriggling into his swimming costume.

'First Lieutenant's report,' I say.

'That was obvious,' says Tommy.

'How deep is one hundred and eighty fathoms?' asks Lash.

'Hundred and eighty times six,' I say.

Lash scribbles the calculation on his pad. 'Ferkin Nora! It's over a thousand ferkin feet.'

'What is?' asks Tommy.

'The depth of water outside. How can anyone swim in that?'

'Same as they do in six feet of water,' I say.

'You don't know what's down there,' says a wide-eyed Lash. 'One thousand feet ... there can be any ferkin thing lurking down there. There could be a whale or anything down there ... or a thingie of whales.'

'A school.'

'Yeah.' Lash clicks his fingers.

I'm the only defaulter to see the First Lieutenant the following day. I've made a special effort and am wearing a clean and ironed white front, shorts with cleaned sandals and a borrowed clean cap.

My appearance doesn't help. As Clink reads out my list of charges I can see the First Lieutenant losing the will to live.

Clink finished with ... 'Leaving his place of work without permission to do so from his Senior Officer namely ...'

The First Lieutenant blinks and looks down at my charge sheet. 'This, Able Seaman Broadbent, is the longest charge sheet I have had the misfortune to encounter. I will have to refer these matters to higher authority, Able Seaman Broadbent. Captain's report.'

Clink clicks the heels of his sandals together and grimaces. 'Captain's report on cap ... lefta tin ... quick march ... wait for me outside the Regulating Office.'

The following day I have to wear white shorts, white front, white knee-length socks, white shoes and a borrowed cap to face the Captain.

I think the Captain is impressed because as Clink reads out all twenty-six of my charges he smiles. 'This was a wager of some kind wasn't it, Able Seaman Broadbent?'

'No, sir ... don't think so, sir.'

'It has the appearance of a messdeck challenge ... with some kind of reward or remuneration.'

I don't completely understand remuneration. 'No, sir.'

'I'm convinced that there is something attached to this stupid and potentially dangerous performance of yours, Broadbent. Any one of these charges could merit a lengthy period of punishment. I have, however, spoken to your Divisional Officer who states that you are a competent Seaman, good at your job and a valued member of the Kumpit Boarding Party. He also says that you have not yet completed the canvassing of the handrails on the Top part of ship. I am therefore prepared to give you one more chance, Broadbent. If I see you in front of me in the future I shall come down on you like a ton of bricks. Do you understand me?'

'Yes, sir.'

'Fourteen days number 9s.'

'Fourteen days number 9s ... on caps ... left tin ... quick march. Report to the Regulating Office,' bellows Clink.

That's it: all finished. Is fourteen days number 9s a reasonable price to pay for two days' tot? I don't know.

Number 9 punishment involves extra work early in the morning, during my dinner hour, after tea and sometime during the evening. Getting up an hour and a half earlier than everyone else is a bit of a nuisance but I get to see beautiful sunrises that are an unexpected bonus.

At dinnertime Apple offers me his tot. I take it and offer him 'sippers'.

He tries to kiss me.

Apparently it's traditional to offer the Rum Bosun 'sippers' but I forget. I know that I'm being watched and that it's normal to down the tot 'in one' so I do. Personally I can't understand what all the fuss is about ... then it hits my stomach and a wonderful glow begins to seep into every corner of my body.

'Well, young Pete,' says Tommy. 'What do you reckon then?'

There is something wonderful going on inside me. 'Brilliant ... absolutely ferkin brilliant.'

The crack of the Tannoy wakes me.

'MAN OVERBOARD. MAN OVERBOARD, AWAY SEABOAT'S CREW. THIS IS NOT AN EXERCISE. I REPEAT THIS IS NOT AN EXERCISE.'

Someone slaps the side of my hammock. 'Throw some clothes on and get up top.'

'Whaaaa?'

Charlie is already halfway up the mess ladder. 'We've got someone overboard. Chop chop.'

By the time I make it to the whaler, it has already been wound out and lowered to deck level.

I step onboard alongside Sooty and Larry.

'Wait for instructions,' says Charlie.

Lincoln is stopped and wallowing.

An officer, with binoculars hung around his neck, appears. He explains to Charlie. 'We have a reported man overboard. The Lifebuoy sentry reported a crewmember dressed in white shorts, white front and his cap jumping over the aft guardrails before he could stop him. He threw a lifebelt overboard, the Ops Room has plotted the position.'

A Communicator appears carrying a radio.

'Sit down aft here,' Charlie says. 'Anybody else, sir?'

'No, speed is off the essence, Coxswain.'

Someone throws a couple of blankets onboard.

'Is the SBA coming?' asks Charlie.

'Can't wait for him,' says Annie Oakley, the Buffer. 'Have you checked communications?'

'Yes, Chief,' replies the communicator.

'Have you got a lamp?' asks Annie.

Charlie scrambles in the locker finds the search lamp, tests that it works and hands it me.

'Let's get you in the water. Lower away,' shouts Annie.

Someone tosses a lifebelt down.

Once in the water we swerve away aft.

As we pass the Quarterdeck we hear ....

'LEADING HANDS AND PRESIDENTS OF MESSES ARE TO VISUALLY IDENTIFY ALL MESS MEMBERS. REPORT ANY DISCREPANCIES TO THE REGULATING OFFICE IMMEDIATELY.'

Charlie ships the radar reflector. The Communicator checks that the Ops Room can see us. Charlie taps the compass to make sure it's working.

The Ops Room directs us to the man overboard point. I sweep the ink black waters with the search lamp. We recover the lifebelt thrown by the Lifebuoy Ghost but can see nothing else.

Charlie switches off the engine and we wallow in silence while I sweep and listen to the undisturbed waters surrounding us.

We do a series of search patterns, but after a couple of hours we are instructed to return to *Lincoln* who is some distance away with all upper deck lights switched on.

Back onboard we learn that the missing individual is a young Stoker who had recently received a 'Dear John' letter from his UK fiancée. He had been depressed for some days and was planning to talk to the Padre later.

I cadge a cigarette from someone as we wait to be dismissed.

'Poor bastard. Let's go and see what's cooking in the galley,' says Charlie.

It's pure good fortune that I finish my punishment the day before we enter Hong Kong. During our way up the China coast we had exercised with *HMS Loch Alvie* and our fresh water evaporators had almost packed in completely. The galleys have priority for what is left of our fresh water supplies, so the rest of us have to go dirty.

Unfortunately Hong Kong has its own fresh water crisis and doesn't have any to spare for us.

Lash, Apple and I stand on the jetty looking down into the brown slurried waters of the harbour that lie static between *Lincoln* and the jetty.

'Fancy a dip?' asks Apple.

'You are joking,' says Lash.

Leaving a pungent trail of three unwashed bodies in our wake, Lash, Apple and myself stroll to the China Fleet Club who have offered the unwashed crew members of *HMS Lincoln* the use of their supply of fresh water. Off the main entrance lobby, the main bar is awash with American sailors. We have a couple of San Miguels and then go up to one of the spare cabins on the second floor for a shower. A little more presentable, we make our way back to the bar where we find one unoccupied table.

Our American 'cousins' occupy every other table. The jukebox is playing rubbish.

Our table is slowly filling with empty San Miguel bottles when we are joined by a freshly showered Tommy.

Apple nods towards the jukebox. 'This is awful stuff, isn't it? They've played the same six ferkin records over and over.'

'It's what they call Country and Western music,' says Tommy.

'And it's crap,' I say.

Lash agrees and signals a young waiter for more beers.

It's this round of beers that does it. Instigated by Apple, we stroll over to the jukebox, unplug it midway through an irritatingly familiar record and push it towards the door.

Everybody looks at us, but nobody moves.

We trundle the jukebox through the entrance lobby, skirting the main reception desk and out through the main door.

We stop on the pavement outside. Passersby ignore us. A jukebox being pushed along the pavements of Hong Kong is obviously not that unusual. 'What the ferk do we do with it now?' asks Lash.

Nobody knows.

'Didn't think that far ahead,' says Apple.

'That's your problem that is, Apple,' I explain. 'Your lack of forward planning.'

'Bollocks.'

Our problem is solved by the arrival of the China Fleet Club Manager supported by a pair of jittery staff. Tommy explains in slow English that it was playing crap music. The manager nods and organises his crew to push the jukebox back up the entrance ramp.

As is the way in Hong Kong, the whole business is immediately forgotten and we politely shake hands before going our separate ways.

We roll down to the nearest bar discussing our collective cheek and wondering why none of our American cousins had tried to stop us.

Ruby isn't in The Old Toby Bar and the working girls make one unfruitful attempt to get us to buy them 'dinks', before leaving us alone to drink. As I try to pay for the second round of drinks, I can't find my wallet. We all search the table area and the heads in the back. The girls help us, but it isn't found. It's a miserable stagger back to the ship.

The following morning Jenny, and a small number of her Side Party, shuffle onboard and start repair work on the bridge top.

I wait outside the Regulating Office while Petty Officer Warden deals with a couple of overalled Stokers in front of me.

Eventually I have his undivided attention. 'Er, PO ... I think I've lost my wallet.'

'You think, lad?' he tosses his pencil into a tray on his desk. 'Able Seaman Broadbent, my favourite high-board diver. Nice to make your acquaintance again so soon. Have you lost your wallet or not?'

'I have, PO – yes.'

'Ashore?'

'Yes, PO.'

'Where did you go last night?'

'China Fleet Club then Wan Chai, PO.'

'Bars?'

'Can't remember which ones exactly.'

'It will help.'

'The Old Toby Bar is one I can remember.'

'Still got your Naval Identity card?'

'No PO, it was in my wallet.'

'How much money was in your wallet?'

'About forty dollars.'

'About forty dollars ... WHAT?'

'About forty dollars, PO.'

'This afternoon, take a walk to The China Fleet Club, find a Chinese member of staff called Mister Armstrong Wong – he's the bloke who liaises with the local gangs. Ask him if anyone has handed in your wallet. It's a long shot but worth a try. You might be lucky and get your wallet back ... it will be empty of course.'

'Thank you, PO.'

'If Mister Wong hasn't got your wallet, put it down to experience. Report to me that you have officially lost your Royal Naval Identity Card and I'll be happy to write out your charge sheet.'

'Thank you, PO.'

I'm midway between the ship and the China Fleet Club when I realise that for the first time I'm in Hong Kong all by myself.

I approach the young lad behind the reception desk of the China Fleet Club gingerly.

'Excuse me. Is Mister Wong here?'

'We goh bags of Mister Wongs ... need more specifi info.'

'Mister Armstrong Wong. I think he may have my wallet.'

'Yew way momen,' and he scuttles away.

I study the sun-bleached grey-and-white framed photographs of Royal Naval ships on the wall behind the desk along with a line of colourful ships crests hung around the entire reception area. I see a *Bermuda* crest but I don't see *Lincoln*'s. The receptionist arrives accompanied by a bloke whose long grey hair is in a plaited ponytail draped over one shoulder.

'Are you Mister Wong, Armstrong Wong?' I ask rather timidly.

'At your service, young man,' he says as he bows slightly. His lack of an accent and his obvious command of English takes me by surprise.

'I lost my wallet last night somewhere ... and err someone onboard suggested I come and see you.'

'Can you tell me what your wallet is like, young sir?'

'Black leather with an outline of the Island of Bermuda embossed in gold on the front,' I explain.

Mister Wong raises a single crooked finger. 'Wait there, my young friend. Just one moment.'

I search for *Lincoln*'s crest: I still can't see it. I complain to the receptionist who has resumed his position behind the desk. 'My ship's crest isn't up there.'

'Wha sheep, sir?'

'Lincoln.'

He disappears below his desk and re-emerges smiling and holding a *Lincoln* ship crest. 'Jus gorra couple of day ago. Purrup layta.'

Mister Wong reappears holding my wallet. 'Is this yours, young sir?'

'Looks like it – yes. Thank goodness.'

'Do you know where you lost it?'

'In one of the bars I suppose.'

'Not exactly ... the receptionist here,' he waves an arm towards the desk, 'took it from your back pocket as you were standing outside with our jukebox yesterday.'

'No!'

'I'm afraid so.'

I hold my hand out and Armstrong Wong returns my wallet with a smile. 'You will find, Able Seaman Broadbent, that a forty-one dollar Hong Kong fee has been charged by The China Fleet Club for the reinstallation of the jukebox. Your ID card is still inside.'

'Thanks,' I smile. 'We didn't like the music.'

'I'm not a big fan of Country and Western music either,' says a smirking Armstrong .

'You didn't take anybody else's wallet did you ... at the same time?'

'No. But you might like to mention to a Petty Officer Cole that I am in possession of his wallet. He has an extremely large-breasted wife and two angelic children.'

'Can I take it ... his wallet?' I hold my hand out.

'Not allowed, sorry. If you can arrange for Petty Officer Cole to come along here after 14:00 tomorrow I'll return his wallet, less an administration fee of course.'

'OK. Thanks, Armstrong ... er Mister Wong.'

'Any time, Able Seaman Broadbent. Safe trip back onboard.'

Back onboard I knock on the Petty Officer's mess door and ask if I can see Petty Officer Cole.

Smokey appears looking a little bedraggled. 'What do you want, Broadbent?'

'Have you lost your wallet, PO?'

His face expands. He looks sheepishly over his shoulder. 'How do you know ... ssshh ... how do you know?'

'I've just met the guy who claims to have it.'

'Where?'

'China Fleet Club.'

'Is my ID card still in it?'

'Don't know. I didn't see the actual wallet, but the bloke says that it is yours and that you have a wife and a couple of children.' I decide that any additional detail would be inappropriate, given the circumstances.

He closes the mess door behind him and with an arm around my shoulders ushers me down the passageway. 'Right then, young man ... where exactly is this bloke who has my wallet and how do I get it back?'

'Go to the China Fleet Club after 14:00 tomorrow and ask for a bloke called Armstrong Wong.'

'And that's all?'

'As far as I know, PO.'

'You've probably saved my life, Able Seaman Broadbent.'

'Apparently there will be an administration fee to pay.'

'That's not important. How much?'

'Don't know. Probably as much as there was in your wallet. That's what it cost me ... to get mine back.'

He gives my shoulder a squeeze. 'Now, young Peter, I will appreciate it if you don't mention this to anyone onboard.'

'Of course not, PO.'

'Honestly?'

'Honestly.'

'I won't forget this, Broadbent.'

Jenny and her girls have stripped the bridge top back to bare metal and applied a couple of coats of Pusser's red lead primer. I'm doing a bit of sunbathing in my spot behind the forward funnel when I see Petty Officer Cole striding over the gangway. On the horizon is a rolling mountain of thick grey cloud heading in our direction and there is a cooling breeze that smells of putrid fish. As the sun disappears behind a large cloud, I collect my bits and pieces and go back down the mess, stretch out on one of the benches and fall asleep. It's an unwritten law in the mess that you don't disturb anybody 'crashed out' on one of the mess benches.

I'm woken by Apple thumping my shoulder.

'They've just piped for you to report to the Petty Officers' Mess.'

I stumble up to the Petty Officers' Mess where PO Cole is waiting outside. He is holding his wallet.

'You piped for me, PO.'

'I most certainly did, young Peter. Thanks to you I've got my wallet back.'

'That's good.'

'Less fifty-three dollars.'

'Blimey.'

'That bloke Armstrong called my missus big-breasted ... cheeky sod.'

Down the mess I tell everybody that Smokey has a picture of his wife in his wallet ... topless.

I'm duty for our final day in Hong Kong. Jenny and her side party have applied a final coat of non-slip green paint to the bridge top. The Buffer complains that not enough drying time has been left between coats.

I watch Jenny's team as they bounce down the brow carrying all their painting equipment. To a young man with a modicum of sexual experience, they are a fit-looking bunch.

We leave Hong Kong at dinner time the following day with everyone onboard.

Today Tansy is promoted to Petty Officer. The first we know about it is when Apple spots him emptying his locker. Leading Seaman Fez Parker is to take over as permanent Killick of our mess.

Tansy passes his tot around everybody in our mess. It amounts to 'sippers' for all of us. He says that as from tomorrow he will be issued with a neat, undiluted tot.

There are handshakes all round. Brick wishes him well in the prescribed Naval manner: 'Best of luck, Petty Officer.'

'Thanks everybody,' Tansy salutes us and leaves.

'DO YOU HEAR THERE, THE INFORMATION OFFICER SPEAKING. LATER TODAY WE SHALL BE ENTERING THE CITY OF MANILA IN THE PHILIPPINES. AN ONGOING INDUSTRIAL DISPUTE IS PREVENTING US FROM ENTERING HARBOUR AS ORIGINALLY SCHEDULED. THERE ARE A NUMBER OF THINGS THAT YOU SHOULD AVOID WHILE ASHORE IN MANILA. THE FIRST THING TO BE CAREFUL OF IS YOUR MONEY. THOSE WHO HAVE CHANGED MONEY ONBOARD HAVE BEEN ISSUED WITH OFFICIAL LOCAL CURRENCY. WITHIN THE PHILIPPINES THERE IS A LOT OF AMERICAN OCCUPATION PAPER CURRENCY IN CIRCULATION THAT IS ABSOLUTELY WORTHLESS. CHECK YOUR CHANGE.'

I flick through my slim wodge of Filipino money and don't find any that looks like American Occupation money; not that I know what it looks like.

'DO YOU HEAR THERE THE PADRE SPEAKING …'

'Now we'll get some interesting information,' says Tommy, who licks the point of his poised pencil.

'MANILA HAS A REPUTATION FOR …' (rustle of paper) 'MANILA HAS A REPUTATION FOR PROVIDING EVERYTHING THAT VISITING NAVAL PERSONNEL ARE THOUGHT TO REQUIRE. SOME LOCALLY BREWED BEER AND SPIRITS ARE SUSPECT AND MADE IN THE BACKSTREETS OF TOWN. PROSTITUTION IS RIFE IN MANILA, AND IT'S REPORTED THAT VENEREAL DISEASE IS RAMPANT …' (cough)

'RAMPANT. THE AREA TO AVOID AT ALL COSTS IS MAKATI. CARE AND COMMON SENSE SHOULD BE EXERCISED AT ALL TIMES. GOD BLESS YOU ALL.'

'Makati. That sounds familiar,' says a smiling Tommy who underlines the word on the back of his cigarette packet. 'Sure I've heard about that somewhere.'

'Lash, go and wet the tea,' says Fez.

'DO YOU HEAR THERE, THE INFORMATION OFFICER SPEAKING. WHEN THE AMERICAN TROOPS LEFT THE PHILIPPINES AT THE END OF WORLD WAR 2, THEIR SURPLUS JEEPS WERE LEFT BEHIND. THE FILIPINOS STRIPPED THEM DOWN, DECORATED THEM WITH ORNAMENTS AND PAINTED THEM WITH VIBRANT COLORS. RECONFIGURED THEM TO TAKE MORE PASSENGERS AND USE THEM AS TAXIS. THEY ARE KNOWN LOCALLY AS JEEPNEYS AND ARE A CHEAP AND REASONABLY SAFE METHOD OF GETTING AROUND TOWN,' (static) 'ERR ... THE PADRE WILL LIKE TO EMPHASISE THAT JEEPNEYS DO NOT RUN TO THE MAKATI DISTRICT.'

Lash pours out a strong cup of tea for everybody at the table. We light cigarettes.

Fez slides the bowl of damp, encrusted sugar towards Apple. 'You lads going ashore tonight then?'

Lash says that he isn't up for it.

I say that I'm doing Brick's duty for him, as he did one for me in Japan.'

'When are we open to visitors?' asks Apple.

'Tomorrow I think,' says Fez.

'DO YOU HEAR THERE: THE INDUSTRIAL DISPUTE ASHORE HAS BEEN RESOLVED ...'

The blokes who berth us alongside a short concrete jetty are a surly bunch. Dressed in shorts, T-shirts and flip-flops they eventually manage to drop the eyes of our ropes over what they think are the correct bollards. We can't explain what they are doing wrong: we assume that they are part of the strike and are berthing us under protest. As soon as the brow is in place we go ashore and relocated the various berthing ropes as Tommy, in his capacity as Navigators Yeoman, says that we can expect a bit of a blow within the next 48 hours. By mid-afternoon Lash and I are the only two people left in the mess. As part of the duty watch I'm given the job of rigging some ropes across various parts of the ship that will be out of bounds to tomorrow's visitors.

Our mess the following morning is a silent and morbid place. Everybody picks and shuffles at the contents of the breakfast tray. Only Lash and I have a smile to greet the day.

'Good run then?' I ask.

'Piss off,' says Apple from below closed eyes.

'Yeah ... piss off,' says Brick.

'Did you get to that place the Padre mentioned?' asks Lash.

'No need ... the whole place is just one big red light district,' grunts Apple. 'I need the heads.'

'Have a sausage, Brick.' Lash waves a cold banger underneath his nose.

Brick swings a dismissive arm, misses everything and spins himself off his seat and flat onto the deck.

'You'd better do mess cleaner this morning,' says Fez. 'You'll be no use to anybody else today. Then after that you can help Tommy take the back off the ladder from the forecastle to the capstan flat.'

The queue of visitors snakes up and down the short jetty hours before we are officially open. The Officer-of-the-Day is organising things so that we can open early, as the local police are getting fractious about the number of people congregating on the jetty.

I'm not duty, but I volunteer to help by hanging around by the brow. It's a great place to be, particularly as the majority of our visitors are girls wearing shorts, vests and flip-flops. Most of these young Filipina girls are beautiful and friendly. Lash and

I chat to a couple of stunningly attractive girls who are wearing next to nothing. They invite us to 'The Furry Feline Bar' that evening and give us both a card with the name of the bar and a simple line map on the reverse. We've cracked it!

Down the mess Popeye is telling us all about what he has learned. 'There's a pink Jeepney on the jetty that will take anybody who is interested to Makati where Dolly, Molly and Polly are ready to entertain you. Pay the driver. He'll run a shuttle service if required.'

'You going then, Pops?'

'Me? Not on your ferkin life.'

'Dolly Molly and Polly eh? Could be related I suppose,' says Lash.

I wave the card. 'We've got dates anyway.'

Tansy looks at my card and flicks it back at me. 'Sure you have, Pete ... sure you have.'

'Beautiful looking girls,' explains Lash.

'Most of them are. Was it worth removing the ladder back?' he asks Brick.

'Can't remember,' Brick splutters.

Tommy grins. 'Very revealing.'

'Perv,' says Apple.

Tommy clips Apple around the ear with the remnants of an elderly, black sausage. Apple collapses on the deck in a burbling heap.

'DO YOU HEAR THERE, MAIL IS NOW READY FOR COLLECTION.'

Everybody looks at Brick as he holds his head in his hands and mumbles something.

The taxi driver looks at the card Lash shows him and whistles long and hard.

The girls we met a few days ago are not in evidence as we stroll into The Furry Feline Bar on Makati Avenue.

In the back courtyard, a Tinkeling competition is underway. We watch with interest as young, beskirted girls hop in and out of a couple of long bamboo poles wielded by young Filipino boys. It's entertaining in a strange way. We are encouraged to try it and we gracefully decline, until that is, we have consumed enough beer to try anything when asked by a pair of attractive bar girls. We don't stand a chance. Lash is the first to collapse in a semi-drunken heap with bruised ankles. I fare a bit better but eventually the bamboo poles get me and I limp away to where a girl with enormous shoulders is massaging Lash's calves and ankles.

I recognise that peculiar mesmerised look on Lash's face and I instinctively know that he isn't going to make it back onboard tonight. My almost empty wallet dictates what I have to do and I'm part-way through the main bar when I'm accosted by Figgy.

'You going back onboard, Pete?'

'Think so. If I have enough for a taxi.'

'I've got some Pesos. Shall we share one?'

'Go on then.'

'Where's your mate Lash?'

'On the Tinkeling sidelines being sorted out by a girl with an enormous pair of shoulders.'

'That'll be Shirley then.'

'Shirley?'

'Yeah. Black hair and brown eyes?'

'Yeah.'

'Shirley is not what he appears to be.'

I turn. 'I've got to get him out of there.'

I search the courtyard but there is no sign of Lash or Shirley.

Figgy inhales deeply. 'We'll just have to hope your mate figures things out before money change hands.'

Despite a cracking Manila hangover and extremely sore ankles the following morning, the first thing I look for is Lash's hammock. It isn't slung. I fear the worst.

As I swing myself delicately onto the mess table, I notice a comatose, fully dressed Lash spread out underneath the table. He is breathing and missing a shoe.

I give his shoulder a gentle shake. Lash opens one eye ever so slowly. 'Shit mate ... that was some run ashore.'

'I came back for you but you'd gone.'

'I was kidnapped.' Lash breaks his morning wind.

'Kidnapped?'

'No, that's not the correct word. I was taken away ... spirited away.'

'By the girl ...' I reassess. 'By the person with the large shoulders?'

'I think so ... yep.'

'So what happened then? That person with the enormous shoulders was massaging your legs the last time I saw you.'

'She wasn't doing it for charity.'

'Wasn't she?'

'When she discovered how much there was in my wallet she left me to find my own way back onboard. I think I missed an opportunity to do battle with something interesting.'

'When you next bump in to Figgy McDuff, ask him about Shirley. Maybe you won't feel so bad about things then.'

'Don't understand. But OK.'

Later in the day Lash discovers that his ID card is missing. 'I'll tell Clink tomorrow.'

Five days in Manila is long enough. It's with a variety of emotions that we unberth and drift gently away from the jetty.

Shirley is among the crowd on the jetty waving us goodbye. Even from a distance, he's an impressive figure.

Lincoln wasn't designed to deal with a Typhoon named 'Wendy the bender'.

'DO YOU HEAR THERE, THE FIRST LIEUTENANT SPEAKING. WE ARE AWARE THAT TYPHOON WENDY IS SOMEWHERE IN THE AREA. ENSURE THAT ALL LOOSE EQUIPMENT IS SECURED AGAINST BAD WEATHER. CLOSE ALL UPPER DECK VENTILATION GRILLS, SCUTTLES, HATCHES AND DOORS. I WILL KEEP YOU INFORMED OF ANY CHANGE IN THE SITUATION.'

As soon as we are out of Manila Bay, Wendy takes us by the stern, twists us and pitches us onto our beam-ends. The main generator fails immediately and as the oncoming sea crashes over the forecastle the water streams in through somewhere, along the main passageway and down into our mess. The main forecastle hatch is the culprit and it takes three of us, sharing two oversized oilskins, to re-clip it. We are soaked by the time we make it back to the mess where everybody is busy baling out water. The red emergency lights cast an eerie red glow over everything.

'DO YOU HEAR THERE, THE FIRST LIEUTENANT SPEAKING. WE HAVE A GOOD IDEA OF TYPHOON WENDY'S INTENT AND ARE ALTERING COURSE TO PUT DISTANCE BETWEEN WENDY AND ...'

The Tannoy sparks, splutters and dies.

'Make sure that those hammocks are out of the way of any slopping water,' says Fez.

'This ferkin water is cold,' explains someone.

'Anybody for Uckers?'

'Yer ferkers.'

'Shall I wet the tea?' asks Lash.

'Check the hammock stowage,' shouts Fez.

'Are the heaters working?'

'Ferk knows.'

Lincoln takes a resounding thump on her starboard side and she swings over, groaning. As she rights herself, she completely blacks out. The emergency lighting fails.

Someone shouts through the emergency mess hatch, 'Report any structural damage directly to HQ1. The telephone system is down.'

Someone from the dark recesses of the mess says, 'Piss off.'

A resounding thump on the port side has us all worried. The cushions on the ship's side bunks fly off over our heads along with a mess fanny, some caps and a stack of plates. There is an alarming rush of wind through the ventilation trunking.

Someone yells down the emergency hatch. 'Emergency damage control parties report to HQ1 immediately!'

'Shit,' says someone from the dark.

'That means we're damaged,' someone else says.

Fez yells. 'Anyone on the damage control roster muster outside HQ1 NOW.'

There is a rush of wind as the main messdeck hatch is opened.

Surprisingly quickly, *Lincoln* settles to a manageable roll and pitch. Some bastard comes down to try and fix our Tannoy. The mess smells of the South China Sea.

After a period of relative calm, *Lincoln* once again shudders, the ladder back vibrates, the air in the ventilation trunking splutters and water pours from the punkah louvres. People are crawling around the soaking deck collecting rolling items. All the cockroaches have disappeared: they obviously have some inbuilt fear of typhoons. *Lincoln* groans as she takes a long slow list to port. We can hear everything in the lockers slide over to one side. The mess trap locker flies open and a bag of sugar arches across the mess table, smashes against Brick's shoulder, who is busy baling out, and explodes.

'Shit,' says Fez, brushing sugar granules from his hair.

The Tannoy crackles. The Greenie trying to fix it gives up and paddles out of the mess after a spout of water from an adjacent vent trunking catches him full on.

Lincoln slews and we are tossed all over the place. Then we hear a distinct difference in the engine tone as we right ourselves and scuttle directly into a series of shuddering 'milestones' that have us creaking and backing.

Slowly the 'milestones' become less regular and we settle down to a long slower roll. We all check our hammocks: a few are wet. Thankfully mine is dry, so I sling it and clamber in. Popeye, whose stomach is historically a little delicate when the ship has some movement on, is 'calling for Hughie' in the mess gash bucket.

10

THE ATTRACTIONS OF RAF GAN

Overnight we put some distance between Wendy and ourselves and *Lincoln* settles down. As we clear the Manila Trench, we rendezvous with the Aircraft Carrier *HMS Victorious* and the Australian Frigate *HMAS Vendetta* who is bound for home waters. We rig for a jackstay transfer: Midshipmen 'Judas' Scariott, who obviously has influence in high places, is to be transferred because he wishes to attend a family wedding in Perth, Western Australia.

When transferring personnel it's normal practice to send over their kit first to test that all the equipment is rigged and working correctly. It isn't that we dislike Judas, quite the opposite: he's an unassuming and reasonably pleasant Midshipman. However, leaving his Pusser's green case in the lobby adjacent to the jackstay transfer point is asking for trouble. A number of us with black pens decorate the top and bottom of the case with balls and chains, prison arrows and some choice, well-chosen words about our Australian cousins. We have the time to do a decent job as both *Lincoln* and *Vendetta* are having trouble maintaining station in an oncoming sea. Apple, who has an artistic flair, adds some creative improvements to our artwork with red and green marker pens.

Finally the jackstay is rigged and Judas stands to one side all harnessed up with his lifejacket on. He waits patiently while his green case is raised onto the jackstay traveller and watches in horror as it is hoisted up and pulled across the turbulent waters towards *HMAS Vendetta*. 'My suitcase has been vandalised,' he says to no one in particular.

As the case lands on the deck of *Vendetta* a couple of large bearded deck hands unhook it from the traveller and examine the artwork.

A worried Judas stands silently looking at the deck, waiting for the traveller to be returned to us. 'I'll find out who was responsible.'

'If you ever do get back in one piece ... sir,' someone mumbles – it sounds like Apple.

Leading Seaman Chaplin and I hook a rather ashen Judas on to the traveller and he is hoisted into the air, legs flailing. He waves a warning arm at us as he slowly begins his journey towards Australian territory. The water between us is unpredictable. Those who have control of the main jackstay wire know exactly what to do and wait until a particularly disturbed and wet section of water comes trundling between the two vessels. The traveller is stopped at the same time as the jackstay wire is slackened, and Judas receives a farewell dunking.

Onboard *HMAS Vendetta* a couple of humongous, unsmiling Aussie deckhands welcome trouser-dripping Midshipman Scariott with open arms and usher him away.

HMS Victorious is a sad and lonely Aircraft Carrier who is in desperate need of a friend to accompany her to Hong Kong, where she's going to stay for a month. We don't have a problem about going back to Hong Kong; so while *HMAS Vendetta* turns south to Perth we are diverted to chaperone our new best friend to the 'Fragrant Harbour'.

Once we are berthed alongside and *Victorious* is anchored close to the *Tamar* mole, we settle ourselves for a reasonably long stay. I plan on waiting until after payday before going ashore. I'm going to re-invite Ruby to the Floating Restaurant and I'm going to explore Kowloon.

I've just got stuck in to Dennis' *The Man Who Killed the King* when ...

'DO YOU HEAR THERE, THE FIRST LIEUTENANT SPEAKING. WE HAVE RECEIVED A SIGNAL DIVERTING US TO GAN. WE SHALL SAIL AT 06:00 TOMORROW, ALL SHORE LEAVE WILL END AT 23:59 FOR JUNIOR RATES AND 01:00 FOR SENIOR RATES. THE SHIP IS UNDER SAILING ORDERS. THE ENGINEERING OFFICER REPORT TO THE BRIDGE.'

'Where is ferkin Gan?' asks Tommy.

'I was ferkin going ashore tomorrow.'

'Bastards.'

'I'll have a look, see if I can find out where Gan is,' says Tommy.

To show our disgust at the wicked way our programme has suddenly been changed, all of us who are not duty go ashore in an attempt to drink the China Fleet Club dry. We fail of course and drift off to the Wanch to say hello to our favourite bar girls and explain why we are leaving so soon. They don't give a shit really.

'They're only interested in those lads onboard *Victorious* who will be here for a month,' explains Tommy. 'It's an uncommonly early departure in the morning – something to do with tides. Gan is an island south-west of Ceylon, just the other side of the equator that will require us to have a 'Crossing The Line' Ceremony. Apparently I'm going to be one of the Bears.'

'What are Bears?' I ask.

'You haven't crossed the line before then?'

'Nope.'

'All will be revealed then, young Pete ... all will be revealed.'

Tommy, Popeye and Fez have all crossed the line before and are given parts in the forthcoming ceremony. Fez is promoted to Major General in the 'Maritime Company of Bears', whatever that is. Tommy and Popeye reportedly are to provide muscle, despite the fact that neither of them have that many.

Lincoln trundles her solitary way south down the South China Sea, heading for the Karimata Strait between Sumatra and Kalimantan.

The last Tuesday in October is devoted to ceremonial preparation as *Lincoln* negotiates the narrow Sunda Strait between Sumatra and the Island of Java before heading off southwest across the Indian Ocean.

The children's party store is emptied of fancy dress costumes. The Scran Bag is opened, and lost or mislaid items of kit are transformed into something out of the ordinary. Coston gun line nylon is unlaid to make false beards and wigs. The galley is cleared of tin foil that is turned into badges of rank and strangely shaped headgear. Those who know how to do it manufacture tridents and swords for the Guard and the Bears. The Petty Officer who is to play the part of King Neptune is kitted out with various impressive-looking trappings as befits his position. His Queen is an Able Seaman with an uncommonly good pair of legs who is 'decked out' in an unattractive dress made from some darken-ship screen material.

I'm part of the team who rig a rubber pool on the awning deck and fill it with water from the Java Sea. Others rig a tipping chair and install the small set of steps that are normally used at the inboard end of the brow.

A raised platform with a protective canvas screen is rigged and after dinner, King Neptune, Queen Aphrodite (with legs unceremoniously splayed) and the Herald take their places and proclaim the official start of the Crossing the Line ceremony. The Bears, brandishing swords and wearing pointed hats, singlet and long shorts, are ordered to scour the ship and to present before King Neptune those who have never 'crossed the line' before.

Before the assembled ship's company, a pair of Officers, resplendent in full mess dress, escort a reluctant Captain to the pool. Traditionally the Captain of the vessel is baptised regardless of how many times he has crossed the line before. The Herald, clad in his cowboy jacket and pork-pie hat, reads out the proclamation. The Constable removes his helmet, declares the charges valid and places the Captain in the poolside chair. The Doctor, kitted out in one of Dagga's white coats with an oversized stethoscope draped over his shoulder, pronounces the Captain fit to be humiliated. The Taster douses the Captain's head and shoulders in a yellowy custard gloop. The Barber, wearing another of Dagga's white coats and a large false moustache, spades a white foam substance over the Captain's face and after shaving it off with a curved, wooden sword, tips him backwards into the pool. He surfaces, spluttering and smiling to the cheers of the entire ship's company. Other Officers follow, their apparent misdemeanours and shortcomings light-heartedly detailed by the Herald. Senior Rates follow.

The Guards take up their protective positions by the King and Queen as the Bears reappear, dragging and carrying reluctant crewmembers to the poolside. I have scurried away to my favourite upper deck lounging place, just aft of the forward funnel. I'm discovered by the ugliest and largest Stoker onboard. He curls a finger at me and escorts me down to the pool area. I wait in line until it's my turn to be placed in the chair. I'm examined in a variety of ways by the Doctor and suitably lathered in an assortment of foul-smelling substances. Someone manages to shove a brush full of something foul-tasting into my mouth and the Barber stuffs something unrecognisable down the waistband of my shorts before I'm tipped over backwards into what is surprisingly refreshing pool water.

I splutter to the surface, which is covered in the remnants of many ceremonial applications. I've officially 'crossed the line'.

The ceremony lasts until almost every member of the crew has been dunked. Only King Neptune survives un-dunked. Queen Aphrodite is submerged more than once because she is wearing a dress and 'her' long yellow wig excites many of those who have been at sea for over a week. According to a member of the Stokers' mess, her shapely legs appear more attractive when glistening wet.

As the sun is going down the stage is unrigged, the pool is emptied over the side and everybody slopes off to their messes. The King struts around in his regalia for a while until the Senior Rates bar is opened and he disappears.

Lincoln stays below 'the line' for a couple of days as she slowly trundles west. It's true that emptied water in a washbasin circles anti-clockwise south of the equator: that's something to tell the folks at home.

'DO YOU HEAR THERE, THE INFORMATION OFFICER SPEAKING,' (rustle of paper) **'WE WILL SHORTLY BE ARRIVING AT GAN, AN ISLAND SITUATED ON THE**

SOUTHERN TIP OF THE VOLCANIC ADDU ATOLL. GAN IS AN RAF BASE AND NOTHING MUCH ELSE. WE SHALL BE HERE FOR APPROXIMATELY THREE WEEKS DURING WHICH TIME WE CAN RELAX AND ENJOY SOME OF THE FACILITIES OFFERED BY AN INDIAN OCEAN ISLAND. THERE WILL BE MANY OPPORTUNITIES FOR SWIMMING, FISHING AND SPORTING ACTIVITIES AGAINST OUR RAF COLLEAGUES. GEOGRAPHICALLY, THE ISLAND IS APPROXIMATELY ONE AND A HALF MILES LONG AND HALF A MILE WIDE.

In early November, we arrive off the Island of Gan, a naturally uninhabited island in the Maldives, many nautical miles south-west of Ceylon, where the Royal Air Force chose to construct an airport.

The RAF consider themselves to be a sporty lot. In response, Gunga has organised teams for almost everything. It's rumoured that he even tries to organise a 'skirmishing' competition, but that doesn't get off the ground. During the first week *Lincoln* win at football, sailing, pulling, rugby, hockey, water polo and swimming. The RAF beat us at indoor skittles, bar billiards and needlepoint. We slaughter them at shove-halfpenny. Cricket is yet to be organised.

The rumour about there being only one female on Gan is confirmed. She works for the WVS and is well over 80. Nobody I know makes any effort to track her down. Apparently she's entitled to a 24-hour, round-the-clock armed RAF guard. It is further rumoured that she knows Sugar of old.

There is never a cloud in the sky above Gan. Lounging around in swimming costume and flip-flops is normal and my colouration is now a rich, deep mahogany.

Once again I'm selected to play for the second eleven cricket team. The RAF are uniformed in freshly laundered whites. You can tell when something is fresh from the laundry as it has horizontal creases in the wrong places. All the RAF team, except one young lad, have underlined their nose with a moustache. One gentleman in particular has a particularly unattractive growth that is hard-waxed and protrudes like the handlebars of a bike. Everybody calls him Sir.

To cut a long cricketing anecdote short, we bat first and win. I bat at number three and hit a couple of boundaries, scoring 21 before an RAF umpire incorrectly gives me out LBW. Boundaries aren't that difficult as we are playing in the centre of a hockey pitch.

The RAF has no answer to our bowling and we scuttle them out for a miserable total of 68 – that's 59 less than our total of 127.

The after-match celebrations are minimal to say the least. 'Sir' makes a speech of congratulations but it's obvious that he doesn't really mean what he says. He doesn't stay for the sausages on sticks or the pork pie slices with a boiled egg in the centre. I know absolutely nothing about the design of food and spend some time looking at my slice and trying to figure out how the hell they get the long egg in the middle.

I ask one of the opposing team, a bloke with an exceedingly bushy moustache, what it's like at Gan with no women. He shrugs his shoulders and replied that it isn't a problem for him.

I have myself another slice of the eggy pork pie and find a *Lincoln* team member to talk to.

I have finished all the canvas sewing and tied my last Turk's Head by the middle of November and am taken off the upper deck, out of the fresh air and given the job of Petty Officers' messman. Along with a few others, it's my job to clean the Petty Officers' mess, arrange meals and be a general dogsbody. Overlooking the slightly servile aspect of the position, it's a good job. I spend most of my time in the little pantry adjoining the mess, where the food is kept warm and tea, coffee etc is made. There are a few perks that go with the job: I'm excused all other duties, I'm able to eat my food in the pantry away from the mess and I get to know all the Petty Officers onboard. The disadvantage is that if I don't keep an eye on it, my upper deck tan will fade.

Gan was never going to be a memorable run-ashore. I don't know what *Lincoln* has done to incur the wrath of Their Lords at the Admiralty, but time rolls on and we remain anchored to the bottom. The delights of Singapore, Hong Kong and Japan are but distant fading memories.

Although the beer is cheap and plentiful in the Other Ranks Canteen ashore, getting showered and dressed to catch a boat to spend a couple of hours in an RAF Canteen becomes less attractive as the time goes on. Those who enjoy fishing love Gan though, and an increasing number take up the pastime. Petty Officer Cole, who considers himself to be an expert at tropical water fishing, holds basic fishing classes on the Quarterdeck every other day except Sunday. Smokey decides which fish are edible and those that are not: he has an illustrated book apparently. Sometimes Smokey gets it completely wrong and the galley prepares something from the Indian Ocean that is dangerously inedible. On the plus side we regularly have swordfish steaks that are brilliant.

Gringo is a surprisingly good chess player and reaches the final of the inter-mess competition. He wins the toss and has home advantage over the Padre for the best out of three final.

The Padre is uncomfortable playing in our mess and is whitewashed 2-0.

Gringo's prize for winning the competition is a travelling chess set, courtesy of a Hong Kong games emporium.

LRO George Wild is an OK bloke. He works hard at keeping us all up to date on news from home and the Malaysian crisis. Personally I'm not very interested in what is going on at home but I do make a point of reading George's notices.

When George hears about anything he thinks will interest the rest of us, he tells us. I'm sitting in the PO's mess pantry one evening, having some quiet contemplative time to myself, when George pokes his head in the door. 'Have you heard that CS Lewis, the author of the Narnia books, and Aldous Huxley have both died today. Coincidence eh?'

'Yeah it is. Thanks George.' To be honest I don't know who Lewis or Aldous what's-his-name are and continue reading *The Man Who Killed the King*.

Within the hour George is back. 'You won't believe it! They say things happen in threes, don't they?'

'Do they?'

'They do, yeah. The President of the United States has been shot. John F Kennedy has been killed.'

It doesn't seem that important at the time but Friday 22 November becomes a significantly historic day.

Sporting competitions between ourselves and our RAF hosts have almost dried up, due to an increasing 'lack of interest'. To alleviate the boredom that is threatening to overrun the ship, a beard-growing competition is held. All the normal naval shaving and not-shaving rules are ignored. Beards from older chins sprout overnight. I don't bother to stop shaving as I obviously have no chance of winning.

The following morning Tansy pokes his chin through the serving hatch.

'You've got a few grey hairs, PO,' I say.

'It'll be bacon grease,' replies Tansy. 'And don't you be so ferkin familiar.'

That's me told.

Eventually Annie Oakley is adjudged to be the winner of the beard-growing competition and is given a glass ashtray as his prize. Annie doesn't smoke so he finds a Petty Officer Writer who is prepared to give him half of his tot in exchange for his trophy.

Once the competition is over I decide to see what I can grow.

'Cultivating on your chin that which grows wild round your arse,' states Apple over dinner one day.

The normal procedure in the Royal Navy to grow a beard is a complicated affair. First I have to fill in a Request Form 'to discontinue shaving'. I'm then cross-examined by my Divisional

Petty Officer and Divisional Officer before the Request Form is signed and passed on to higher authority. If it is decided at this early stage that an individual is not capable of growing an acceptable beard, then permission to discontinue shaving can be refused. The Royal Navy have strict rules regarding the style and appearance of facial hair and trimming or styling any growth is not officially allowed. The Higher Authority, previously mentioned, is the First Lieutenant who deals with all the facial hair requests.

'Do you think that you can grow a decent-looking set then, Able Seaman Broadbent?'

'Don't know, sir.'

'You ever grown one before?'

'No, sir.'

'Didn't you compete in the recent beard-growing competition?'

'No, sir.'

'So you have no idea what will surface once you discontinue shaving?'

'No, sir.'

'Well then, request granted but I want to assess the results in two weeks time to see if you are able to grow an acceptable set.'

'Thank you, sir.'

Petty Officer Warden clicks his sandaled heels together. 'Request granted. To be re-assessed in two weeks time!' Leftaa tin ... qwicka ... march.'

Between the second and sixth days my chin and cheeks really itch. Those in the mess with many years of experience of not shaving are not that encouraging.

'Thought you'd stopped shaving, young Pete.'

'Piss off.'

Someone strokes my chin. 'That's not going anywhere.'

'It's only been six days.'

'It's got to get going soon otherwise ...'

'I can see a few little black hairs there.' Popeye pokes a finger in my left ear. 'Sorry, Pete ... missed.'

'They're just not coming out are they?' asks Fez.

'Not yet they're not.'

'Give it up as a bad job, mate,' says Lash. 'Looks untidy anyway.'

'And when it does eventually grow into a dense bushy set, say this time next year, your chin will be white as the sun won't penetrate,' explains Tommy.

'I'm shaving the ferkin thing off then,' I decide.

'Make out your request form,' says Fez. 'I'll get Conway to sign it.'

'What do I write?'

'Request to re-continue shaving.'

The First Lieutenant looks at both sides of my chin. 'Not much happening is there, Able Seaman Broadbent?'

'No, sir.'

'It's a brave attempt however, Broadbent. I suggest you wait a few years before trying again.'

'Aye aye, sir.'

'Request to re-continue shaving granted.'

Petty Officer Warden clicks his heels. 'Request to re-continue shaving granted!' Leftaa tin ... qwicka ... march.'

The EST (Euchre Standardisation Team) that has been meeting periodically since last February is officially disbanded. According to the team's fourth Chairman, LME 'Bungy' Williams, none of the team can agree on the published rules of a game that no one onboard understands.

We leave Gan on the first Sunday of December and head north for a quick visit to Male, as it's rumoured that Midshipman Scariott – who we transferred to *HMAS Vendetta* – is waiting for us.

At Male we are officially informed that nobody of that name has arrived on the island. We leave the following day apparently bound for Singapore to celebrate our second successive Christmas Singapore style.

Once again we are berthed at the far end of Sembawang dockyard. Rumour has it that the Captain of *HMS Albion* has something to do with the allocation of berths. Apparently he hasn't forgiven *Lincoln* for the football match they almost lost.

Midshipman Scariott finds his way back onboard this evening. His green case is still emblazoned with anti Australian graffiti.

Once again, we are accommodated in *Terror* for the festive period: apparently there is something technical and disruptive to be done onboard. On Christmas Day we are allocated a time in the Dining Hall for a slap-up Christmas dinner. Traditionally our Officers and Senior Rates serve us, clear our plates away and generally skivvy for us. The whole experience is brilliant. After dinner we repair to the Armada Club for cigarettes and beer. In traditional style we pour pint after pint of Tiger on top of our ceremonial dinner.

Tommy, who is drinking gin and tonic, is the first one to collapse under the table. Traditionally, we leave him where he is and use him as a rather comfortable foot-rest until Fez declares him fit enough to be taken back to the mess. Lash and I take half of Tommy each and we struggle with him all the way uphill to the mess. We dump him fully clothed and breathing onto his bunk and scamper back to the Armada Club before anyone scuppers our unfinished pints.

The remainder of the day is a blur. I vaguely recall a nighttime visit to the nearest Monsoon Drain: appropriate I suppose.

The last day of 1963 begins well enough. It continues well into the afternoon until Fez finds me sitting on the mess balcony reading the final chapter of *The Dark Secret of Josephine*.

'Heard the football results for the Christmas period, Pete lad?' he asks, a smirk starting to materialise.

I haven't, so I shake my head.

'Boxing Day at your place, you scored against us for the first time in ages.'

'Great ... thanks.'

'But we scored as well, so it was a 1-1 draw.'

'That's OK then. Honours even.'

'Not exactly, because your bunch of no-hopers came up to Roker Park a few days later.'

'Yeah?'

'And we ferkin trounced you two nil.'

'It's only a game.'

'You always say that when you get beat.'

'It's only a game of football.'

'You always say that as well.'

I point my nose at my book.

We return onboard *Lincoln* once our technical problem has been resolved.

I'm given my draft-chit: details of my next 'ship'. I am to do an RP2's course at *HMS Dryad*. From what I understand, this course is for relatively experienced RP3's who have proved themselves competent. I haven't gained much Radar Plotting experience onboard *Lincoln* having spent most of my time steering the ship, sewing canvas, tying Turk's Heads, doing boats crew, along with other Seamanship-like things, and getting drunk. I certainly haven't made much of an effort to prove myself during my short spells in the Ops Room. However, it's a shore draft in Pompey for at least six months so, despite the fact that the course is thoroughly undeserved, it's good news. I recall my *Dryad* afternoons with Wilco.

We leave Singapore at 17:00 in the middle of a unseasonably late monsoon downpour. Some of us reckon that our time of departure was calculated to see how the upper deck Seamen operated under heavy rain conditions. Others blame *HMS Albion*'s skipper for everything.

We relieve *HMS Cavalier* on Borneo Patrol in early January. The Kumpit Boarding Party has been disbanded as officially the smuggling threat is no longer considered to be a problem. That's why, as Petty Officers messman, I'm no longer boats crew.

We are pleased to have a five-day break alongside the wooden jetty at Tawau. It's a normal evening at Blinkers Bar that turns into something quite different and embarrassingly ridiculous. Lash and I consume a little more alcohol than normal and, as we are staggering back towards the jetty, one of us notices a severed bull's head lying up against a mud wall.

Bloody hell, what's that?'

'It's a head.'

'A head of what?'

'A cow.'

'It's got horns.'

'It's a whatsit then ... a bull then.'

'It will look great on the mesh bulkhead, won't it?'

'Fabulous ... ferkin fabulous.'

So we grab a horn each and stagger on.

'Where shall we shtow it ... until tomorrow?'

I jab a knowing finger at Lash. 'There's a shpare locker below mine ... empty.'

As we approach *Lincoln,* we discuss the problem of getting the bull's head onboard, unseen by the gangway staff. We squat down behind a discarded trolley opposite the brow.

'Do you think they'll let ush take it onboard?'

'No ferkin chance.'

'How we goin' to get it onboard then?'

'Dunno.'

'There's got to be a way.'

'Leave it with me. Fag?' I ask.

'Don't smoke ... never smoked. You know that.'

'OK then.'

'How we going to get it onboard then?'

'Dunno.' I light my cigarette.

Lash looses the toss and gets the job of distracting the Quartermaster while I slip up the brow with the bull's head. I lose my fifty cent coin.

Lash is brilliant. He staggers up the brow and at the top, he pretends to collapse. Both the Quartermaster and the Bosun's Mate rush to help him.

With their backs to the gangway I skip up the brow unnoticed and toss the head inside a screen door. I then join the group who have managed to get a recovering Lash to his feet.

'You sure that you're OK, Lash? asks the Quartermaster.

'Sure,' replies Lash. 'Jusht lost my feet ... footing for a shecond that's all.'

We make it back down the mess giggling and chuffed to bits with our trophy. Everybody is asleep as we manage to squeeze the head into the spare locker and close the door. We sling our hammocks and turn in, satisfied that we will be the envy of all the other messes in the morning.

Fez is violently shaking my hammock. 'Get out.'

My eyes are stuck closed. 'Whaaa? ...'

'Don't you what me.'

'Sorry.'

'Get out of your stinking pit now. Feet on the deck.'

As I slide to the floor one of my eyes opens and I notice a rivulet of blood and quivering maggots seeping from the bottom of the spare locker. There is a strange smell.

Fez drags a drooping Lash over to the locker. 'What's in there?'

'Nothing,' splurts Lash.

'Don't piss me about. What have you two adventurers put in that locker?'

Lash looks at me. I look at Lash and decide to come clean. 'It's a bull's head. It ...'

'A WHAT?'

'A bull's head. We thought it would look great on the mess bulkhead, I splutter. 'It's a complete head with horns and everything.'

'Get it out. Ditch it and then start cleaning. I want this area spotless and the mess smelling like a virgin's gusset before breakfast ... understand me?'

Unbreakfasted and unwashed, we drag the suppurating head out of the locker and wrap it in rolls of strong paper. We tie the paper with good strong lines of Coston gun line, carry it to the upper deck and give it a float test. We watch in silence as the bull's head bobs away on what we hope is an ebbing tide.

'Was that a great idea or what?' I ask.

'It was ferkin ridiculous,' replies Lash.

'It was yeah.'

'I mean. It was riddled with crawling stuff.'

'And snot.'

'And snot yeah.'

'What made us think it would look great on the bulkhead?'

'The booze probably.'

'Yeah ... probably."

'I think the tide is coming in, not going out.'

'Ferkin isn't, is it?'

'Think so ... yeah.'

'Shit.'

The mess is empty. The smell of the now departed bull's head still remains.

'What did you do with it?' Fez asks from over the other side of the messdeck.

'Gave it a float test.'

'You didn't.'

'We did yeah.'

'It may have been a village relic or something.'

'Never thought of that.'

'Part of some sacrifice or something.'

'Never thought of that.'

'This mess has to be sparkling before you pair go ashore again.'

We both nod. A stressed-out Lash violently breaks wind.

'That'll help clear the atmosphere,' says Fez. 'You know where all the cleaning gear is. Get to it.'

It takes us more than three hours to clean the inside of the spare locker and the surrounding area. Collecting the wriggling maggots is difficult and unpleasant: they're clever little buggers.

Neither Lash or I are in the mood to go ashore by the time we finish.

'You any idea what a virgin's gusset smells like?' I ask Lash just on the off-chance.

'Dunno. What is a gusset exactly?'

'I think it's that bit of the knickers that ...'

'Oh I know,' says Lash clicking his fingers

'Probably doesn't smell as pleasant as this locker though.'

'Probably not ... no.'

Before dinner we attract a few visitors to the mess who come down specifically to take the piss out of me and Lash. Surprisingly we are both offered 'sippers' at tot time.

The following evening we have something else to talk about.

We have consumed a few Tigers in Blinkers when we notice that Blinker, and a large group of villagers, are standing outside scanning the eastern skies and excitedly flapping their arms at each other.

A few of us can't ignore such an unexpected and animated display, so we sidle outside with our beer. Down the track are dozens of other villagers all looking east. A few are holding large nets.

A flapping sound gradually grows louder and I scan the eastern skies, not knowing what is approaching.

Suddenly there appears a dark swarm of large winged insects, obviously attracted by Tawau's handful of lights. Thousands upon thousands of huge winged moths land everywhere: on roofs, the ground, the walls ... and us. Our shoulders and heads become the perfect landing place for these huge colourful creatures. I suppose they all measure at least nine or ten inches across. The wings are every colour of the rainbow. They have small bodies and long, thin antenna. Apart from the occasional flapping of their wings to maintain their balance, they are gentle and composed once settled. It's quite a pleasurable experience.

The invasion of the giant moths lasts about an hour. Then, as a choreographed swarm, they launch their way west and away. A few stragglers strut and flap around the bar. Blinker has netted one that he puts into a wooden cage behind the bar. It's admired by a few village visitors who come around to marvel at the giant moth who sits morose in a corner of the cage, its colourful wings folded. They poke it with sticks. I wish I'd had my camera with me, because nobody back home will believe the size of those Tawau flutterbys, but the one thing you don't take on a night-time 'run ashore' is your camera.

Gringo has had a suit made by Sew-sew onboard. It's green-grey with a scarlet lining, fits him beautifully and didn't cost that much. Compared to the relatively expensive grey John Collier's suit I had brought with me, it's brilliant. I decide to have Sew-sew make a suit for me. My choice from Sew-sew's limited onboard materials is a dark blue mohair mix.

Before we leave Tawau, Gringo and Tommy decide to release Shoe-shoe's parrot. It has spent the last fourteen months in a small cage outside Shoe-shoe's cabooch. They feel sorry for the bird and decide that it would be a fitting end to the commission to give the bird its freedom. They wait until Shoe-shoe goes down to the laundry where the Chinese contingent eat the last meal of the day and play Mah Jong. They open the cage door; the parrot cowers under its perch and they have to drag it out. Tommy ceremonially kisses its head before launching it towards the jungle south of Tawau and its long-awaited freedom. The parrot drops like a stone into the harbour waters, sinks and is not seen again.

'It probably never learnt to ferkin swim,' says Tommy.

'Yeah probably,' agreed Gringo. 'Or fly.'

'Poor little sod.'

Lincoln is relieved of our final Borneo patrol duty and we skip past Singapore on our way to Hong Kong. The weather is kind to us; there are no typhoons with girly names waiting around Filipino corners to surprise us.

After a few daily fittings, I am the proud owner of a lightweight, blue mohair suit that fits me perfectly and will impress everybody in Pudsey, particularly Mrs Shufflebum. There is little room for growth. I buy myself a special plastic suit cover for an extra Singapore dollar.

Down the mess, Fez asks me to model my new suit but I manage to talk my way out of it.

On arrival in Hong Kong the mail is issued and we are all surprised that Brick hasn't got any. Once again he casually puts it down to a glitch in the mail system, saying that Polly's letters have probably gone to Tawau. I secretly think that he's pleased he hasn't got a fresh consignment of letters to reply to. I have one from Mum that was written three weeks ago. I also receive a short note from Wilco telling me that she is still progressing her transfer to the Singapore NAAFI. She can't resist putting something disgustingly sexual on the bottom.

We are the only Royal Naval ship in Hong Kong. We have the whole of Wan Chai to ourselves for a couple of days until *HMS Albion* is scheduled to arrive and both the attitude and price of the girls will change.

Lash and I go ashore with Brick to collect Polly's engagement ring from the jeweller's at the junction of Stanley and Lockhart Road. It must be a popular jeweller's as there is a bloke standing outside wearing a turban and cradling an enormous rifle. Lash and I stand politely to one side as Brick takes delivery of Polly's ring and hands over a wodge of money to the smiling gentleman behind the counter.

We have a drink in the Old Toby bar and Brick shows Polly's engagement ring to us. Both Lash and I say it's nice.

One of the girls is attracted by it and asks if she can handle it.

Brick refuses. 'It wouldn't be right would it?' he asks me.

I know nothing about the etiquette of engagement rings, but say, 'Not really ... no.'

We are officially presented with our individual Crossing-the-Line certificates. They are colourful enough and someone who can write skilfully has carefully inserted our names in the appropriate place. Mine reads ...

Neptune Rex – Ruler of the deep, Sovereign of the Oceans and Lord of the Seas bear witness that

Able Seaman Peter Broadbent

of Her Majesty's ship Lincoln did on this thirtieth day of November 1963 cross The Line at Long 74º East and that the aforesaid having observed the proper rites of ceremony, is baptised at the hand of His Most Gracious Majesty King Neptune, who according to the Law of the High Seas, pronounced him a Son of Neptune thereby permitting him to cross the Line at any future date unmolested by any creature of the Deep. Certified this day above written and given under our hands and seal.

Signed Neptunus Rex.

The following day George Wild points out that the certificates are incorrect and that we had actually crossed the line a month earlier than shown. Diplomatically, George blames King

Neptune's backroom staff who apparently have a lot on their plate at the moment. So we all have an incorrect certificate – we just have to live with it.

'DO YOU HEAR THERE THE PADRE SPEAKING. ON BEHALF OF KING NEPTUNE, QUEEN APHRODITE AND THEIR STAFF I WOULD LIKE TO APOLOGISE FOR THE CLERICAL ERROR ON THE CROSSING THE LINE CERTIFICATES. THE WRONG DATE DOES NOT INVALIDATE THE CERTIFICATE IN ANY WAY.'

There is a general cheer down the mess. I unroll my certificate and sure enough it proclaims clearly that I had Crossed the Line a month later than I actually did.

'DO YOU HEAR THERE, THE FIRST LIEUTENANT SPEAKING. IT'S THE PADRE'S FAULT. IT'S THE PADRE WHO HAD THE JOB OF ARRANGING THE PRINTING OF THE CROSSING THE LINE CERTIFICATES.'

The following day Brick has a letter from Polly. He turns white, screws the single page letter into a ball and tosses it into the full mess gash bucket. 'The bastard!' he shouts as he kicks a convenient locker.

'Is that Polly then?' asks Popeye, pointing to the gash bucket.

Lash farts and sneezes more or less simultaneously.

Fez springs over to where Brick stands staring at nothing in particular. He places a comforting arm on his shoulder. 'What's the matter, Brick ... bad news?'

'Nothing.' He takes a really deep breath.

'Is it a 'Dear John'?'

'More than ferkin that.'

'What then?'

'She's called everything off.'

'The engagement?'

'Everything.'

'It happens to the best of us, Brick,' says Popeye.

'Shit, shit.' Brick thumps his locker door. 'And buckets of shit.'

'If I have a quid for every Dear John I'd received I'd be a rich man mate,' explains a sorrowful-looking Popeye.

'How many have you had then?' asks a straight-faced Apple.

'A couple.' Popeye nods towards Brick.

'How does a couple of quid make you a rich man then?' asks Apple.

'Piss off.'

'Right then lads,' Fez claps his hands. 'Stand-easy is over, back to work. Pete, it's your turn to ditch the gash.' He taps Brick on the shoulder. 'Take your time, Brick. I'll tell your PO that you're doing some work for me.' He gives him a friendly pat in the centre of his back.

I struggle into my overalls and we leave Brick, who is rummaging in his locker.

'It's best not having girlfriends in this man's Navy,' declares Fez.

I'm about to ditch the gash in the shoreside bin when something glints and catches my eye within the static, putrid yellow stuff known as custard. It's Polly's engagement ring: I put it in my pocket. Back down the mess I decide to keep it in my locker rather than give it back to Brick who, in his present state of mind, will probably throw it away again.

I'm duty messman the last night in Hong Kong so Lash and I decided to go ashore the day before and say a final and fond farewell to the Colony.

'DO YOU HEAR THERE, THE INFORMATION OFFICER SPEAKING. TODAY IS A SPECIAL DAY IN THE CHINESE CALENDAR. TODAY IS THE FIRST DAY OF THE CHINESE NEW YEAR, THE 2ND FULL MOON AFTER THE WINTER SOLSTICE.

THIS IS THE YEAR OF THE GREEN WOOD DRAGON. IT WILL BE POLITE FOR ANYBODY GOING ASHORE TONIGHT TO WISH THE LOCAL CHINESE A 'KWONG HAI FAT CHOY' WHICH IS CANTONESE FOR HAPPY NEW YEAR. IF YOU'RE LUCKY YOU MAY RECEIVE A FREE DRINK.'

'I got that,' says Apple tapping his writing pad with a pen. 'Kwong hai fat choy'. That could get us a free drink or something in the bars. Kwong hai fat choy.'

I make a note of it on the palm of my hand.

Later that afternoon Lash and I are sitting in the China Fleet Club's main bar having a few cold ones and planning our Wan Chai evening when Lash, who is facing the entrance door, says 'Ferk me, Pete mate: who's the very last person you would expect to walk into this bar?'

'Marilyn Monroe.'

'Seriously.'

'Gina Lola whatsit.'

'Seriously, Pete,' he leans back and raises his arms. 'Wha ... aa ... aha.'

Before I can answer, a familiar arm drapes itself firmly over my shoulder and someone kisses me on the back of my neck.

I turn to face a beaming Wilco.

'Told you I'd do it, didn't I?'

'Wha?'

'Got myself a transfer didn't I? I know my timing's awful. I know you're leaving the day after tomorrow.'

'And I'm duty tomorrow.'

'Get a sub then. I've got a brilliant little room on the third floor overlooking the harbour.'

Lash stands and winks at me. 'I'm going to the Old Toby. I'll leave you alone. Enjoy yourselves.'

'OK mate,' I say. 'Say a few Kwong Hai Fat Choys for me then.'

Wilco looks at me.

'It's Chinese New Year today,' I explain. 'And Kwong Hai Fat Choy is 'Happy New Year' in Chinese ... apparently.' I show her what is written on my hand.

Wilco snakes a hand over the table and grips mine. 'I arrived in Singapore a week ago to do my acclimatisation course and am not officially due to take up my position until next week. I told the Manager in Singapore that I have a special friend onboard Lincoln … '

'Special friend?'

'Yeah. I told him that you're onboard Lincoln and that you are going to be in Hong Kong until tomorrow. So he cut short my course, organised me an RAF flight and got me here before you leave me again.'

'Nice of him.'

'Very nice.' She smiles her special Wilco smile. 'I've got a tattoo.'

'You haven't?'

'I have.'

'Where?'

'In Pompey.'

'No, I mean where is your tattoo?'

'That's for you to discover, sailor.'

I finish my drink with a splutter. 'Lead on.'

The lift is unbelievably slow: it takes ages to get us to the third floor. As the metal grill doors slowly open she kisses me. 'You'll never guess who was on the same flight as me from the UK.'

"Who?'

'Your mate Tug.'

'Yeah?'

'Shortly after you left he was drafted to the dockyard sailing school. He came back to Dryad about a month ago and was drafted to the Sailing school in HMS Terror.'

'Blimey.'

We stroll arm in arm down a short passage and stop outside the door numbered 33. I put my hand on her backside and give it a stroke as she places her key in the lock. 'I've missed your gentleness.' She swings the door open. 'According to Mister Armstrong downstairs this is a lucky room … thirty three is doubly lucky apparently.'

'It will be if you play your cards right,' I joke.

'A game of cards is most definitely not on the menu.'

We scatter our clothes all over the place. I throw my socks at the rotating ceiling fan and miss.

A very naked Wilco scrambles into bed first. What follows is a brilliant hour of sexual exercise. Little has changed since we have been apart: I'm much darker of skin and Wilco has put on a little extra ballast around her upper thigh area.

'Where's this tattoo then?'

She sits up and pulls the sheet over her breasts. 'Do you mean you haven't noticed … what you been looking at for the last hour or so?'

'Wasn't looking for tattoos.' I pull a sulky face and try to recall some of our more recent activities, but I can't remember seeing a tattoo.

She lies back with her head on her pillow and the covering sheet held tight in both her hands. She lowers it slowly to reveal both her breasts and looks questioningly at me.

I examine both her breasts but find nothing unusual. 'Err … no tattoos there.'

She slowly lowers the sheet until it's in line with her belly button. 'See anything unusual?'

This is an awkward moment. 'Can I have a cigarette?'

'Sure.'

I light my cigarette, but I still can't see a tattoo. I double check. 'Nothing there apart from a magnificent pair of tits.'

She flaps the sheet.

I notice something and with my forefinger I pull the top of the sheet a little further down to reveal a strange-looking tattoo about an inch square and three or four inches below her belly button. 'What is it?'

'NAAFI logo.'

'NAAFI logo?'

'Yeah.'

'Why?'

'Why not?'

'Dunno.'

'Kiss mi logo then.'

So I do. I extinguish my cigarette and everything kicks off again. It's dark before either of us comes up for air.

We stand in front of the window looking out over the harbour with the twinkling lights of Kowloon reflected in the dark harbour waters and the silhouette of the mountains of the New Territories as a backdrop. The fluorescent wakes of the numerous craft plying their trade in the harbour silver-line the waters. What a way to celebrate Chinese New Year.

'Who'd have thought,' she says as she strokes my spine, 'that we would be looking out over Hong Kong harbour together?'

'On Chinese New Year?'

'Yeah, that as well.'

'How long will you be in Singapore then?'

'As long as I like, I think. They haven't said anything about length of contract or anything. I could be working in Hong Kong or Singapore.'

'I'm going back to Dryad.'

'When?'

'Next month. Going to do a 2's course.'

'Thought you said that you were crap at that Radar Plotting stuff?'

'I am.'

'So what are you doing on a 2's course then?'

'Don't ask me.'

'So you'll be in Dryad and I'll be out here?'

'Unless I can stay out here,' I say as I envelope her in both arms.

'Could you?'

'Dunno. I'll ask.'

'If you can't, I'll resign and go back to Dryad. They said they would keep my position open for me.'

'I'll ask.'

'Before tomorrow?'

'I'll try.'

It's a stagger back onboard from the China Fleet Club in the early hours of my last day in Hong Kong. The smell from the fish market is particularly intense at sunrise.

Fez Parker gives me a smile as he hands me my Station card. 'Heard that your NAAFI girl turned up unexpectedly.'

'Who told you that?'

'Lash.'

'Shit ... I forgot all about Lash.'

Down the mess, I'm subject to some friendly banter ...

'You look like you've have an entertaining night,' says Popeye.

'Looks shagged out to me,' declares a smirking Tommy.

'Did you give her my regards?' asks Lash.

'Too busy giving her my own ... sorry.'

That gets a laugh.

Apple appears with the tray full of breakfast. He slaps me on the shoulder. 'You lucky bastard. Heard that you screwed the NAAFI ... again.'

I don't know why, but I need to keep my position as the centre of attention going, 'She's had a NAAFI logo tattoo.'

'What?' asks Lash.

'A ferkin NAAFI logo ... where?' asks Apple.

'Can't tell you that. It wouldn't be gentlemanly.'

'What, you a gentleman?'

Fez appears, dives into the breakfast tray and extracts himself a couple of sausages. 'You dirty, lucky bastard,' and gives me a clip around my ear.

'Who should I see about staying out here instead of going back to the UK next month?' I ask.

'Oh ... I see,' says a smiling Fez. 'Bit of the 'you-can't-bend-it' and you want to go all Oriental.'

'Just a possibility.'

'Not allowed,' says Tommy. 'Rule is that you have to go back as planned and then put in a request to be drafted out here again once you're back in the UK.'

'Is that right?' I ask.

'Yep,' says Tommy.

Fez nods agreement.

'Shit.'

'Did anyone manage to get a free Chinese New Year drink with a kwong hai fat choy?' Asks Fez.

Nobody says yes.

Later in the day I ask Petty Officer Cole the same question about staying in the Far East and get a similar reply. I decide that if I want an official answer I'll have to ask someone in the Wardroom. I don't fancy doing that, so I reluctantly decide that the simplest thing is to get Wilco to resign her position.

I arrange with one of the other messmen to do my duty today in exchange for a tot that I'm due to start getting in a few days time.

There is no need for me to go into detail about my final eighteen-and-a-half hours in Hong Kong: it's mainly spent in the privacy of room 33 at the China Fleet Club.

Wilco and I stroll back towards *Lincoln* hand in hand, arriving at the bottom of the brow at 06:58 the following morning. Despite my asking her not to, Wilco walks up the gangway behind me and tells the Officer-of-the-Day to make sure that he looks after me on the way back to Singapore. Then she flings her arms around my neck and kisses me long and hard before skipping back over the brow where she arranges herself cross-legged on top of a large dockside bollard.

The Officer-of-the-Day looks at me as he hands me my Station card. I think he smirks. 'Chop chop, Broadbent. Down the mess and get changed for leaving harbour.'

'DO YOU HEAR THERE, THE OFFICER-OF-THE-DAY SPEAKING. NOW THAT ABLE SEAMAN BROADBENT HAS RETURNED SAFELY BACK ONBOARD, HMS LINCOLN IS OFFICIALLY UNDER SAILING ORDERS AND IS SCHEDULED TO DEPART HONG KONG FOR THE FINAL TIME THIS COMMISSION IN

FORTY-FIVE MINUTES. SPECIAL SEA DUTY MEN WILL CLOSE UP AT 07:20. UPPER DECK SEAMEN WILL FALL IN AT 07:30.'

As *HMS Lincoln* drifts away from the jetty at exactly 07:45, Wilco, still perched on top of a bollard blows me, and *Lincoln*, a farewell kiss.

After we leave the Fragrant Harbour for the final time there is a miserable silence throughout the ship. The silence in the mess is disturbed ...

'ABLE SEAMAN BROADBENT REPORT TO LIEUTENANT CONWAY IN THE WARDROOM.'

'Shit,' I say as I grab my cap and shuffle up the mess ladder. 'Wonder what this is all about.'

Lieutenant Conway is standing outside the Wardroom Pantry smoking a cigarette.

I stand to attention.

'Stand at ease, Broadbent.'

I stand at ease.

'Tell me, Able Seaman Broadbent, that the young lady who perched herself on a dockside bollard ... the young lady who told the Officer-of-the-Day to look after you ... is related to you in some way.'

'No, sir.'

'What do you mean ... no?'

'She's not related to me ... sir.'

'Then who the devil is she?'

'Daughter of a Diplomat, sir.' I don't know where that came from, but it sounds impressive.

'And the name of the Diplomat is?' says Lieutenant Conway scrabbling in his back pocket for something to write on.

'Never got around to surnames, sir ... sorry.'

'Pardon?'

'I didn't ask her for her family name, sir. Didn't seem that important.'

'I believe she flew in from Singapore a few days ago,' he clicks his pen.

'That's correct sir.'

'For what reason?'

'So we could spend some time together, sir.'

Lieutenant Conway coughs and stares wide-eyed at me. 'All the way from Singapore?'

'Yes, sir.'

'On an RAF flight?'

'I believe so … yes, sir.'

"That's all, Broadbent,' he waves a dismissive arm. 'Back to work.'

'Thank you, sir.' I come to attention, turn right and slouch away.

Down the mess, I tell Fez and the others that I have just been cross-examined about Wilco.

'What did you tell him?' asks Tommy.

'Told him that she's a Diplomat's daughter.'

'You didn't?'

'Did he believe you?' asks Popeye.

'I think so yeah.'

At exactly 08:05 the following day, with the dark green mountains of China on our starboard side …

'ABLE SEAMAN BROADBENT REPORT TO LIEUTENANT CONWAY IN THE WARDROOM IMMEDIATELY. ABLE SEAMAN BROADBENT.'

Lieutenant Conway is standing outside the Wardroom Pantry with his cap on.

I stand to attention facing him.

'Stand at ease, Broadbent.'

I stand at ease.

'You, Able Seaman Broadbent, are a liar of the first water.'

'Pardon, sir?'

'You, young man, are a stranger to the truth.'

'If you say so, sir.'

'I could charge you will wilful insubordination and lying to a Senior Officer.'

'Yes, sir.'

'You are a story-teller, Able Seaman Broadbent. What are you?'

'A story-teller, sir?'

'You should write a book.'

'I might do that one day, sir.'

'She wasn't ... isn't a Diplomat's daughter, is she?'

'Not exactly, sir.'

'What is she? The truth this time.'

'She works for the NAAFI, sir.'

'Managerial position?'

'I don't think so, sir.'

'Then what?'

'She serves drinks, rolls, sandwiches and things, sir.'

'Just a bog-standard NAAFI girl then?'

'Yes, sir.'

'Dismiss,' he waves a hand at me and turns away.

I considered myself lucky, having escaped with nothing more serious than a half-hearted bollocking.

Down the mess, George has posted his latest report that is entitled 'The Final Malaysian Crisis Report'.

Malaysian Crisis Report #6

The Indonesian Air Force has been 'buzzing' towns in Sarawak. In retaliation, Malaysia has declared an Air Defence Identification Zone and the RAF have started periodic fighter patrols along the border using Javelin and RN aircraft.

RO George Wild.

Have a safe journey home.

I'm still working as a Messman when I draw my first tot on my 20th birthday – 16 February 1964. It's a landmark day; I'm no longer a teenager and old enough at last to be issued with my daily ration of 'Nelson's Blood'.

Because I'm Petty Officers Messman, my tot is issued with the rest of the Petty Officers mess ... undiluted

Petty Officer 'Tansy' Lee pours me my fist legal tot and, along with a bunch of other Petty Officers in the mess, watch me.

'A first tot has to be downed in one,' declares Tansy.

'Honestly?'

'It's tradition.'

You don't argue with a Petty Officer, particularly one who has a judo black belt.

Nelson's blood hits my stomach like a battering ram. I don't move for a while. Then it hits my equipment, then my knees, then my feet ... and finally it does an about turn and reaches my eyes. For a brief moment the world is an unfocussed place.

'Enjoy that?' asks Tansy.

'Please give me a minute,' I cough.

I'm already looking forward to tomorrow dinnertime.

Four days later, we arrive back in Singapore. Once again, we are berthed at the far end of the Dockyard: the Captain of *HMS Albion* has a long memory. Along with everybody else, I pack my kit, say a quiet farewell to the messdeck and move into *HMS Terror*. We are all in the same, first floor mess as before.

I regret not having said a fond farewell to *Lincoln*. She has been a great little ship having taken me to a handful of interesting places and battled us through a series of female typhoons.

Tot time in Barracks is a matter of queuing up at a table, being 'ticked off', collecting a diluted tot, drinking it under the watchful eyes of members of the Regulating Branch, placing your empty glass on a rotating glass washing machine and leaving. There certainly isn't any ceremony to it and the exchange of rum is impossible. The whole process is a disappointment to me as I had begun to enjoy my 'neaters'.

I'm enjoying a cold Tiger in the Armada Club with Lash and Gringo when I see Tug.

I wave my hand high in the air. 'Hey! Tug you ugly old bastard ... over here!' He is neither ugly, old nor illegitimate but this is the prescribed way of welcoming old friends in the Royal Navy, particularly those you haven't seen for a while and who are ex-*Ganges* boys. Of course you never greet those of your mates who are actually ugly, old or illegitimate in the same way.

Tug almost runs over to our table. 'Someone told me you would be down here. How's things?'

'OK. What you doing here?'

'Got drafted to the Sailing Club here at Red House. Ship's company.'

'Terror ship's company?'

'Yep. Got my draft chit a couple of months back. Got here about a week ago.'

'That's why you look underdone,' says Lash.

I introduce Gringo telling him that Lash, Tug and I were in the same mess at *HMS Ganges* and onboard *HMS Bermuda* together.

'Terrible smog in London when I left,' says Tug.

I look up at a clear blue sky. 'That's a bastard then.'

Tug waves a piece of paper, 'I've got to go, finish this joining routine.'

'We must organise a run ashore.'

'Of course. Wilco sends her love by the way. I've got a letter for you. I'll give it to you when I've unpacked the rest of my kit.'

'I met her in Hong Kong.'

'You didn't?'

'Had a few days together at the China Fleet Club. She's trying to get transferred back to Dryad.'

'Why?'

'Because, for some strange reason I've been put on a 2's course.'

'You ... you on a ferkin 2's course?'

Tug's accommodation is much more civilised than ours. It's fully air-conditioned and they have local cleaners. He is going sailing for a week to get the lay of the surrounding waters so we postpone our run ashore in Singapore until he gets back.

On our final payday, those of us who have grown to love Lakki's Bar make a big deal out of our final visit. All the girls understand that we are on our way home and generally ignore us because there are tables full of pasty-faced new arrivals to work on. The gorgeous Burma isn't around. Suzie Right is sulking because Sugar had left Singapore a few days earlier. Even Lash can't make her smile.

Part-way through the evening I notice Burma beckoning me from the backroom doorway. I scuttle away as though on my way to the heads. Mama San ignores me. Burma beckons me to a hidden doorway. Inside she stands in front of me and looks sad.

'Goodbye, Burma.'

'Pita,' she holds a slim hand out to me.

I kiss it and give her one my smiles.

She looks confused – my smiles sometimes do that to girls.

I open my arms and hold her shoulders. She is wearing an elaborately embroidered turquoise cheongsam and her shoulders stiffen.

I stroke the side of her face and kiss her cheek.

She gently pushes me away; there is a glint of a tear in her eye.

The Mama San shoulders the door open and breaks us up. She looks from Burma to me and back again. Without saying a word she waves me away and Burma back to work.

Back at our table, we ceremonially finish our final drinks in Lakki's Bar. The girls wave us away as we stagger towards the door. Burma raises her broom in salute and smiles that wonderful smile of hers. Mama San gives her a poke in the ribs and points at the floor.

I spend some time in either Sembawang or Neesoon village, buying 'rabbits' for those back home. I buy myself a large brown leather-look suitcase.

It's taken a week, but Brick is slowly beginning to emerge from his dark and abandoned place. Tomorrow we fly home and I decide that a well-timed piece of good news is exactly what he needs to bring him back into our world. I'm a little apprehensive, as I don't know how he will react.

I give Polly's engagement ring a bit of a polish and choose my moment. I hand it to him over the mess table as he finishes a cup of tea. His initial shock quickly turns to grudging acceptance. He takes it with a grimace. 'It's Polly's ring ... my ring. Thanks a bunch, mate.'

'I saw a glint as I was ditching the gash the day you got your letter from Polly,' I explain. 'Thought I'd save it for you.'

Brick studies the ring for a moment. He smiles. 'That's it then lads,' he holds it aloft. 'Bukit Timah Road pawn shops first ... then the farewell run down Bugis Street is on me.'

'Count me in,' says Popeye.

'And me,' says Tommy.

'Thanks Brick. I didn't know how you would react.' I say.

'No use hanging onto Singapore dollars,' Brick explains.

Gringo declines the invitation. He says he has an upset stomach that he puts down to the excitement of going home.

Popeye suggests that we delay our entrance into Bugis Street by a few hours, so that those of us who have long wanted to see the sun come up at 06:00, can. It's agreed that we should stay onboard until 21:00 so that we can catch the pawn shops before they close and hit Bugis Street sometime after midnight.

I invite Tug who has heard about Bugis Street but has not yet been there.

Brick accepts the first offer from the only pawn shop still open on Bukit Timah Road and we pile into a couple of fast-blacks.

'Bugis Street, John.'

'Yes John, Bugis Street ... quick as you can.'

Bugis Street at 23:35 on a Friday night is in full swing. We make an entrance, telling those we recognise that we are flying home the following day. We order a Mami Soup for Lash and Nasi Gorengs for the rest of us. Brick's bulging wallet immediately attracts a stunningly attractive Kai-Tie who plonks herself on his lap. She has great legs. Brick nuzzles his face in amongst her overflowing breasts and declares noisily that he doesn't really want to leave Singapore.

'What about Polly then?' asks Popeye.

'Who?'

'Polly.'

'Who?'

An elderly blonde lady and her husband join us at our table. 'Are you really flying home tomorrow?'

'Midday tomorrow ... yep,' says Popeye.

'Him as well?' asks her husband pointing at Brick.

'Him as well.'

A gaggle of Kai-ties, rejected by an adjoining table, home in on us. A Eurasian-looking individual wearing an almost totally transparent short dress asks us if we are really going home tomorrow.

The one occupying Brick's lap waves them all away.

Tug hasn't closed his mouth since we arrived. 'That's a bloke, right?' he asks, nodding at the one on Brick's lap.

'Fraid so,' I say.

'I don't believe it.'

'And don't play noughts and crosses with the kids, they're experts and you'll never win,' says Lash.

Brick makes the fatal mistake of opening his bulging wallet. The information flies around the Street and by 02:30 our table is the centre of attention. We are hosting half a dozen of the most desperate of the Street's regulars who were buying their own drinks until Brick offers to buy them.

By 04:00 things are beginning to calm down. The unoccupied folding tin tables and chairs are being stacked away. Some of the lights are turned off and the woks extinguished. We explain to the guy who is serving us drinks, that we are determined to see the sun come up. We have a few photographs taken to show those back home who will never believe that our companions aren't real females. Generally they are happy to have their pictures taken even though Tommy, who is the self-proclaimed photographer amongst us, is a bit on the slow side getting things in focus.

Tommy and I continually check on Brick's wallet.

Tug has gone all floppy under a combination of Tiger, heat and excitement. We bundle him into a taxi with a couple of blokes from *Loch Alvie* who promise to make sure that he gets back to *Terror* safely. I gave him a long farewell hug: I won't see him again until goodness knows when. It's a poignant moment – two *Ganges* friends saying a drunken, dribbling farewell to each other in Bugis Street.

You tell me ...

Eventually, those of us who want to see the sun come up are alone. All our guests have staggered away, drunk at Brick's expense. Our drinks are coming very slowly now. Our heads are flopping and secretively I'm looking forward to seeing a yellow glow appear from somewhere.

'Which is west?' I ask. 'You're the Navigator's Yeoman Tommy ... which way is west?'

'Ask someone who gives a shit.'

'Right then, I will.' I look around the table. 'Which way is wesht then? Where will the shun appear?'

Nobody is interested, so I give up.

Ten minutes after my last bottle of Tiger a yellow glow appears behind the toilet block. It's exactly 06:02. Brick officially declares that we have achieved our goal. Bugis Street is completely empty apart from us.

There is only one taxi at the end of the Street. The driver is asleep on the back seat as we bang on the door.

He flops himself behind his wheel, finger-combs his tousled hair and lights his breakfast before setting off.

'HMS Terror, John.'

'Quick as you like, John ... HMS Terror.'

Brick counts the money in his wallet. 'Still got a fair amount left. Hope I can change it for proper money before we leave.'

We all nod silently. I have a couple of Singapore dollars in change ... nothing much to worry about. The remainder of last fortnight's pay packet is in Sterling and safely tucked away in my locker.

As we drive slowly through a deserted Sembawang I manage to focus on a shuttered Lakki's Bar and wonder where Burma is. Even in my inebriated state, I recall the feel of her shoulders beneath that silky cheongsam.

11

HOMEWARD BOUND

Fortunately all my kit is packed. I manage a few hours sleep before Lash wakes me at 10:45.

'Whaaaa?'

'Got to get our kit onto the wagon, mate.'

It's a struggle but I manage to drag my kitbag and my new leather-look suitcase down the stairs and into the back of an RN truck with some help from Lash.

Our transport to *RAF Changi* leaves *Terror* at 13:00 exactly and I blink a farewell to *Terror* barracks as the bus crosses the Parade ground and through the main gate without stopping.

In the assembly lounge at the airport, those of us who have seen the sun come up over Bugis Street form an exclusive bunch in a quiet corner and sprawl in a serious hung-over stupor. Although we don't realise it, the RAF could refuse to transport us because of our condition.

My walk to the plane is a blur. I sleep through take-off and don't wake until I'm offered food half an hour before we are due to land at Bombay. I'm not at all sure that last night's escapade had been a sensible way to spend our last night in Singapore.

At Bombay we meet a group of guys who are travelling east. It's strange to see pasty faces again: direct from a UK winter their complexion looks distinctly unhealthy.

A lot of the younger eastbound lads are wearing collarless jackets that look most odd. On investigation we are told that this is the style now – everybody back home has gone Beatle mad: Beatle wallpaper, Beatle toilet seats, Beatle knickers for the girls; apparently you can't avoid Beatle everything.

Figgy McDuff and I have a chat during the short time that we are both awake between Bombay and Istanbul. He lives in Bradford and we agree to have a night out on the first Saturday home. Figgy convinces me that he knows a bar in Bradford City centre where the local girls are queuing up for a 'good time' with blokes like us. I can't offer anything comparable in Pudsey, so Bradford next Saturday night is confirmed. We exchange telephone numbers and shake on it.

I've grown to love the Far East during the last eighteen months. On reflection, it's definitely been the most enjoyable time of my life. I've had no commitments, other than looking after myself. I've sent Mum a small monthly allowance that has been automatically taken from my pay: everything else I have spent on myself. I've enjoyed the company of my mates, visited exotic places and generally had a whale of a time. I really don't want to go home to Pudsey, but all good things have to come to an end in this man's Navy ... so the older guys say.

I arrive at RAF Stanstead on the first day of March 1964 and after I clear immigration, I naturally head for the small bar with most of the others. There is a bewildering array of strange, unknown keg beers. I order a pint of Watneys Red Barrel that I find terribly gassy and difficult to drink. I don't finish it before we are all ushered onto the London-bound coach.

The weather is good for the time of year, the early Spring sunshine bringing some 1960s colour to the Capital. We gaze intently out of the coach windows taking in sights not seen, or considered, for a year and a half. The girls of London are all wearing much shorter skirts. Unbeknown to us, not only has there been a revolution in popular music during the past 18 months, there has also been a much-appreciated raising of hemlines. The most appreciated British invention of the century, the mini-skirt, has made an appearance during our absence. Shapely knees, curvaceous ankles, slinky calves and vast lengths of long upper thigh are displayed with each feminine stride. For a guy just turned twenty, London – on a warm spring day – has sexuality everywhere. Top of the Hit Parade is *Diane* by The Bachelors, which isn't to my taste. I desperately hope that the mini-skirt fashion has reached Pudsey.

It takes days for me to relate most of my experiences of the past eighteen months to Mum and my brother Tony. Some details I keep to myself. What does impress them is my Chinky underwear. When pegged on Monday's washing line they bring a well-needed splash of colour to the Pudsey skyline. Neighbours the length of Robin Lane pop into the shop to welcome me home, marvel at my tan and comment on my remarkably interesting underwear.

The large brown leather-look suitcase I had bought in Sembawang begins to fall apart when exposed to the West Yorkshire climate. Mum explains that it's actually made from compressed paper made to look like leather.

Mrs Shufflebottom and Mum are impressed with my new blue suit. Shufflebum couldn't believe that it was made in less than a week by a little Chinese bloke called Sew-sew.

There are a few so called mini skirts in the centre of town but they don't have the cut or hang of those I saw in London.

I phone Figgy to confirm that our Saturday night out in Bradford is still on.

I catch a Sammy Legard's double decker bus into Bradford and we meet in the town's bus station. Once again Figgy tells me that Bradford city centre on a Saturday night is awash with young, single girls looking for well-travelled and experienced young Yorkshire lads like us.

We select a bar that Figgy says he knows is promising: the strains of Beatle music are enticing. After the bars of Singapore and Hong Kong my first impression of this Bradford bar is less than inspiring. It's dingy and, apart from us, completely empty. The only thing moving is the stylus of the jukebox. Figgy and I stand at the bar and wait; there is a clinking of glasses from somewhere in the back.

Eventually a well-proportioned gentleman drying his hands on a grimy blue and white dishcloth waddles into view.

'Two pints of Red Barrel please, Frank,' says Figgy.

He looks from Figgy to me and back again. He tosses his dishcloth onto the top of the bar. 'Yew can 'ave a pint Figgy but yewer Paki pal can sling his 'ook.'

'He isn't a …' blurts Figgy.

'You lot aren't allowed to drink are ya?' He looks directly at me.

I don't know what to say. This is unexpected. I don't know what is going on.

'Dew ya?' The bloke leans closer to me and stares straight into my eyes.

'He's from Pudsey, Frank,' says Figgy.

'Well the weather over there must be a lot 'otter than it is here then.'

I understand what is happening. 'I'm a Yorkshire lad. Born and bred here. I've just got back from the Far East. I'm in the Navy with Figgy.'

'Piss off,' he spits.

'It's true.'

'Is it?' The barman asks Figgy .

'Yeah, we're both back home after eighteen months in Singapore.'

'But he's black.' He waves an arm at me. 'And you … you're well you're a sort of a sickly yeller colour.'

'I'm a Chef. I work in the galley. He's an upper deck Seaman and works in the sun.'

The barman picks up a couple of pint glasses and waves them at me. 'Sorry, lad … terribly sorry. I thought you are one of those Pakistani Indians. Have a pint on me.'

I forgive him immediately.

The Red Barrel is no better than the one at Stansted; if anything it's worse.

'Do the girls still get in here on a Saturday night, Frank?' asks Figgy, looking around the still empty bar.

'Girls? Naah, not in 'ere now.'

'Who put the music on the jukebox then?'

'I did. I like those Beatle lads.'

In recognition of *HMS Lincoln*'s contribution to what is officially termed 'The Malaysian Crisis', I am awarded the General Service Medal with a Borneo clasp which I receive on 5 November 1965.

I'd done my bit.

If you've enjoyed *A Singapore Fling*, then you'll want to discover Peter Broadbent's other top-selling naval memoirs, *HMS Ganges Days* and *HMS Bermuda Days*.